Cú Chulainn's Death:
A Critical Edition of
Brislech Mór Maige Murthemni

Revised Edition

Bettina Kimpton

CONTENTS

FOREWORD

This volume presents a revision of the author's first critical edition of Cú Chulainn's death tale, published in 2009 in the Maynooth Medieval Irish Text series. The author wishes to thank John Carey, Johan Corthals, and David Stifter for comments on this edition; Kim McCone for comments on the first edition; and Calvert Watkins and Tomás Ó Cathasaigh for comments on the dissertation from which these editions were developed. Remaining errors and oversights are the author's responsibility alone.

INTRODUCTION

Brislech Mór Maige Murthemni, the earlier version of Cú Chulainn's death tale, survives only as an acephalous copy in the Book of Leinster (119a–123b) (Best and Bergin 1956: 442–457) and in a series of glossed excerpts preserved in Trinity MS H.3.18. The latter conclude by identifying the tale as *In Brislech*, indicating that the earlier version was already known by this title (Thurneysen 1912–1913: 18). It has been partially translated by Stokes (1877), D'Arbois de Jubainville (1892), Dottin (1926), Guyonvarc'h (1968), and Carey (1994), all of whom omit most of the poetic portion. A translation without edition of the surviving text was published by Tymoczko (1981). This revision of the current author's previous edition (Kimpton 2009) aims to clarify passages, expand the analysis, and provide a more engaging translation that may capture some of the metrical qualities of the text's verse portions.

As Thurneysen observes (1921: 548), excerpts from the tale in Cormac's Glossary demonstrate the tale's existence in the ninth century. He notes (ibid.: 548–549), as does Pokorny (1919: 123), that some linguistic forms indicate eighth-century composition and others later reworking.

Themes and Structure
Brislech Mór Maige Murthemni tells the tale of the slaying of the warrior hero Cú Chulainn, his avenging by Conall Cernach, his resurrection and prophecy of Christianity's arrival in Ireland, and his lament by his wife Emer. Kelleher (1971) uses the depiction of Cú Chulainn's death in this text as evidence for an association drawn in annals and saga literature between Cú Chulainn and Christ. McCone (1990: 25) further places this association within the context of an overarching goal of *comúaim n-ecalsa fri túaith* ("sewing together of Church and State"). Radner (1982) cites this text as an example of the use of Ulster tales in the interest of joint Uí Néill and Armagh propaganda. The text conveys these ideas through narrative and poetic devices that demonstrate the power of the spoken word; address the conflict between destructive and protective aspects of war; and transform a tale of vengeance into one of pacifism, social cohesion, and Christian salvation.

3

The Slayer Slain

The theme of vengeance generates much of the tale's action. The alliance of Murthemne's invaders is led by children of warriors slain by Cú Chulainn: Lugaid son of Cú Roí, Erc son of Cairpre, and the children of Calatín. Upon Cú Chulainn's death, Erc admonishes the warriors for not immediately taking the slain hero's head in vengeance for that of his own father (§26, ll. 383–385), and Cú Chulainn's arm is struck off in vengeance for that of Lugaid, which had been struck off by Cú Chulainn's falling sword (§27, ll. 393–395). Cú Chulainn and Conall Cernach make a promise to avenge one another (§30, ll. 430–435), a promise duly fulfilled by Conall Cernach.

This cycle of slaying in vengeance and Cú Chulainn's role suggest the tale's association with the Indo-European myth of the slayer slain (Watkins 1995), the reciprocal iteration of the dragon-slaying myth. In Lebarcham's speech inciting Cú Chulainn to battle, the use of forms of the verb *gonaid* ($*g^w hen$) to describe the hero's slaying in vengeance (*cot-gní Lugaid lánchlemnas/goin fris-gegna gním*, §3, ll. 29–30) and the reference to the subject's companions (*lánchlemnas*, l. 29) (Watkins 1995: 301–302) indicate the tale's continuation of elements of this myth. Word order— with forms of *gníid* framing two forms of *guin*—highlights the action of reciprocal killing.[1]

According to Watkins, the dragon-slaying myth "is a symbolic victory of growth over stagnation or dormancy in the cycle of the year and ultimately a victory of rebirth over death" (Watkins 1995: 299). Savior of the Ulaid, the warrior hero Cú Chulainn has also been argued to play a rejuvenating role in a seasonal myth (Ó Broin 1963), and his death on the first of August (*ata-mbebai...i cétlathiu fogomuir*, §40, ll. 605–606) is in accordance with this tradition. The Christianization of his tale of death and rebirth, effected

---

[1] If the figure of Cú Chulainn continues a tradition associated with Fíacc, son of Fergus, narrated in the seventh-century poem *Conailla Medb míchuru* by Luccreth moccu Chiara (see Carney 1971: 79), his death tale may also have origins in Fíacc's slaying, also committed in vengeance.

by the narrative parallel drawn between him and Christ, is advanced by this mythological significance.[2]

The text's structure emphasizes the opposition of slayer against slain through replication, by which Lugaid's portrayal partly mirrors that of Cú Chulainn. Also a personage with hound associations, Lugaid bathes himself before death, as does Cú Chulainn, and fights Conall Cernach with one hand and with an injury to his side, also like his opponent. This injury is itself inflicted by a being with a hound aspect, Conall Cernach's horse (*cend con furri-side*, §35, ll. 486–487). As in *Orgain Denna Ríg*, as Ó Cathasaigh has demonstrated (2002: 13–16), narrative symmetry reflects the action of vengeance.

This theme of reciprocal violence is balanced against a theme of intervention. For example, toward the beginning of the tale, Cú Chulainn expresses remorse at not intervening on behalf of crying women and children. Also, Conall Cernach is away from Ulster on an expedition to aid Cormac, and his horse helps him prevail over Lugaid in single combat. Even Cú Chulainn's undoing is brought about partly by this motive as he is asked to intervene in a trio of quarrels staged by the enemy troops.

A related theme is that of deliverance from exile. Three of the tale's characters (Lebarcham, §3, ll. 24–27; Cú Chulainn, §38, ll. 544–545; and Emer, §43, ll. 686–688) refer to Cormac's absence in exile and Conall

---

[2] The episode in the *Táin* bearing the title *In Carpat Serda 7 In Breslech Mór Maige Murthemne* (O'Rahilly 1976: ll. 2072–2234) parallels this tale in its account of the hero's warrior feats in battle (ll. 2292–2334) and three-day regenerative slumber through the healing efforts of his divine father Lug (ll. 2109–2144), suggestive of Christ's resurrection. The following episode, *Túarascbáil Delba Con Culaind so*, also mirrors the vision of Cú Chulainn (in earthlier guise) appearing to the woman-troops after his death. Perhaps, just as the death tale draws on elements of the *Táin* such as the *Boyhood Deeds* and the hero's defense of Ulster against the provinces of Ireland (and perhaps these episodes themselves) from an earlier version of the epic, so the *Táin* episode may draw on (a version of) the death tale. Such a borrowing would be consistent with the *Táin*'s use of other texts—for example, the motif of metamorphosis into deer that appears in Muirchú's *Life of St. Patrick*, which Carey (2013) considers to have been borrowed in the reverse direction; the death of Fráech (see Meek 1984); and perhaps the single combat between Aeneas and Turnus, in the borrowed version of which, however, the vanquished warrior's life is spared. Both the death tale and the *Táin* episode may also of course draw on an earlier seasonal regeneration story involving the hero.

Cernach's absence because of his mission to protect Cormac. Also, Cú Chulainn's prophetic poem before his death possibly refers in ll. 219–221 to Christ's deliverance from exile in Egypt upon Herod's death. The echoing of the theme of exile may serve two functions: further highlighting Christ's role as redeemer of humankind and calling attention to the problem of exile itself as a disruption in social order.

Violence and Social Order

The tale thus presents an opposition between benevolent and malevolent aspects of physical violence. In contrast with the vengeful slaying of Cú Chulainn, Conall Cernach's vengeance for his companion is recounted with emphasis on his loyalty, presenting a positive aspect of martial force. And Cú Chulainn manages within his own person the protective and destructive forces of violence associated with wolvishness (McCone 1984: 14–17; Ó Cathasaigh 1986: 159–160; Ó Cathasaigh 1977: 37–38). As in the *Boyhood Deeds*, he is immersed in vats of cold water to cool his battle ardor (§1, ll. 4–5), here for his own protection rather than that of Ulster. His prohibition from eating his namesake's flesh and his slaying by another hound personage also reflect the destructive aspect of his own nature.

The text counters the destructiveness of violence in part by emphasizing the importance of social bonds. Lebarcham's poem inciting Cú Chulainn to battle (§3) appeals to his kinship ties and patriotism. Entreating him to protect Ulster, she identifies him through his rearing and lineage (*gein Loga soalta*, l. 18; *uí Chathbad*, l. 32) and reminds him of the importance of kinship: Cormac's distance from his kindred while in exile renders him unavailable to assist, and Conall Cernach is likewise unavailable because he is protecting Cormac. She points out that Lugaid and his alliance have no such kindred affection for Cú Chulainn (ll. 28–30). Repetitive alliteration of *c/g* on words expressing core themes of the poem— preparing for and fighting in battle (*comérig, churad cathchlessu*), protecting Ulster (*cobairthe*), slaying in vengeance (*goin fris-gegna gním*), kinship ties and filial piety (*gairi, gein Loga*), and Cú Chulainn's own name—links these themes and reinforces the urgency of Lebarcham's message. Although Lebarcham's second poem asking Cú Chulainn not to leave (*nán-fácaib*, §10, l. 98) appears to send a contrasting message, it

6

nevertheless continues emphasis on the warrior hero's honor and noble bearing (*gnúis cnedach*, l. 103) and praises his regal march to battle (*céim rígairech*, l. 110), even resuming her first poem's sound pattern with an alliterative chain of words beginning with *c/g* (ll. 100–104) and interlaced alliteration (see metrical analysis below) involving this sound throughout.

Similarly, the tale's depiction of the war goddess reflects the contradiction between the protective and destructive aspects of war. References to the Mórrígan in Cú Chulainn's poem addressed to Líath Macha (*fechuir fiach*, l. 82; *suilig*, l. 91) express the complementary aspects of her role as "guardian of [Cú Chulainn's] death" (Herbert 1996: 146), apparently malevolent while also protective (Lysaght 1996: 162).

In addition to heightening the dramatic effect of prophecy and fulfillment, the tale's verbal echoes and structural symmetries reinforce social ties. For example, Cú Chulainn's prediction of his encounter with the witches (*ammiti túathcháecha*, §12, l. 142) and his description of foreboding events leading to his death (*delg/ad-chumben chness/co tuitt...duirn*, §7, ll. 60–65) are echoed in Emer's lament (*millsit ammaiti*, l. 608; *co farnaic ammaiti túathcháecha*, ll. 626–627; *at-cummai a delg*, l. 622; *ara torchair a scíath*, l. 620). Cú Chulainn's poem before death (§12) and the final section of Emer's lament (§43) both begin by referring to the mourning over his loss, using similar phrases (*it brónaig banchuiri*, l. 130; *bit brónaig Delguin dílachtai*, l. 682). The closing lines of Cú Chulainn's and Lebarcham's prophecies of his loss in battle also echo each other almost exactly (*día már/des Maig Murthemni dim és*, §7, ll. 68–69; *díe mór/Maige Murthemne dit éis*, §10, ll. 112–113). Also, the poems addressed by Cú Chulainn (§9) and Conall Cernach (§31) to Líath Macha are similar in structure and content. In the same meter (lines of two to three stresses each) and heavily alliterative, they both describe Líath Macha's damaged appearance and encourage him to set forth to battle, creating a parallel between the heroes that reflects their social bond.

The poems of Cú Chulainn and Níab in §§4–6 are also linked through verbal echo and structural symmetry. The poems in §§4 and 5 begin with an address in the vocative, proceed to a sentence in the negative, include a subordinate clause introduced by *ar*, and end with a negative sentence.

7

Forms of the verb *imm-goin* (*ní imgén, imgona*, §4, ll. 36 and 38; *ní imgonat*, §5, l. 46) also link the two passages. Further, Cú Chulainn's expression of determination to enter battle in defiance of Níab's taunts (*cíabam trú-sa ním-tharraid cubés*, l. 51) echoes his earlier expression of reluctance to fight (*cíabo bidbu imnedach ní imgén m'óenur*, l. 36), highlighting the transformation in his mood.

Cú Chulainn and Christ

Crucially, at this point in the tale, the preeminent Ulster hero is motivated solely by honor and personal pride. Níab's taunts stir Cú Chulainn's battle ardor whereas Lebarcham's appeals to kin loyalty fall flat. As the tale progresses, however, Cú Chulainn's character undergoes development. One of the tale's primary means of transforming a story of vengeance into one of salvation and pacifism is through the representation of Cú Chulainn himself—through parallels with Christ's death and resurrection and through Cú Chulainn's own personal redemption.

In addition to the obvious parallels the text draws through Cú Chulainn's Crucifixion-like death and his rebirth to utter prophecies of Christ and St. Patrick, the poems delivered by Cú Chulainn and others further his Christian associations. In the opening lines of §38, Cú Chulainn appears to refer both to himself and to Jesus as the lamb that has been slain (*úaine ortae*, l. 521). In §7 the word denoting the brooch that pierces Cú Chulainn's skin (*delg*) recalls the crown of thorns placed on Christ's head—for example, in the poems of Blathmac (*coronn delccae*, Carney 1964: 18, ll. 201–202)—and the discussion of the brooch's culpability (*is bidba delg*, l. 60) recalls that of Pontius Pilate's culpability in Christ's death (*ba bibdu cech cruth/ar buith oca dílsiuguth*, Carney 1964: 24, ll. 287–288). And Cú Chulainn calls these foreboding events "a warning" (*robud*, l. 59), the same word he uses to denote the vision the elements will present before Christ's death (*dall taidbsiu do doínib robud ría mbás bias*, §39, l. 564).

Cú Chulainn's description in §12 of the aftermath of his wounding (ll. 175–188) may also resemble the narration of the Crucifixion as seen in Blathmac's poems (parting drink: l. 233; Christ crying out to His father in momentary despair: ll. 239–240; the elements responding to Christ's

8

death: §§61, 62, 65; the division of spoils (*noíbfodb*): ll. 215–216) (all line numbers from Carney 1964). Amid her taunts to incite Cú Chulainn to battle, Níab refers to his being sacrificed for the Ulstermen (*renar ar Ultaib*, §5, l. 43). And Emer describes Cú Chulainn in terms that echo his own description of Christ (*ar chenél féchid...seiss for dindaib flatha/in ri*, §39, ll. 550 and 561–562; *séol n-óir úas dindaib...ar fáebraib féchad*, §40, ll. 591–592) and refers to Cú Chulainn as *nél find* (l. 590). Erc also explicitly identifies Cú Chulainn with Christ and refers to him/Christ as *flaith findnélach* (§16, l. 281).

Further, the placement of Cú Chulainn's narration of his death and heroic past (§38) between prophecies of Patrick (§37) and of Christ (§39) and these passages' connection through linking alliteration (*Emain/Úaine*, ll. 519–521; *Cride/Críst*, ll. 547–549) suggest an association of the two figures' salvific roles. Verbal echo between poems and prose passages also links the two figures. The reference to Christ's Harrowing of Hell in §39 (*tria erscartad iffirn*, l. 571) echoes the description of Cú Chulainn's attack on the invading hosts in Mag Murthemne (*do urscartad na slóg*, §18, l. 298). Resonances of the poems of Blathmac, a text of Christian lament, in Emer's lament further strengthen this association (*ba méite...frassaib fola*, ll. 674–677).[3]

In addition, Cú Chulainn undergoes personal Christian redemption. Upon accepting his fate and setting out for battle, he recites a prophetic poem (§12) in which he condemns covetousness (ll. 151 and 165), greed (ll. 213–214), and battle violence (ll. 203–208) as marks of an unjust king (ll. 200–202) and admonishes his audience to worship Christ and observe Christian law (ll. 222–223). He expresses remorse over his own pride and a desire

---

[3] The lines of influence could perhaps also have extended in the reverse direction. Parallels between this death tale and Blathmac's poems, both texts from the early to mid-eighth century and likely of northern provenance, suggest a connection between them or at least mutual familiarity. In addition to phrasal echoes between them, the death tale portrays its hero as a figure of Christ; features, like Blathmac's poems, a long, complex lament in which all are exhorted to join in "perpetual keening" (*bithchoíniud*, l. 676); and contrasts, as do Blathmac's poems, its this-worldly lament with a revelation of eternal life. The texts also share a set of terms associated with lament (e.g., *gubae, gol, coíniud, cíid, dirsan, mairg, ar-cessi*) (see also Hollo 2005: 84). See also note to l. 586.

to have followed Christian law himself (ll. 224–227). In battle, he defends his kin and his province from the threat of satire, leaving himself vulnerable to attack. In §9 he appeals to Líath Macha through empathy, reminiscing on their long rides together and admitting his own reluctance to set out for battle. In §38, recited after his death, he reveals the importance to him of his personal kinship ties—to his wife (l. 532); his mortal mother (l. 534) and divine father (l. 539); his son, whom he had unknowingly slain (l. 541); his charioteer (l. 542); and his fosterbrother and fellow Ulster warrior Conall Cernach (l. 544). This poem also represents Cú Chulainn's relationship with his divine father in the framework of both Christian piety and the warrior ethos. He describes Lug, whom he says he would invoke for divine assistance in battle (*ad-muindfind mac nEithnend*, l. 539), as being "everywhere in every form" (*cach cruth cach leth -robae*, l. 540), ascribing to Lug the Christian God's qualities of omnipresence as well as protection (*dim-emed art úasal*, l. 535). He describes his journey after death as one "on blessed paths to the fort of joy" (i.e., Heaven) (ll. 532–533), and his final poem (§39) concerns only Christ and Christian devotion.

The Christian associations of Cú Chulainn's path to redemption are underlined by possible echoes of phrases and ideas from Columbanus's *Sermons*, which also consider "this life…as a way and an ascent" (Walker 1957: 87; see also Stancliffe 1997: 131). For example, the expression of the ineffability and inscrutability of God and the Trinity in Cú Chulainn's devotional poem on Christ (§39)—*in rí…óenaib dédaib trédaib/tria chumachta nát érglond, nád écgut, nád érbur* ("the king…as one, as two, as three, through powers I cannot examine, I cannot utter, I cannot describe," ll. 562–563)—recalls phrases from *Sermon* I.2 (*Deum unum ac trinum…totus invisibilis, incomprehensibilis, ineffabilis*, "God one and three…wholly invisible, inconceivable, unspeakable," Walker 1957: 60–61) and I.3 (*Nullus itaque praesumat quaerere investigabilia Dei, quid fuit, quomodo fuit, quo fuit. Haec sunt ineffabilia, inscrutabilia, investigabilia*, "Therefore let no man venture to seek out the unsearchable things of God, the nature, mode, and cause of His existence. These are unspeakable, undiscoverable, unsearchable," ibid.: 62–63). This poem's final phrase (*i mbethu tria bithu*, "alive through ages," l. 577), though perhaps a common one, resembles the closing words of each of the

10

Sermons (*in saecula saeculorum*), most closely Sermon 5 (*qui vivit...in saecula saeculorum*, "who lives...unto ages of ages," Walker 1957: 86–87). The use of rhetorical questions in this poem and others in the text, though perhaps a common convention, may also parallel Columbanus's frequent such usage in the *Sermons* (e.g., *Quis est ergo Deus?*, "Who then is God?" Sermon I.4, ibid.: 62–63; compare *cía rí seo, cía tuili...?*, l. 558).

Also, one of the witches who force Cú Chulainn to break his *geasa* taunts him using a modifed version of a (perhaps proverbial) phrase found in the Sermons, Letters, and Rule for Monks (and originating in the writings of Sulpicius Severus) (Stancliffe 1997: 98–99), *cui pauca non sufficiunt, plura non proderunt* ("The man to whom little is not enough will not benefit from more," Sermon III.4, Walker 1957: 78–79): *Ní túalaing mór nád fulaing nó nád geib in mbec* (l. 241, "He who doesn't endure or accept something small isn't capable of anything great"). The phrase, which Stancliffe (1997: 98) calls a "favourite" "tag" of Columbanus, also appears in Sermon I in the saint's discussion of faith in the Trinity—*cui haec pauca de Deo Trinitate non sufficiunt, plura [iuxta Scripturam] non proderunt* ("For the man to whom these few words on God the Trinity are not sufficient, will not [according to Scripture,] be profited by more," Walker 1957: 60–61)—and in I.4 on seeking divine understanding (*quia in maioribus idoneus esse non potest, qui prius minora non investigavit, et cui in minoribus non creditur, in maioribus quomodo credendum est?*, "because none can be competent in the greater if he has not first explored the less, and when a man is not trusted in the lesser, in the greater how should he be trusted?" ibid.). The phrase's occurrence in this context (assuming the writer drew the phrase from this source) would—for an audience familiar with the sermon—reinforce the tale's focus on Christian faith and the link the tale draws between Cú Chulainn's journey and that of the individual soul.

Another possible echo of the *Sermons* is Cú Chulainn's drink "from a gushing, wholesome stream" after his wounding (*Íba srúaim sruthbarr slán*, ll. 175–176), which may draw on Sermon XIII.3 (*ut ibi et ego...vivam undam vivi fontis aquae vivae biberem*, "so that there I too...might drink the living stream of the living Fount of living water," Walker 1957: 118–119). The blindness of the witches in Cú Chulainn's path might also recall

11

the *Sermons* (e.g., Sermon III.4 "Unbearable blindness!" Walker 1957: 77), and VII.1 "Blind madness...human will," ibid.: 92). The text may also be drawing on Columbanus (and other sources) as the saint likens the soul's struggle with vices to a battlefield: *certaminis sanguineo solo....Pugnandum ergo hic est et certandum cum vitiis nostris, ut alibi coronemur*, "in the bloodstained soil of battle....We must fight and struggle with our vices, that we may be crowned elsewhere" (Sermon X.3, Walker 1957: 104–105). Cú Chulainn's battle activity in the tale may thus also be interpreted as the soul's fight to live a virtuous life to achieve salvation.

Just as Cú Chulainn is portrayed as a Christian figure, Christ is depicted as a warrior hero. In §39 (*De Adventu Christi*) Cú Chulainn describes the Harrowing of Hell (*tróethfaid Ísu iffern*, l. 555) and refers to Christ as a fort for His kindred on their journey to Heaven (l. 552) and as a battle-victorious king (*in rí íar mbúaid chatha*, l. 562). By merging the portrayals of Christ and the warrior hero Cú Chulainn, the text both furthers its expression of the link between divine and human manifested in the Trinity and strengthens the impact of the tale's pacifist message. As Herren and Brown (2002) observe, "It is only the Christ who with his own hands can overcome the cosmic dragon who can earn the reverence of heroes and kings" (160).

Kingship and Peace
Cú Chulainn's reference to Christ as a battle-victorious king also reveals the text's concern with kingship itself. Cú Chulainn is called the king of chariot-fighters (*rígeirr*, l. 594), just as Lóeg is the king of charioteers (*rí arad*, l. 342) and Líath Macha the king of horses (*rí ech*, l. 594). Cú Chulainn's poems after death express devotion to Christ the King presiding over all other kings (ll. 558–563) and foretell the arrival of priests who will pray on humanity's behalf to the King of High Heaven (ll. 514–515). By contrast, his prophetic poem before battle (§12) describes an unrighteous king and his downfall, invoking the concept of *fír* (truth) (*cloífid fír*, l. 202). The unjustness of this king's rule is emphasized through syntactic parallelism and crossed alliteration (interrupting the pattern of linking alliteration) (*bith dáer a acille/bid dorcha a amser*, ll. 195–196). Like the ancient Egyptian concept of *Maat*, *fír* encompasses the

12

idea of cosmic order, which the king is responsible for upholding. According to the description given in Cú Chulainn's poem, a just kingship would be characterized by peace, absence of greed, and observance of Christian law.

A striking reference to kingship also appears as Lugaid mac Con Roí concedes victory to Conall Cernach (ll. 493–495), demonstrating the text's concern not merely with ideals of peace and just kingship but specifically with peace and social order under the Uí Néill and Armagh. As Thurneysen (1921: 549) observes, the tale's plot recapitulates that of the *Táin* by setting the provinces of Ireland against Ulster and its solitary defender, Cú Chulainn. Ulster's ultimate victory over these forces asserts Uí Néill supremacy. Likewise, in Cú Chulainn's death tale, Ulster emerges victorious over the provinces of Ireland. Repetitive use of the intensive prefix *mór-* in the final section of the tale (five times within the section's twenty-three poetic lines) emphasizes Ulster's dominance. However, in this case, the representation of Cú Chulainn's downfall allows the Uí Néill kings to both appropriate the incomparable warrior hero's valor and glory and assert that his reign (as "king of chariot-fighters") is over—the Ulster kings have been forever displaced by the Uí Néill. One may speculate whether the text may specifically recall the defeat and decapitation of Áed Róin, the king of Ulster, by Áed Allán in the battle of Fochart in 735 and/or Domnall's hosting of Leinstermen in 756 against his challenger Níall, Áed Allán's half-brother (see Charles-Edwards 2015: 95).

Perhaps the tale's most critical use of verbal echo occurs in its closing lines. Just as St. Patrick's host will, as Cú Chulainn foretells, pray for humanity's salvation through a transcendent utterance, understood here as "prayer" (*alchél*, §37, l. 515), Emer declares through a transcendent utterance, understood here as "proclamation" (*alchél* §43, l. 699), that all kingdoms should unite in lamenting the fallen hero, as would be expected in commemoration of one's lord (Breatnach 2015: 108). The subsequent contrast between the lament's final line and Cú Chulainn's parting words, using different forms of the same verb (*con-ricc*), reveals this action's greater significance. Whereas Emer mourns that she will never meet Cú Chulainn again (*ní chomraicfem nach laithiu aile*, §43, l. 703), Cú Chulainn bids farewell "until we meet again" (*co comairsem*, §37, l. 519)

13

in the afterlife. Although Emer's statement seems to limit her perspective to the secular realm, her words effect a link between social and divine order. Through parallel (*alchél*) and contrasting (*co comairsem*/*ní chomraicfem*) verbal echoes, her words translate a divine concern for peace to the human political realm, conveying a key message of the text: that to attain salvation, worldly kingdoms must uphold peace and social order. That is, peaceful action binding kingdoms under a just (Uí Néill) ruler is in accordance with Heavenly law and will reap rewards of eternal life. When Emer claims a right to peace (*dlegmai scur sáetha*, §43, l. 698), she thus declares that society deserves not only relief from turmoil and violence but also lasting freedom from earthly troubles and that the former will lead to the latter.

Emer

Although Emer appears only in the final sections of the tale and is represented only by her lament for her husband, this lament nevertheless plays a crucial role in the tale and exhibits a magnificent range of metrical patterns and poetic features (see metrical analysis below). As discussed above, verbal echoes between her lament and poems delivered by Cú Chulainn earlier in the tale link her with her husband, expressing their bond as well as her equal importance. They also further the link between Cú Chulainn and Christ in their salvific roles and forge a parallel between human and divine concerns. As Cú Chulainn makes the transition to the afterlife, Emer mediates between divine and human realms through her words to deliver the text's message of pacifism.

In so doing, Emer may be seen to "occup[y] [the lamenter's] marginal position between the worlds of the living and the dead" (Bourke 1988: 289). Her lament indeed displays some typical features and fulfills some essential functions of traditional lament poetry.[4] She praises her husband's valor and physical beauty (*eirr caín cumachtach cathbúadach*, §40, l. 588; see Bourke ibid.: 288) and expresses great sadness and grief at his loss (*dom-chommart a chuma....ním-thá ní íarum*, §42, ll. 669–673; see

---

[4] In its use of stressed, alliterative meters and of repetition and syntactic parallelism as organizing principles, the lament shares features with the Middle Irish *caíned* in the *Leabhar Breac*, analyzed by Hollo (2005).

14

Bourke ibid.). She perhaps also censures his fellow Ulster warriors for their absence at his death considering the many battles he has won for them (§42, ll. 662–663; see Bourke ibid.). Her lament contrasts Cú Chulainn's noble qualities with images of his downfall at the hands of witches (*millsit ammaiti…crúancern Con Culaind cathbúadaig*, §40, ll. 608–611; see Bourke ibid.: 289). It also facilitates the grieving process of others as she asserts that all eyes must weep for him and all hearts break (§42, ll. 674–677; see Bourke ibid.: 288–289). Bourke explains that "at times of social disruption…the lamenter helps to define (or actively does define) the boundaries of human life and culture following a death" (ibid.: 290). Indeed, as performative speech acts, her declaration uniting kingdoms in Cú Chulainn's lament and her statement of the right to an end of turmoil actively set the terms for continuation of life after his loss.

Emer's portrayal in her husband's death tale thus aligns with her representation in other tales as a "model of…eloquence" (Findon 1997: 55) and a "voice of moral order" (ibid.: 99) associated (despite her expression of emotion in her lament) with "the realm of reason" (ibid.: 105). As in *Fled Bricrenn*, she extols her husband's rank and valor. As in *Aided Óenfir Aífe*, she recommends a wise course of action against the prevailing warrior ethos. As in other tales, her role and her words, though situated within the patriarchal norms, transcend the social limitations traditionally placed on women. Though performing an expected role as hero's wife in lamenting Cú Chulainn, she uses her position to steer social action through her speech acts.

As in other tales, Emer also plays a human rather than an otherworldly role. In contrast with female characters associated with the Otherworld (such as in *Echtrae Chonnlai* and *Immram Brain*) and often seen as representing sovereignty (Findon 1997), she is portrayed as a real rather than allegorical character. Moreover, in her lament, she clearly expresses autonomy, asserting control over her own destiny by stating that she will never marry again (*níba fri céili aile íarum nom-accfither*, §42, l. 679). On the other hand, given the text's concerns with kingship and social order, perhaps this assertion still carries a resonance of representations of sovereignty.[5]

Allegoresis

In its portrayal of Cú Chulainn and in its delivery of Christian messages, Cú Chulainn's death tale exemplifies the use of allegorical technique, drawing on the fourfold sense of Scripture—literal, typological, tropological or moral, and anagogical—as outlined in Cassian's *Conferences* (Conference 14 "On Spiritual Knowledge," Luibheid 1985: 155–173). As discussed above, Cú Chulainn's literal representation as warrior hero who rises from the dead, itself perhaps an embodiment of a seasonal regeneration myth, also typologically represents Christ and His resurrection. In addition, the hero's journey of personal redemption—and perhaps his battle against the illusoriness and vices of mortal life— tropologically represents the individual soul's path toward salvation, a sense underlined by Cú Chulainn's counsel to follow Christ's law (*adraid in mac cona recht*, §12, l. 222) and by Emer's appeal to cease strife in the mortal world to attain salvation in the eternal world (*dlegmai scur sáetha*, §43, l. 698). Finally, the text fulfills its anagogical function through its depiction of Cú Chulainn's death and resurrection and through the hero's explicit prophecy of the arrival of St. Patrick and Christianity.

Like the Christian allegories *Echtrae Chonnlai* and *Immram Brain*, the tale expresses the priority of the immortal over the mortal world (see McCone 1990: 82). It conveys its principal message, however, by expressing the link between them and urging the importance of living a Christian life to achieve immortality, as taught, for example, in the *Sermons* of Columbanus. Its method of portraying Christ's prefiguring of Christianity both literally and allegorically enacts this link and places the allegorizing

---

[5] In examining female representations of sovereignty, it may be beneficial to consider not only how historical circumstances may motivate their use but also how these circumstances may shape or relate to the representations themselves. For example, it is possible that Adomnán's Law of Innocents in 697 protecting women, children, and clerics influenced representations of a sovereignty goddess (e.g., in *Echtrae Chonnlai* and *Immram Brain*) associated with an Island of Women characterized by peace, sinlessness, and immortality— that is, in addition to Christian adoption of the traditional sovereignty goddess figure to represent the Church (McCone 2000: 103–104).

inclinations of early medieval Irish writers further beyond doubt (see Hollo 2011).

The Power of Language

As much as vengeance and the countering pacifist message of divine salvation and worldly social order generate the tale's action, so do speech acts themselves. Indeed, Cú Chulainn's downfall itself can be attributed to the power of language through the threat of satire. The tale's poems strongly attest to the perceived power of the spoken word—they incite, taunt, sympathize, foretell, admonish, lament, command, and express devotion. And as the above analysis argues, features such as verbal echo in and among poems and between poetry and prose further the tale's themes. The poems achieve their goals partly through their intricate artistry.

The Poems

Passages with metrical structure and/or poetic features such as alliteration, preposed genitives, final-verb constructions, parallelism, asyndeton, and expressive word order constitute a large portion of the text. The most common metrical patterns are two- to three-stress lines and cadenced lines. Syntactic parallelism is frequent, and all poetic passages are intricately ornamented with both simple and complex line-internal and linking alliteration.

In addition, many poems exhibit a special kind of alliteration that is termed here interlaced alliteration. Although the individual interlacing pattern may vary from one manifestation to the next, the principle of this alliterative technique remains the same: sounds introduced within an alliterative series recur in a following series in an interlaced, braid-like fashion to create a brilliantly evolving but unbroken alliterative chain. The effect may resemble that of a melodic line in which ornamental turns surround some individual notes before the melody proceeds. In some instances, an alliterating initial sound may act as a pivot around which subsequent alliterative sounds recur in altered order before the alliterating initial moves to a new group of sounds and then recedes, recurring after a new alliterating initial commences (e.g., ll. 17–19: g-l-n-g-n-l-g-s-l-t-s; ll. 130–132: b-r-n-g-b-n-ch-r-b-d-n-b-d-r-d-r-n). In the following analyses,

17

the first few instances of interlaced alliteration are described in detail; thereafter, instances are identified by line number.

The poems are tentatively analyzed as follows. In passages with metrical structure, syntactic units, meaning, and the prevailing metrical pattern (e.g., linking alliteration, number of stresses per line, parallelism) were used to determine line divisions.

§3.   Lebarcham's poem inciting Cú Chulainn to battle is structured in mostly heptasyllabic lines punctuated by lines of five syllables. (See the textual notes for discussion of syllable count in individual lines.) All the longer lines have trisyllabic cadences, all but one of which alliterate with their preceding words. Two of the shorter lines also display alliteration between the final word and its preceding word. There is linking alliteration between every line except ll. 21–22 (though see below), where there is, however, compensatory alliteration in l. 21 (see Kelly 1973: 5, also quoted in Carney 1981: 261), and internal alliteration in most lines. There is occasional complex alliteration (Sproule 1987) and an instance of compound alliteration (*cathchlessu*, l. 19) (see Stifter 2018: 228), and interlaced alliteration occurs throughout. Beginning in l. 15 with an alliterating series on *c*, *l* and *n* are introduced and then *m* and *r*, followed by a return of the (now voiced) guttural (*g*). In l. 16 *m*, *r*, and *g* return and *t* is introduced as the initial alliterating sound moves to *m* and then to a vowel, after which *r* returns, *g* reappears as the next initial alliterating sound, and *l* and *n* then recur. The three sounds *g/c-l-n* thread ll. 17–20 (*Gaileoin/a gein Loga soalta/soí frit churad cathchlessu/a Chú Chulaind*) in an interlaced fashion, enabling the alliterative series to pivot to another without a break in the chain. From *g-l-n* the pattern moves to *g-n*; *l* then returns, after which the chain moves back to its starting point on *g*. A new consonant (*s*) is then introduced, after which *l* returns once again before the new alliterative link on *s* is established in the following line (*soí*). The sounds *r* and *t* (*frit*) then reappear and are repeated after the (again voiceless) guttural returns (*churad*), followed by a return of *l* and *s*. As alliteration continues on *c* with a repetition of l. 15, the alliterating initial moves to *b* with a return of *r* and *t*, followed by a return of *s* and *l* (perhaps compensating for the lack of ordinary linking alliteration between these lines). Similarly, the same groups of sounds recur and recede and again

18

reappear in an interlaced manner throughout the remainder of the poem so that alliteration continues unbroken and individual words resonate with each other through alliterative echo.

§4.   Cú Chulainn responds to Lebarcham by reminding her that he is not the only warrior in Ulster. This poem is structured in lines of three to five stresses each. Like Lebarcham's poem, it uses alliteration to emphasize its point, especially through the alliterative chain in the final line. There is internal alliteration in every line and linking alliteration between every line except the final two, where internal alliteration compensates (Carney 1981: 261). There is interlaced alliteration throughout, in which the sounds *d-m* (*dím*) appearing between two alliterating words (vowel plus *n*: *-an, ingen*) in the first line return in the following line after a continuation of alliteration on *n* and *r* (*óenur...do-miul-sa*); *d* and *r* return after introduction of *c* and *b* (*Chonchobuir cóiced*); *c, b,* and *d* return in *cíabo bidbu*; and *im-, n,* and *d* return (*imnedach, ní imgén*), followed by a recurrence of *r, d,* and *m* in the next line as a new alliterating sound (*s*) is introduced, leading to a final chain alliterating again on an initial vowel and repeating *im-* twice.

§5.   In contrast with Lebarcham, Níab incites Cú Chulainn by taunting him. This poem is structured in lines of two or three stresses each with linking or compensatory alliteration between every line and frequent internal alliteration.

§6.   Cú Chulainn's poem in response to Níab consists of four lines of two or three stresses each with both linking and internal alliteration in every line (assuming that *ro-* in the first line was considered prevocalic). Line 54 displays complex alliteration and l. 51 displays complex, chiastic alliteration or "inverse echo" (Travis 1944: 95),[6] also termed mirrored alliteration (De Vries 2015). The poem also employs syntactic parallelism. The verbal position in the final two lines in Tmesis II (Greene 1977) yields parallel sentences with trisyllabic cadences (though in the first line the subject is interposed and in the second line the object is interposed). Here as elsewhere such parallelism can emphasize the message (see Carney

---

[6] Quoted in Bisagni (2019: 178). Another example can be seen in ll. 102–103.

1981: 259, where he remarks that in *Félire Óengusso* "syntactic and verbal parallelism…connotes emphasis and intensity").

§7.   Cú Chulainn's poem on his ominous faulty brooch is structured in lines of two to three stresses each (except for the final line with four stresses) with linking alliteration between almost every line. Where linking alliteration is lacking, there is compensatory internal alliteration. In two instances—ll. 63–64 (*scánfaiter fuidb/scarad fáebuir*) and ll. 68–69 (*día már/des Maig*)—linking alliteration takes the form of what Carney (1981: 259) refers to as crossed alliteration, citing examples from the seventh-century poem *Tiughraind Bhécáin* (Kelly 1975: 70). This device is termed paired alliteration by Hollo (1990: 78–79), who provides additional examples. There is complex alliteration linking ll. 58–59 (*bratt/beres*) and ll. 59–60 (*robud/bidba*) and in l. 62 (*tria thraigid*) and l. 63 (*scíath for scánfaiter*). Interlaced alliteration appears throughout. Syntactic parallelism also links the first two pairs of lines.

§9.   Cú Chulainn's poem addressed to Líath Macha is structured in lines of two or three stresses each with linking alliteration between every line and some internal alliteration. There is complex alliteration linking ll. 80–81 (*Líath/leithe*) and in l. 82 (*fechuir fiach*), l. 85 (*mmuige mag*), and l. 90 (*suidmis suide*). Asyndeton in ll. 87–89 reflects and reinforces the passage's meaning as Cú Chulainn describes the dismantled chariot.

§10.   Lebarcham's second poem to Cú Chulainn consists of lines of mostly two or three stresses each with linking alliteration between every line and some internal alliteration. If *dano* in l. 110 represents a later interpolation, all lines follow the two- to three-stress pattern. (The gloss *nó cichme* appears above the line in the manuscript.) There is complex alliteration in l. 101 and linking ll. 101–102 (*gartach do gruad/goirthech*) and ll. 103–104 (*cnedach/caín*), and verbal echo and complex, chiastic alliteration link ll. 102–103 (*caíngnúis/do gnúis cnedach*). There is also verbal echo in the link between ll. 105 and 106 (*mairgfem/Mairg*), preceding a series of three lines joined through syntactic parallelism. Interlaced alliteration occurs throughout the poem. Beginning with *n* in the first line (l. 98), the sound pattern proceeds through *f-c*, with *c* providing linking alliteration with the following line. This line's final word

20

introduces the consonant *l* and then returns to *n*. The *l* recurs unstressed in the first word of the following line (*fíal*), a link strengthened by stressed linking alliteration with the first line (*fácaib*/*fíal*).[7] The consonant *n* from the first line thus recurs in the second, and the consonant *l*, appearing as a new strand between *c* and *n* in the second line, recurs in the third. After introduction of the voiced dental *d*, the guttural consonant returns voiced, along with a recurrence of *n* (*gnúis*), both providing simple linking alliteration with the following line (*gartach*) and participating as a pivot in the complex alliteration (*g-r-t*) in that line and the next, which again returns to guttural plus *n* (*caíngnúis*). Meanwhile, the voiced and voiceless dental sounds introduced in ll. 100 (*do*) and 101 (*gartach do*) thread through the following lines to emerge in l. 104 as the stress-bearing alliterating sound in the next chain (*tocad*), which also returns to *c* and then *r* before resuming (*tocad ardo díth*/*dubae dia*). After the next consonant (*m*) is introduced, *r* and *g* return, the three sounds echoing over the following three lines as syntactic parallelism pauses the poem's motion to heighten the expression of grief. After the final line in this series introduces *s*, it reverts to *l* (*súle*) before linking with the following line through alliteration on *s*; *r*, *d*, and *g* return (*sír do guba*, also echoing *dubae* from l. 105) and then *m* (*múiche*) before the pattern returns to an alliterative chain on *c*/*ch* (*cichsi*). *M* and *r* return interlaced with *c* (*céim rígairech*) as this alliterative chain continues to *d*, itself interlaced in the series before appearing as an initial alliterating sound (*rígairech*/*don chath ara mbebat airdde*/*díe*). *M* and *r* again reappear to initiate another complex alliterative series (*mór*/*Maige Murthemne*) before *d*/*t* and *s* return to close the poem.

§11.   Cú Chulainn's poem addressed to Lóeg consists mostly of five lines of two stresses each exhibiting syntactic parallelism and internal

---

[7] In the *retoiric* in *Aided Chonchobuir*, alliteration skips over a vocative phrase (Corthals 1989a: 54). See also Schrijver (2005: 94, 95, 99) on omission of the vocative for purposes of stress count and alliteration in *roscada* passages in the *Táin*. Here, as elsewhere in this text, the vocative phrase is part of the metrical structure; it displays linking alliteration with its previous line and its stress count aligns with the rest of the poem. However, the alliteration between two unstressed sounds may not be acceptable for linking alliteration with the following line. The admissibility of omission of a vocative phrase, combined with the presence of interlaced alliteration linking the three lines, perhaps enables the initial alliterative link between *fácaib* and *fíal* to be heard more strongly.

(sometimes complex) alliteration in every line as well as linking alliteration between almost every line.

§12.   Cú Chulainn's prophetic speech before death may be analyzed in lines of two or three stresses each with linking alliteration between almost every line and frequent internal alliteration and syntactic parallelism. In the few instances where linking alliteration is lacking, there is compensatory internal alliteration, verbal echo (*ní ciat súli/ní nád aiccet*, ll. 154–155), or crossed alliteration with syntactic parallelism (*bith dáer a acille/bid dorcha a amser*, ll. 195–196). Lack of ordinary linking alliteration after this couplet is perhaps compensated for by alliteration between the initial stressed sound of l. 196 and the initial sound of l. 197 (whether *togáethfaid* or earlier *do-gáethfa*). Complex alliteration links ll. 156–157 (*sírechtach/sercfid*), ll. 159–160 (*fír fer/forgoba*), ll. 187–188 (*comarbae/cumachta*), ll. 192–193 (*gand gein/gignithar*), and ll. 217–218 (*fair/i forciund*) and appears in l. 159 (*fír fer*), l. 170 (*la dulu dílúba*), l. 182 (*chuirp crí*), l. 186 (*tríuin tormaid*), and l. 192 (*gand gein*). Interlaced alliteration appears in ll. 130–132, 137–139, 162–167, 175–177, 209–211, and 213–216.

The long alliterative chain in ll. 149–150 (*díchra aige/eblas eirr óencharpait*) reinforces the sense of the chariot-fighter's intensity. In addition, the two successive lines of internal alliteration (as well as interlaced alliteration) in ll. 163–164 (*ro sía dígail díriuch/lorg Léith Macha*) call greater attention to the event of Líath's wounding and pivot to another topic. The poem also shifts phrase and sentence length to vary the semantic rhythm and pivot to another theme. For example, the series of single, two-stress parallel phrases in ll. 201–212 pivots through a sentence straddling two lines (ll. 213–214) while maintaining linking alliteration as the topic moves from violence and materialism to deceit and treachery.

Lines 222–223 constitute a rhyming couplet with irregular syllable count. Lines 224–227 constitute a quatrain in *rannaigecht* (5^2 6^1 5^1 6^1). See Breatnach (1991: 203–204) for use of syllabic poetry in combination with stressed nonrhyming verse.

§14.   Cú Chulainn's reply to Lóeg is structured in lines of two to three stresses each with linking alliteration between every line, internal alliteration in l. 251, compound alliteration in l. 250, and verbal echo between ll. 252 and 253 (*remi-tuit a ré/ar mo-thuittet*). There is complex alliteration in l. 251 (*clár clé cleithe*) and ll. 252–253 (*remi-tuit a ré/ar mo-thuittet*) and interlaced alliteration throughout.

§15.   This later descriptive passage is heavily alliterative.

§16.   This later poem exhibits alliteration, syntactic parallelism (*mairg...suthchern*, l. 280), and tmesis (*imma- nár néoil -slecht*, l. 283).

§28.   This rhymed syllabic poem consists of stanzas with the following metrical structure:
  1. *deibide* 7/1, 7/2, 7/1, 7/2, followed by a rhyming couplet 7/1, 7/3
  2. *deibide* 7/1, 7/1, 7/1, 7/1, followed by a rhyming couplet 7/1, 7/3
  3. *rannaigecht* 7/3, 7/3, 7/3, 7/3
  4. *deibide* 7/1, 7/2, 7/2, 7/1
  5. *deibide* 7/1, 7/2, 7/1, 7/2

§31.   Conall Cernach's poem addressed to Líath Macha is structured in lines of mostly two or three stresses with linking alliteration between almost every line and frequent internal and complex alliteration. There is interlaced alliteration throughout.

§37.   Cú Chulainn's three poems after his death—§37, the poem on St. Patrick's arrival; §38, *Síaburchobra Con Culaind*; and §39, *De Adventu Christi*—are connected through linking alliteration (*Emain/Úaine*, ll. 519–521; *Cride/Críst*, ll. 547–549). In their use of varying syllabic structure and of occasional rhyme, these poems may resemble Hiberno-Latin verse compositions such as *Precamur patrem* (see Lapidge 1985: 116 and Stevenson 1999: 343).

The poem in §37 consists of lines of mostly six, seven, or eight syllables arranged in couplets (*leis* in l. 515 may represent a later addition). There is a rhyming couplet of eight-syllable lines at ll. 512–513. Most end words alliterate with their preceding words and some also with their following

23

lines (e.g., *Eoraip Elpae/Di-uiscebthar*, ll. 511–512; *Succet sáiliu gil/Gigsit*, ll. 513–514). In ll. 510–511 (*trebfait íathu Emna/Ticfat de Eoraip*), crossed alliteration replaces ordinary linking alliteration. Linking alliteration is lacking between ll. 512 and 513, ll. 516 and 517, and ll. 517 and 518 (*frim/anair*); however, there is compensatory internal alliteration in each line (complex in ll. 513 and 517). In addition, many lines exhibit alliteration between the first stressed word and the following word or phrase on either a stressed or an unstressed syllable (e.g., *oll olleith*; *talcind trebfait*; *slúagaib Succet*; *gigsit co*; *alchél coton-*). Interlaced alliteration appears throughout.

§38.   This poem is structured mostly in six-syllable lines with disyllabic endings and occasional end-rhyme—for example, *ngubae/subae* (ll. 531–532) and *iliu/firu* (ll. 525–526), with rhyme between palatal and nonpalatal medial consonants, for which see Carney (1971)—and internal rhyme (*óen/lóeg*, ll. 525–526), concluding with a quatrain of seven-syllable lines. The poem is also fused with (often complex) alliteration, and interlaced alliteration is frequent throughout. Most lines exhibit line-internal alliteration, and there is linking alliteration between almost every line. From l. 521 to l. 522 and l. 523 to l. 524, linking alliteration skips over the repeated word (in the vocative) *Emuin*. Where linking alliteration is lacking, there is compensatory alliteration. The first several lines are further linked through syntactic parallelism and repetition. Two repeated lines (l. 521 repeated in l. 527 and l. 528 repeated in l. 537) perhaps set off units of the poem.

§39.   This poem is organized into five stanzas. The first consists of lines of ten or eleven syllables each (ten each if *dún* in l. 552 is the result of dittography), with imperfect rhyme between the end-words of the second and fourth lines. The stanza could also be arranged in shorter lines with a syllable count of 4/6/5/5/6/4/5/5, with rhyme (of unstressed final syllables, for which see Carney 1971) between the end-words of ll. 3 and 4 and of ll. 7 and 8 and consonance between the end-words of ll. 1 and 2. In the second stanza, there are either eight or six (with elision of *a* and with *nia* treated as monosyllabic) syllables in the first line; nine syllables each in the second and fifth lines, each of which can be divided into cola of four and five syllables; and twelve syllables each in the third and fourth lines. There

24

is rhyme (of unstressed final syllables) between the end-words of ll. 555 and 556. The third stanza consists of lines of mostly twelve syllables each. If *foirm* in l. 560 was originally a dative plural (*foirmib*) and *chumachta* in l. 563 originally accusative singular (*chumacht*), all lines are of twelve syllables. The stanza could also be divided into shorter lines of six syllables (given the same alterations) with one instance of end-rhyme (*flatha/catha*). The fourth stanza consists of lines of two to four stresses each, four of which are linked through syntactic parallelism of final-verb constructions. The fifth stanza consists of lines of two or three stresses each, most of which are linked by syntactic parallelism.

There is linking alliteration almost throughout the poem; where it is lacking, internal alliteration compensates. In ll. 556–557 (*formdig ingair/fris failtniget*) the alliteration skips over a word in an alliterative chain (see Carney 1981: 259) (also linked through syntactic parallelism), and in ll. 557–558 it skips over a word in a semantic unit (*recht nime/cía rí*). In ll. 574–575, the alliteration is crossed. There is internal alliteration in almost every line, sometimes complex. Interlaced alliteration links the entire first and third stanzas. Under the current line division, there is perhaps *aicill* rhyme between *flatha* and *catha* (ll. 561–562). The poem also employs merism (*fris mbet formdig ingair/fris failtniget, fris ráidfet recht nime*, ll. 556–557), perhaps evoking the encompassing reach of Christian law (see Kelly 1975: 77 for the use of contrasting phrases in *Tiughraind Bhécáin*).

§40.   Emer's lament, comprising three sections (§§40, 42, and 43), displays a combination of metrical patterns and poetic features. The most common patterns are two- or three-stress phrases and cadenced lines of variable length; sometimes a series of short phrases builds momentum leading to a long, cadenced line.[8] Variations in line length may express the

---

[8] See Marlow (2007) for discussion of a lament in Classical Hebrew poetry (the Lament over the River Nile in Isaiah xix: 5–10) that uses parallelism and accumulation of phrases to build momentum toward a conclusion, emphasizing the dramatic effect. In drawing upon an ancient Egyptian literary genre depicting "national distress," this lament is also instructive for its presentation of the breakdown of cosmic order (*Maat*), parallel to Irish *fír*.

emotional turmoil of grief. The lament makes extensive use of parallelism as well as anaphora, and complex alliteration is frequent throughout.

This first section contains seven stanzas organized by topic and structure and joined by linking alliteration. The first stanza, in which Emer expresses grief at seeing Líath Macha without Cú Chulainn, proceeds from four short parallel phrases to two short parallel negative relative clauses and closes with a longer negative relative clause consisting of an alliterative chain ending in a trisyllabic cadence. Where linking alliteration is absent, there is internal alliteration or syntactic parallelism.

The second stanza, describing Cú Chulainn, consists of a single sentence containing three lines of relative clauses in the imperfect tense in nominativus pendens construction followed by their verbal clause. All four lines end in cadences alliterating with their preceding words. Three of the cadences are trisyllabic (one consisting of two words) and two are dependent verbal forms in final-verb construction. The second and third lines exhibit parallel noun and prepositional phrases and verbal tmesis. Each line displays both linking and internal alliteration. Complex alliteration links the second and third lines and is found in the final line.

The third stanza, poignantly describing Cú Chulainn's absence as it would be felt by his horse, contains an introductory sentence, two parallel prepositional phrases, and three parallel sentences beginning with the same verb. Each line ends with a trisyllabic or equivalent disyllabic cadence, most of which alliterate with their preceding stressed words. In the first three lines, the cadence consists of an unstressed word combined with a disyllabic stressed word. Each line also displays both linking and internal alliteration. Word order and alliteration in the first line link Cú Chulainn (*rígeirr*) and Líath Macha (*rí ech úas echaib*) on either end of the connective phrase *sceo bás*, expressing their close bond.

The fourth stanza, describing Emer's experience of her husband, consists of four sentences in the past tense, the first three containing two stresses and in the imperfect tense and the fourth containing four stresses and in the preterite with tmesis. There is internal complex alliteration in the first line (*-benad a bunad*) and a four-word alliterative chain and trisyllabic cadence in the fourth line. There is linking alliteration between all lines except the second and third, where possible alliteration between the final words of each line (along with syntactic parallelism) perhaps compensates.

The fifth stanza, describing Cú Chulainn's fall in battle and the witches responsible, consists of two sentences over five lines of three to six stresses each with a trisyllabic cadence on each line. Again, each line is marked by both internal and linking alliteration. The final three lines show alliteration between the cadence and the preceding word.

The sixth stanza, extolling Cú Chulainn's incomparable valor and honor, contains three sentences over seven lines of four or five stresses each. The first sentence, a question, is marked by a series of alliterative chains. Syntactic parallelism links the following three lines. There is internal alliteration in almost every line, and where linking alliteration is lacking there is compensatory alliteration.

The seventh stanza, narrating the ominous events before Cú Chulainn's death, his encounter with the witches, and his fighting in battle, consists of lines of two or three stresses each with linking alliteration throughout except between the second and third lines, where there is both compensatory alliteration and syntactic parallelism. Complex alliteration links ll. 622–623, 632–633, 636–637, and 638–639. Between ll. 637 and 638 there is crossed complex linking alliteration as well as internal (*deibide*) rhyme between *Dub* and *adbul*. Interlaced alliteration appears throughout.

§42.   Syntactic parallelism and anaphora organize each of this passage's three stanzas. The first stanza (quoted by Bergin 1938: 200 in illustration of final-verb constructions) consists of lines of variable length, most of which end in final-verb cadences alliterating with their preceding words, beginning with either *aprainn* or *dursan* (in alternation) followed by a negative relative clause. Lines ending in nouns (*n-écomlund*, l. 662; *ilairbriu*, l. 663) also alliterate with their preceding words. The second stanza contains three parallel sentences beginning with a past-tense verb followed by a sentence in the present tense. The third contains four sentences beginning with *ba méite* with a verb in the past subjunctive,

27

followed by a sentence in the present tense and three negative sentences in the future tense. In both the second and third stanzas, each line exhibits both linking and internal alliteration. Each line of the third stanza also has a cadence, most of which are trisyllabic (or disyllabic with medial consonant cluster), alliterating with its preceding word or phrase. In addition, linking alliteration binds the three stanzas together.

§43.   Emer's closing poem contains two stanzas. The first consists of lines of variable length, most of which end in a trisyllabic cadence, frequently with (sometimes complex) alliteration between the cadence and its preceding word (*Delguin dílachtai*; *búad bantrochta*; *daltae dígáirsi*). There is linking alliteration between almost every line; where linking alliteration is absent, there is compensatory alliteration. The second stanza consists of lines of three or four stresses joined by linking alliteration. Interlaced alliteration appears throughout the poem.

The tale thus employs a wide range of metrical patterns, sometimes within the same poem. Metrical variation and similarity across and within poems can serve an expressive function. For example, using similar forms for separate poems draws parallels between them, and shifting metrical patterns within a poem can signal a shift in topic. Variations of line and phrase length within the same metrical type can emphasize a passage, heighten emotion, pivot to a new subject, or simply provide shifts in rhythm, to which both poet and audience would have been highly attuned, just as they were sensitive to alliterative variation. According to Bergin (1921/1923), "[W]hat Irish poets aimed at was not identity, but similarity combined with variety" (82).[9]

Expressive use of metrical shifts within a verse passage can also be seen in a so-called *roscad* from the *Táin* discussed by Corthals (1989a, 1989b). Corthals points out that two verse-lines in a meter distinctive from their surrounding text convey the warning the Mórrígan wishes to impart to the black bull of Cúailnge (1989b: 215). Although Corthals considers the surrounding text nonmetrical artistic prose (ibid.), it can also be analyzed as verse, portions of which appear to adhere to the common two-stress

---

[9] See also Tristram 1995.

accentual meter—for example, *"táthum rún ro-fiastar Dub...meldaid slóig scoithnía[b] Boidb. Bó geimnech, feochair fiach..."* (ibid.). The connection of the two lines conveying the secret with the surrounding text through linking alliteration (ibid.) supports this interpretation. Another example of the use of metrical shifts can be found in the legal text *Immathchor nAilella 7 Airt* (Corthals 1995, also discussed in Stacey 2007: 130–134), where changes in meter mark distinct steps in a legal process.

Despite the metrical diversity in Cú Chulainn's death tale, the poems share some stylistic features. For example, several use questions as a rhetorical device (§§3, 5, 10, 12, 39, 40). The poems also frequently use intensive prefixes such as *ath-*, *for-*, *mór-*, *im-*, and *lán-*. The occurrence in several poems of a particularly intricate type of alliteration—here termed interlaced alliteration—also helps establish a consistent poetic style. Too frequent in this text to be accidental but irregular in its occurrence, it may constitute a stylistic feature of its own.[10] In addition, almost all poems that contain vocative phrases (§§4, 5, 9, 10, 11, 37, 38, 40, but not 3) include them in the metrical structure (see footnote 7). And as discussed above, verbal echo links poems together and with the tale's prose sections.

It is tempting to consider the possibility that the tale originally consisted of individual poems, possibly with short prose introductions, as Thurneysen mentions (1921: 549), especially as some of the surviving text's poems narrate partial episodes of the story. And identification of some of the poems by title (e.g., *De Adventu Christi*, *Núallguba Emire*) both in the manuscripts themselves and in later glossaries suggests the possibility of their recognition as independent compositions. However, stylistic consistency, verbal echoes, structural symmetry, and thematic repetition demonstrate that the text as it took shape already in the eighth century (see discussion of possible stages of composition below) must be viewed as a unified, carefully crafted composition.

---

[10] Further investigation may reveal whether this type of alliteration occurs in other texts and, if so, whether it is more common at specific times or in specific genres. Perhaps less widespread poetic devices such as this may help with dating of texts or even serve as distinctive marks of a single composer.

Some of the text's poems are accompanied in the manuscript by the symbol .r., usually interpreted as *retoiric* or *roscad*. The substantial scholarly controversy surrounding these terms has greatly influenced investigation of the literary forms they have been associated with.[11] Once considered artifacts of pre-Christian oral composition, these forms have been clearly demonstrated as literary works of Christian provenance (e.g., Breatnach 1984; Carney 1955; Corthals 1989a). And as McCone points out (1990: 197), poems in Cú Chulainn's death tale that prophesy the arrival of Christianity obviously were composed in a Christian context. Indeed, explicit expression of Christian sentiment in this text occurs only in passages that would be categorized as *retoirics* or *roscada*.

As Corthals (1996) observes, so-called *retoirics* can be considered "adaptations of Latin literary art into the vernacular" (26) and "simply a special form of elevated literary art" (ibid.: 20). Indeed, although poetic features such as "abnormal" word order have sometimes been interpreted as evidence of a deliberately obscure, prophetic style, one need look no farther than classical Latin poetry, with which the early Irish *literati* were very familiar, for abundant examples of expressive, artistic use of word order. Some examples of expressive use of syntax in Cú Chulainn's death tale can be found in §§3, 9, and 40 (see above discussion and metrical analysis).[12]

As Watkins (1963; 1995: 255–264) has shown, *retoirics* may also continue elements of inherited tradition in both content and form. The preservation of Indo-European myth may be seen, for example, in Lebarcham's poem in §3 (see discussion above and textual notes). Continuities of Indo-European metrical forms can also be attributed, however, to the influence

---

[11] As Melia (1990) points out, the symbol .r. may not have stood for a poetic term at all.
[12] Another remarkable example of expressive word order in combination with alliteration in early Irish poetry can be found in the first stanza of Bécán mac Luigdech's poem on Colm Cille *Fo réir Choluimb* (Kelly 1973: 9, l. 2), in which the word order—*find for nimib snáidsium secht* (= *snáidsium find for secht nimib*)—reflects the soul's frightening journey and produces an alliterative series linking words denoting the saint's spiritual protection and the difficult path itself (*snáidsium secht/sét fri húathu…*). The poem is analyzable both syllabically and accentually.

of Latin meters, which imitated Greek meters (Corthals 1996: 28). According to Corthals, early Irish *retoiric* forms may have arisen in imitation of Latin models (ibid.: 36).

Such views of course need not be mutually exclusive. "Native" meters may have evolved under the influence of Latin meters (McCone 1990: 41). In an examination of Celtic versification systems, Stifter (2016) considers "a basic type of stress-counting metres with alliteration" as "the core of an inherited Insular Celtic tradition of versification" (84). Upon this core, both internal developments and external models, such as Latin syllabic poetry, could have exerted influence. As Bisagni (2019) observes with respect to the poetic device of parallelism, both Biblical models and native traditions could have served as sources (182). Biblical models also use verbal echo extensively (Alter 2011).

But regardless of the origins of various metrical forms, as Robin Chapman Stacey (2007: 11–12) has pointed out and as the term *retoiric* itself indicates (if it was indeed associated with particular literary forms), verse passages such as those in this tale were viewed and portrayed as verbal art to be spoken. Furthermore, especially in poetic composition, in which sound patterns serve as structural principles and convey meaning in themselves, written language does not lose its connection to speech. It may thus be beneficial to resist stark oppositions between oral and written. Oral and literate traditions "were in constant contact with each other" (Ní Dhonnchadha 2010: 556), and views of orality and literacy developed in continual negotiation (Nagy 1997).

Especially as the terms *retoiric* and *roscada* at this point often suggest more about ongoing scholarly controversy than about the compositions themselves, this edition refers to all such passages as poems; regardless of their formal origins and diversity, that is what they are. It may be helpful to consider Jakobson's discussion of poetry as language in which the poetic function is dominant—that is, in which the focus is on the message itself. Through the poetic function, "equivalence is promoted to the constitutive device of the sequence" (Jakobson 1960: 356).[13] In early medieval Ireland, a wide variety of metrical types—both syllabic and accentual—and poetic features evidently flourished in a continuum that allowed for experimentation and variation.[14] Critically, as this text and others demonstrate, more than one metrical type may appear in a single poem, and some poems exhibit attributes of both (Breatnach 1991: 203–204).

The complexity of metrical definition need not therefore exclude some compositions from the realm of poetry and assign them to an opposing realm of prose or even artistic prose (*Kunstprosa*, as it is termed by Corthals 1989b: 215), as has been suggested (Bisagni 2019: 198). Indeed, as argued above, such variation can be viewed as an expressive malleability. Adopting adherence to a single meter or metrical pattern as a defining characteristic of poetry or of a category of poetry risks obscuring significant, meaningful forms, techniques, and differences. It may be helpful to distinguish between metrical types or patterns and poetic features on the one hand and the compositions they constitute on the other. In many compositions the two may correspond exactly, but the distinction may further the analysis of poetic passages that combine metrical forms or patterns and/or poetic features. Such analysis may also help identify functions and techniques associated with particular forms and their combination.

It may also be beneficial to resist stark oppositions between verse and prose. Some compositions may be viewed as "transitional" (Jakobson 1960: 369). And as verbal echo and structural symmetry in Cú Chulainn's death tale demonstrate, verse and prose may influence and interact with each other. Further, given the early date of poetic composition in Irish and the use of prosimetrum from the beginning of narrative writing in the vernacular, it is possible that poetic features such as parallelism and verbal echo influenced the development of the early Irish narrative technique of

---

[13] See Bisagni (2019: 187–198), where Jakobson is also cited, for a discussion of definitions and views of poetry in historical perspective.
[14] Stevenson (1999: 341) notes that "both syllabic and accentual verses were flourishing in Ireland by the end of the sixth century, suggesting that early medieval vernacular poets were flexible and tolerant of innovation."

iteration or variation on themes explicated by Ó Cathasaigh (e.g., 1981, 1983). Biblical models, however, may also have sparked these techniques' development directly (see Alter 2011 and McCone 1990).[15]

Probably only comprehensive analysis of the many early Irish poetic forms in their various manifestations may yield the information needed for reliable categorizations and terms. As investigation of these forms continues, one looks forward to a time when early Irish poetic compositions are viewed as less of a puzzle and can be appreciated even more richly as examples of poetic art.

Language, Date, and Composition

Date of Composition: The *L* text appears to present an early eighth-century core that received reworking later in that century or the early ninth century, followed by later Middle Irish updating and interpolation. Instances of early Old Irish features (see below) in both verse and prose passages suggest an original date of composition of at least some portions of the text in the early eighth century. Excerpts quoted in Cormac's Glossary confirm composition of the text no later than the ninth century. In many places, Old and Middle Irish forms, sometimes of the same verb (e.g., *tuitfid* and *do-fáethsad*, ll. 363–364; *fo-thruci*, l. 377, and *fothraicid*, l. 426), appear side by side. Some sections show a greater concentration of Middle Irish forms; even these sections, however, contain some Old Irish and early Old Irish forms, such as suffixed pronouns, preservation of the neuter gender, and pretonic *to-*, pointing to greater expansion and/or updating in these sections rather than entirely new composition (except for passages in §§15 and 16 at least partly replacing earlier *retoiric* material).

Middle Irish forms appearing in some verse passages do not necessarily constitute evidence against composition of these passages at an earlier date as restoration of earlier forms does not disturb the metrical pattern. In fact, such restoration can sometimes improve the metrical pattern, providing alliteration where it has been lost through updating—for example, in §7, l.

---

[15] Berlin (2008) summarizes types of and approaches to Biblical parallelism, citing Kugel's emphasis on progression and difference rather than sameness—"'A, what's more B'" (155)—and observing the effectiveness of the "creative tension between them" (156).

61, where *ad-chumben,* restored from *athchummas*, alliterates with *chness*. In §12, l. 197, *togáethfaid* could be emended to *do-gáethfa* without changing the alliterative pattern. Furthermore, as McCone (1985) explains, some Middle Irish forms are not necessarily to be assigned to dates beyond the Old Irish period.

The appearance of both Old and Middle Irish forms of the same verbs, the appearance of Old Irish and early Old Irish features in both prose and verse sections, and verbal echo between verse passages and between verse and prose passages point to a unified composition. This observation, however, does not exclude the possibility of multiple stages of composition. Indeed, the text appears to present evidence of reworking (both in the Old Irish period and later) of an earlier composition. For example, verse passages display a few instances of what may represent glosses on an earlier text. In §10, l. 109, the gloss *nó cichme* is written above the line. Other possible instances are identifiable only through discontinuities in the metrical pattern. For example, in §38, l. 544, *Conall* may be a gloss clarifying the identity of Cú Chulainn's *chaurchobraid.* Removing this addition yields a metrical pattern that aligns with the following lines (see textual notes). Similarly, in §40, l. 635, *ainmem Líath* may have been added to specify the horse referred to in that line (*co torchair a ech*). In this case, some words appear to have been transposed for metrical reasons to accommodate the gloss (see textual notes), disrupting, however, the possibly original, more intricate alliterative pattern and poetic word order. As the word order presented in *L* appears the same in the corresponding fragment from *H* (no. 51), the change may have been copied from a source in which the glosses and reworking had already been incorporated unrecognizably into the text.

There is also an example of possible misplacement of a line. In §12, l. 183 (*clú im cathu canis-n-immarburt?*) appears in the *L* text between l. 191 (*slab comdetae*) and l. 192 (*gand gein*), where it is clearly out of place in the verse's narrative (see textual notes). Such a misplacement may have arisen in the process of revising or adding to an earlier composition (although it may also be due simply to transcription error). As in l. 635, however, the alteration reveals attention to metrical considerations as the line does display linking alliteration with the preceding line (*comdetae/clú*).

Indications of conscious storytelling, such as references to other Ulster Cycle tales (e.g., the narrator's reference to the *Macgnímrada* in l. 3 and *Aideda Ulad* in ll. 398–399) and comments such as that appearing in ll. 337–338 (*amal at-rubramar remaind*), may also represent additions to the original text. Later Middle Irish forms in some passages, including (as already noted) §§15–16, indicate an additional, later layer of scribal modernization and interpolation. It may be impossible to determine precisely how much reworking has been added to the text as some forms may reflect either new composition or mere updating.

Examples of the preservation of the Old Irish verbal system include the following:

- deponent forms: *-fordámar* l. 1; *-mbúretar* l. 21; *-comathar* l. 42; *con-róetar* l. 52; *líagair* (?) l. 637
- strong preterites: *reraig* l. 402; *sephaid* l. 688; *siachtum* l. 692
- *ro* in "fixed" preverbal position: *-fordámar* l. 1
- *s*-futures: *cichsi* l. 110; *riris* ll. 201, 348; *con-bóssad* l. 674
- earlier relative form of the substantive verb: *file* ll. 9, 381
- early Old Irish pretonic *to-* and *di-* (secured by alliteration): *to-rét* l. 531; *dim-emed* l. 535
- suffixed pronouns: *téite* l. 76; *léicthi* l. 346; *siachtum* l. 692

Examples of later features of the verbal system include the following:

- spread of the *s*-preterite: *ro ling* ll. 55, 94
- simple verbs for earlier compounds: *ro taiscélad* l. 2; *athchummas* (*L*) l. 61; *ro chunnig* l. 294
- narrative use of the augmented preterite: *ro gab* ll. 55, 70; *ro scaíl* ll. 76–77
- formation, with *–(a)ig*, of the denominative verb from the verbal noun: *nom-airfitiged* l. 74
- the 3 sg. present indicative ending *-enn*: *cuirend* l. 269; *-drónand* l. 310
- the 1 sg. copula forms *nídam* l. 38 and *cíabam* l. 51

35

- spread of the *f-* and *é-*futures: *-chunnécha* l. 293; *tuitfid* l. 363; *nom-accfither* l. 679
- spread of the 1 sg. future ending *-at* and 1 sg. present subjunctive ending *-ur*: *aírfat* ll. 333, 356; *-thísiur* l. 374

Early Old Irish Features: Examples include pretonic *to-* and *di-*, secured by linking alliteration in §38 (ll. 531, 535) (with another possible instance in l. 512); final *-th* (*sreith* l. 328); declension of *dún* as an o-stem (l. 579); and, in the rhymed syllabic poem (§28), preservation of final *-o* (l. 417), secured by rhyme.

The syllabic poem in §28 exhibits evidence of composition in the late seventh or early eighth century. For example, in stanza 4, as mentioned, final *-o* in *Temro* is secured by rhyme with *dó*. However, this instance may be due to petrification of a common phrase. In stanza 1, rhyme between *clith* and *Lugthig* could be evidence of composition before voicing of final palatal *-ch*; it could also, however, be a metrical exception, also seen in the rhyme between *forceth* and *fer* in stanza 4. Trisyllabic *Sualtaim* may also provide evidence of an earlier date of composition. In stanza 5, the final *-i* of *Tethbai* (dat. sg. of *Tethbae*) is secured by rhyme with *rí*, providing evidence of composition before the ninth century.

Final Vowels: Except in the syllabic poem in §28, there is no preservation of the distinction between final *-a* and final *-o*; however, final *-(a)e*, *-(a)i*, and *-u* are sometimes preserved.

Definite Article: The neuter article is frequently preserved, with three instances in the nominative and seven in the accusative; exceptions are nominative singular *in biad* (l. 239), accusative *in mbec* (l. 241), nominative *in mag* (l. 304) beside accusative *a mmag* (ll. 456, 459), and nominative *in cend* (l. 501) beside nominative and accusative *a cend* (ll. 497, 498). The plural of the article is represented mostly by *na*; exceptions are two instances of masculine nominative plural *int* (ll. 396, 424) and one instance of masculine genitive plural *inna* (l. 695). There is loss of *-b* in the dative plural of the article before a nonlabial initial: *forna* (l. 3), *forsna* (l. 12), *dona* (ll. 287, 291), *isna* (l. 487) (see McCone 1985: 89–90).

Syntax: Verse passages contain examples of independent datives such as *dígáirsi* (l. 689), *buidnib* (l. 131), *frassaib* (l. 677), and *díb lámaib comlánaib* (l. 650); preposed genitives such as *churad cathchlessu* (l. 19), *Chonchobuir cóiced* (l. 35), and *Cormaic comaitecht* (l. 688); and final-verb constructions such as *nít- charpat Conaill -comathar* (l. 42), *ní- mmo guin -immgabaim* (l. 54), *-comarnic* (l. 650), and *-comairlestar* (l. 651).

The text contains several otherwise unattested words, including the verbal compounds *fris-guin* (l. 30), *con-táilgi* (l. 24), *for-cing* (l. 136), and possibly *di-fen* (l. 172); the nouns *alchél* (ll. 515, 699), *luing* (ll. 545, 686), and *díchimmid* (l. 609); and the adjectives *díairle* (l. 37) and possibly *dílúib* (which might alternatively be a verbal form *di-lúba*; see textual note) (l. 170).

Editorial Procedure
As the text survives only in one manuscript (except for the fragments in H.3.18) and clearly shows more than one stage and time of composition, this edition has not attempted to restore an "original" text, the existence and boundaries of which cannot be determined with certainty. Middle Irish forms and spellings are mostly left beside Old Irish ones. However, where metrical considerations clearly call for it, Old Irish forms are restored. These instances are identified and explained in the textual notes. All emendations for clarity are noted by providing the *L* readings at the bottom of each paragraph. Instances where readings from *H* are adopted are also identified in the textual notes. The *H* fragments are presented in an appendix with translations provided of the first nine fragments (corresponding to the missing portion of the *L* text). Where needed, the edition presents suggested emendations based on the syntactic, semantic, and metrical context. They are intended, however, as proposed solutions rather than certain conclusions.

To the transcript of the *L* text are added punctuation, length marks, word division, and hyphenation of verbal forms and enclitics and after nasalization. Paragraph divisions and line divisions of poems are my own.

Translation

The translation attempts to provide a close rendering of the text in idiomatic, engaging English. Idiomatic Irish phrases are often translated in idiomatic English equivalents, and the historical present is translated in the past tense. At times, words are left untranslated (e.g., some instances of "et" at the beginning of sentences); at others, words or phrases are supplied for clarity (e.g., personal names replacing pronouns). Translations of the poems at times attempt to capture something of the structural principles and sound patterns of the original where possible. In many places where the translation diverges significantly from the original, a more literal translation is provided in the textual notes. More literal renderings may also be arrived at by consulting the glossary. Alternative translations of some passages may be found in the textual notes.

TEXT

1. "...nád fordámar-sa gol ban 7 mac cen etráin forru cosindiu." La sin do-cing in .l. banrígan ara chind 7 tornochtait a cíche friss. Is accu ro taiscélad ar tús cíchi ban do nochtad .i. forna Macgnímradaib 7 oc fastud Chon Culaind i nEmain Macha. Et do-bretha na téora dabcha usci do díbdud a brotha. Et ní
5 tarlaiced a llaa-sin dochum in chatha.

2. "At-chíu ní thic Cú Chulaind úaib indiu, a maccu Calatín, tresin ceird toṡúigthi fil lib," or Lugaid. "Is cían dond fir fil sund ó Dún Chermnai 7 ó Beluch Con Glais 7 ó Themair Lóchra 7 ó Chombur Trí n-Usce beith fri Béolu Menbolg. Is olc in chelg toṡúigthe file lib. Is cían cu tic Cú Chulaind," or
10 Lugaid. "Ticfa úain-ne imbárach." Ro bátar and co arnabárach. Et dolbit clann Chalatín na slúaig im Emain Macha combo óensmúit forloiscthe in Macha uile. Et coro cuired Emuin Macha forsna slúagaib. Et co torchratar na gascid dia n-adlennaib. Et do-breth a mífoclad do Choin Culaind.

3. Conid and as-bert Lebarcham:
15 .R. "At-raí, a Chú Chulaind, comérig.
   Cobairthe Mag Murthemne
   ar firu Galeoin.
   A gein Loga soalta,
   soí frit churad cathchlessu.
20 A Chú Chulaind, comérig
   co mbúretar basa
   lia indrid Murthemni.
   Móra airdi, óic do níth.
   Náchit Cormac cotalgad
25 admuintire i céin Chonchobuir.
   Nít-tá Conall, comnesam
   Cormaic, arndin-nderóemad.
   Ar ní tria gairi
   cot-gní Lugaid lánchlemnas
30 goin fris-gegna gním.
   Gaib immut, a ándrennuig.
   A huí Chathbad, comérig. At-raí."

39

Nít-tá] Ní tá *L*; arndin-nderóemad] ar nin eróemaid *L*; cot-gní] cotob gní *L*;
ándrennuig] andremuig *L*

4. Conid and at-bert Cú Chulaind:
.R. "An dím, a ingen.
35 Ní mm'óenur do-miul-sa Chonchobuir cóiced.
Cíabo bidbu imnedach ní imgén m'óenur
ar is díairle íarna scís mo scís.
Nídam eirr imtholtanach accobrach imgona indiu."

5. Is and at-bert Níab ingen Cheltchair ben Conaill Chernaig:
40 .R. "Deithbir duit-siu ón,
a Chú Chulaind.
Nít- charpat Conaill -comathar.
Cain róg renar ar Ultaib?
I n-áthaib búaderthaib -bíth
45 conid úanchend airm inid accid
ar ní imgonat na aill.
Ní gním ní chenae
acht a fíthis móir
meic Amairgin."

Cain] caín *L*; imgonat] imgonaid *L*

50 6. "A ben ém," ar Cú Chulaind.
"Cíabam trú-sa ním-tharraid cubés.
Con-róetar m'ainech.
Ním- ág -archelad.
Ní mmo guin -immgabaim."

55 7. Íar sin ro ling Cú Chulaind fora gaisced. Et ro gab fathi immi. In cétna fathi
ro gab immi ro meth fair co torchair a delg asa láim. Conid and at-bert Cú
Chulaind:
.R. "Ní bidba bratt
beres robud.
60 Is bidba delg
ad-chumben chness
co tuitt tria thraigid

40

scíath for scánfaiter fuidb
scarad fáebuir
65 fri desláim mo duirn.
Mos-baim fuil n-anabaid
créchtnaigfit formnai fer.
Airchisfither día már
des Maig Murthemni dim és.”

ad-chumben] athchummas *L*; n-anabaid] anabaid *L*

70 8. Íar sin ro gab a fathi immi. Et ro gab a scíath co fáebur chondúala fair.
Conid and at-bert fri Lóeg mac Riangabra, “Innill dún, a phobba Laíg, in
carpat.” “Tongu do día a tonges mo thúath,” or Láech, “cía no beth cóiced
Conchobuir immon Líath Macha nís-tibritis dochum in charpait. Ní erbart frit
cosindiu. In menma nom-airfitiged do grés ní hé dom-riacht. Maso áil duit tair
75 féin da acallaim ind Léith fadessin.”

9. Téite Cú Chulaind a dochum. Et ro impa int ech a chlé friss fo thrí. Et ro
scáil in Mórrígu in carpat issind aidchi remi ar nírbo áil lé a dul Con Culaind
dochum in chatha. Ar ro fitir noco ricfad Emuin Macha afrithisi. Conid de as-
bert Cú Chulaind frisin Líath Macha:
80 .R. “Níbu gnáth, a Léith,
leithe for clé frim.
Fechuir fiach fondat-gaib
im gním do-tluchemar éc.
Ní thintlaig mo menma
85 i mmuige mag
diandot-imrédinn cíana.
Éssi derga imchíana,
eich sceo ruith scarad
creta cungai fortche
90 forsa suidmis suide.
Suilig rodon-baí
Badb i nEmuin Macha. Níbu gnáth.”

leithe] lithe *L*; fondat-gaib im] fonat gaibim *L*; do-tluchemar] donothlogmar
L; thintlaig] thintla *L*; diandot] dianot *L*

10. La sodain do-dechaid in Líath Macha co tarlaic a bolgdéra móra fola fora díb traigthib. La ssin ro ling Cú Chulaind in carpat et do-curidar bedg de fodes
95 íar Sligi Midlúachra. Co n-accai in n-ingin ara chind .i. Lebarcham ingen Auae 7 Adarci, .i. mug 7 cumal, ro boí i tig Conchobuir, i. Auae 7 Adarc. Conid and as-bert Lebarcham:
.R. "Nán-fácaib, nán-fácaib,
a Chú Chulainn.
100 Fíal do gnúis.
Gartach do gruad.
Goirthech caíngnúis
do gnúis cnedach.
Cain in tocad ardo díth
105 dubae dia mairgfem?
Mairgg ar mná.
Mairg ar maccu.
Mairg ar súle.
Sír do guba múiche. (*nó cíchme*)
110 Cichsi dano céim rígairech
don chath ara mbebat airdde.
Airchisfither díe mór
Maige Murthemne dit éis."
Et cumma as-rubairt-si 7 as-bertatar na trí coícait ban baí i nEmuin Macha ó
115 guth mór.

Cain] Caín *L*; ara-mbebat] ara mbebad *L*; airdde Airchisfither díe] airdde díe *L*; Cichsi] cichseo *L*

11. "Ba ferr ná fácbaitis," ar Lóeg, "ar iss ed náro śáraigis cosindiu nert ceníuil do máthar."
"Acc amae," ol Cú Chulaind.
"Geib leic, Loíg.
120 La araid airitiud.
La errid imdegail.
La cunnid comairle.
La firu ferdacht.
La mná mifre.
125 Tair rium don chath.
Ná frithái l in n-airchisecht nachit-chobradar."

To-ssuíther in carpat éis for desel. La sin do-beir in banchuire gáir guil 7 golgaire 7 bosschaire. Ro fetatar nícon ricfed co Emuin Macha.

ferr] fer *L*

12. Béochobra Con Culaind isind ló fúair bás:
130 "It brónaig banchuiri
  buidnib dér
  diar n-apthaib di maigib
  díe dall.
  Fríth fo-n-úair
135 fas-cíurat ceirn
  co for-cingiu dinn drisib.
  Rot-bith-mairg ro fáthatar
  flathi fer
  íar mbuntáib bethad.
140 Gamain íath
  imm-derga éssi.
  Ammiti túathcháecha
  táircébat mo milliud.
  Mór n-Ulad atom-chuínfet.
145 Con-cechalsat búada
  a n-at-mbélat eslabrai
  a baccaib ráth.
  Randfaider domun deslámaib.
  Díchra aige
150 eblas eirr óencharpait
  ét im thúaith
  téora forránu.
  Fo-nena níthu.
  Ní cíat súli
155 ní nád aiccet.
  Aithguba sírechtach
  sercfid brú
  in churad ó ingnasaib.
  Con-coillfither fír fer—
160 forgoba óenfir,
  écomluind ili.

Eter dá roth
ro sía dígal díriuch
lorg Léith Macha.
165 Mairg ét i ssídib.
Sies ingantu adderga
úane urchraide.
Nós níbu thais
arcu ech n-aignech
170 la dulu dílúba.
Ata-bíu-sa fri écraitiu aithber.
Aithber íarum díthide
lathe Maige
Murthemni atharda.
175 Íba srúaim
sruthbarr slán
lam brond begdolb crú.
Íar feis nom-fothraicfe
níth nemnech
180 nél sorcha somlas
sémite fuile
form chuirp crí.
Clú im cathu canis-n-immarburt?
Bibsaitir cretta fuidbechta.
185 Fúaim talman
tríuin tormaid.
Ecnaithi ad-rainnfet comarbae
cumachta beca.
Bérthair i th'aimserdaib
190 díth slabrae,
slab comdetae.
Gand gein
gignithar gair
ría ndomuin díth.
195 Bith dáer a acille.
Bid dorcha a amser.
Togáethfaid sochaide.
Soífid iliu.
Is é ro fiastar

200 i mbo cen athfír.
　　Riris goí.
　　Cloífid fír.
　　Fessair cathu.
　　Carcair airchind,
205 imdibe ball,
　　brisiud cnáma,
　　cumma tuinne,
　　todlach súla,
　　sáebrechta úabair,
210 ór urraib,
　　arget ar crannaib,
　　gemma a leccaib.
　　Línfait saint
　　sléibe glainithe.
215 Gressach taircsiu,
　　sáer díamlad.
　　Ar ro-fessamar fair
　　i forciund a dála.
　　Lathe dia mbáidfider
220 bith móras doíne dúib
　　dúile dia cennach.

　　Acht adraid in mac cona recht.
　　Is ferr dúib co fa ṡecht.
　　Os mé im úabor
225 imma-rordus a leic.
　　Do-génaind bad ḟerr
　　a ro mbeth mad cet bith.
　　It brónaig."

Íar sin túargabtar in banchuire gáir guil 7 golgaire ar ro fetatar nách ricfad co
230 Ulto Cú Chulaind.

fas-cíurat ceirn] fascíugrat ceirm *L*; for-cingiu] forcingi *L*; bethad] bethaed *L*;
imm-derga] imderga *L*; n-Ulad] Ulad *L*; a n-at-mbélat] at-mbélat *L*; óenfir]
oenfer *L*; nós] noes *L*; Maige] Mag *L*; sruthbarr] sruthborr *L*; brond] broind *L*;
sémite] sémide *L*; crí/ Clú im cathu canis-n-immarburt/bibsaitir] cribsaite *L*;

45

ad-rainnfet] adrainfet *L*; comdetae/Gand] comdetae clú im cathu canis nimarburt gand *L*; ndomuin] ndomun *L*; Is é] hé *L*; todlach] tadlach *L*; díamlathat] diamlaid ar

13. Ro boí tech a mumme rod-n-alt-som ara chind forint ṡligid taidled-som beos in tan na théiged fora érim secci fades 7 aness. Lestar co ndig lee-si ara chind-som do grés. Ibid dig 7 do-cumlai ass 7 celebraid dia mummi. Téit ass íar Sligi Midlúachra íar Maig Mogna. Co n-accai ní na téora ammiti
235 túathcháecha ara chind forint ṡligid. Orce co nemib 7 epthaib fo-noíset for beraib cáirthind. Ba do gessib Con Culaind cen adall fulachta dia chathim. Geiss dó dano carna a chomanma do ithi. Rethid 7 ba do dul seccu. Ru fitir níbu 'c dénam a lessa ro bass and. Conid de as-bert friss ind ammait, "Tadall latt, a Chú Chulaind." "Ní adliub ém," ol Cú Chulaind. "Até in biad cú," ol sí.
240 "Diambad fulocht mór no beth and," or sí, "ro adelta. Úair is bec fil and ní thaidle. Ní túalaing mór nád fulaing nó nád geib in mbec." Ata-ella-som íarum 7 to-n-indnaig ind ammait leithi in chon dó assa láim chlí. Ad-etha Cú Chulaind íarum assa láim 7 da-mbeir fo ṡlíasait clí. Ind lám rod-n-gab 7 int ṡlíasait fo tarat ro gabtha ó chund co fond conná rabi a nnert cétna indib.

rod-n-gab] rod gab *L*

245 14. Do-cumlat ass íarum íar Sligi Midlúachra timchell Sléibe Fúait fades. Conid and as-bert Cú Chulaind fri Lóeg, "Cía facca dún, a phopa Loíg?" Conid de as-bert Lóeg, "Troich imda 7 mórchoscuir." "Fé amae," ol Cú Chulaind.
"Fúaim immairic,
250 eich dubderga comrethi,
clár clé cleithe
remi-tuit a ré
ar mo-thuittet eich i fochluib.
Fé. Cían ad-ráigsemar
255 messchuiru fer nÉrend."

cleithe] clithi *L*; ré] rae *L*

15. In tan do-chuaid Cú Chulaind for Sligid Midlúachra fodess co 'mma-n-accai dó 7 a ndúnad boí i mMaig Murthemne. Is and as-bert Erc mac Carpri:

46

.R. At-chíu-sa sund carpat cóem crichid cumtachglan co pupaill úanicda co
mórsaide do chlessaib cliss gascid i carput chaín chlessamna colgatchaín. Is
260 amlaid atá in carpat-sain for dá n-echaib cendbeca cruindbeca corrbeca,
crúeich bedgaich bolgsróin bolgroisc uchtlethnai brondlethnai. Cidat cuibdi
comríata inn echrad-sin nídat comdatha. Indala ech díb luglíath lémnech
maignech tairngech torandchlessach stúagmar fótmar focursid. Int ech aile
immurgu círdub cennand brúmár co mbrúaib duba dorchaide. Dá chuing ardda
265 forórda foraib. Fuil fer findcass foltlebor issin charput-sin. Luinech derg
daigerda na láim ar derglassad. Énblaith (.i. lón gaile) etarlúamnach úasa erra
óencharpait. Folt dúalach trí ndatha fair .i. folt dond ra tuind cind, folt cróderg
íar n-irmedón, mind órda ra tuigedar díanechtair. Caín cocarus in chind 7 ind
fuilt-sin co cuirend téora imsrotha de immo chend. Comba samalta ra tétaib
270 órsnáid dar or n-indeóna fo láim suad saincherda ná ra buiderad ris taitni grían
i llathi samrata i mmedón mís maí taídlech cecha fadmainni d'fuilt ind óclaig-
sin.

óencharpait] óenchairpait L; cuirend] uirend L

16. "A séin chucund. In fer-sin, a firu Érend, no frithalid." Turgabad fert
fótbaig fo Erc mac Carpri in tan-sin. Et do-ringintea lébend scíath imbe. Et
275 do-rónta trí catha cróda comchóire do feraib Érend in tan-sin 7 at-bert Erc,
"Frithalid, a firu Érend, in fer-sin .i. Coin Culaind," 7 ro ráid na bríathra-sa:
.R. "Comérgid, a firu Érend. At-raígid. Fil sund Coin Culaind costodach
coscarach claidiubderg. Iraichlid, eraichlid. Airégid. Íactbatir cind de sein.
Ailfitir aichthi. Cosc n-admait dítnui taclaid fert fair. Óenni sin amáin mac Dé
280 mac duini. Mairg mindóene, mairg séis, mairg sreith, mairg suthchern. Aid-
gén in flaith, flaith findnélach fornélach fossad fíchda fírchlich feromail ra
hart in domuin dédenaig. Boí dano noí mís fo chleith ingeni détlai bunaid.
Machait Macha imma- nár neóil -slecht. Mairc ro chaith slecht. Bud adbur
anmich airchind dia-n-tic. Do-cer Cú. Comérgid. Comérgid."

taclaid fert] taclaid ferg L; íactbatir] íachtbadir L; détlai] détlaind L; machait]
machit L; do-cer Cú] ba cher Cúa L

285 17. "Cinnas fuirechlem? Cinnas aurisfemmar clessu?" ol firu Érend. "Ní
andsa. Is í mo chomairli-si dúib," ol Erc, "na cethri chúicid filet sund di
chóicedaib Érend dénid óenbuidin díb 7 óenchlár dona scíathaib immon
mbuidin-sin anúas 7 immacúairt 7 foraib. Et tabraid triar cacha arda immon

47

mbudin-sin 7 días oc imessarcain do neoch as tressiu dont ślúag 7 cáinte co
290 culluaisc accu co rragbat álgis dia gaí-seom féin .i. Blad ar Bladaib a ainm-
side 7 dano co rragbat álgis dona gaib indlithib do-lléicter fair beus. Atá i
tairngere dia gaí-seom rí do marbad de mani gabthar álgis de. Et tabraid gáir
guil 7 éigmi. Ní géba in fer ara bruth 7 forbruth na n-ech. Et ní chunnécha
comlund chucaib amal ro chunnig oc tánai bó Cúalnge." Do-gníther aní-sin
295 amal ro rádi Erc.

álgis dia gaí] álgis dia gaíb *L*; do-lléicter] dolléicther *L*

18. Do-tháet trá Cú Chulaind dochum na buidni 7 do-rat na trí torandchless
forsin carpat .i. torandchless cét 7 torandchless trí cét 7 torandchless trí nónbur
do urscartad na slóg di Maig Murthemni. Tánic Cú Chulaind cusin mbudin 7
gabaid glés n-immberta a airm forru. Is cumma no imbred na gaí 7 in scíath 7
300 in claideb 7 na clessa comtar lir gainem mara 7 renna nime 7 drúcht cétamuin
7 lóa snechta 7 bommand ega 7 dulli for fidbaid 7 budi for Bregmaig 7 fér fo
chossaib grega i lló samraid a lleithchind 7 a llethchloicne 7 a llethláma 7 a
llethchossa 7 a cnáma derga comscáilte íarna n-esrédiud fo Mag Murthemni
et ropo líath in mag-sin dia n-inchinnib íarsin tress díberge-sin 7 imberta arm
305 do-rat Cú Chulaind forru.

19. Íar sin co n-acca in dís ocond immessorgain cena n-etarscarad. "Is mebol
duit, a Chú Chulaind, cen etargaire na déssi-se," ar in cáinte. La sin trá ro
thairling Cú Chulaind chucu 7 do-beir buille dia durn i cend chechtar de co
tánic a n-inchind dara clúasaib 7 dara srónaib immach. "Da-rónais a n-
310 etargaire," or in cáinte. "Ní drónand nechtar de olc ria chéile." "Ní betis na
tost tria impide forru," ar Cú Chulaind. "In gaí-sin dam-sa, a Chú Chulaind,"
or in cáinte. "Tongim-se a tonges mo thúath nách mó a ríchtu a lessa duit-seo
andás dam-sa. Ataat fir Érend form sund 7 atú forro dano." "Not-aírub-sa dano
mani thuca," ar in cáinte. "Nírom-áerad-sa dano riam i cinaid mo
315 drochthidnacuil nó mo dothchernais." La sodain ro díbairg in ngaí dó 's a
urlond reme co ndechaid triana chend 7 coro marb nónbur friss anall.

20. Do-dechaid Cú Chulaind triasin mbuidin co forcend. La sin ro gab Lugaid
mac Con Ruí in tres ngaí n-indlithe ro boí oc maccaib Calatín. "Cráet do-fáeth
don gaí-seo, a maccu Calatín?" ar Lugaid. "Do-fáeth rí din gaí-sin," or meic
320 Calatín. Íar sin ro theilg Lugaid in ngaí forsin carpat co tarlai i lLáeg mac
Riangabra co tarlaic a mbuí do innib ina medón co rrabi for fortchi in charpait.

48

Is andsin ro ráid Láeg, "Goirt rom-gáet." Íar sin trá do-beir Cú Chulaind in ngaí ass 7 celebraid Lóeg. Conid and at-bert Cú Chulaind, "Bam eirr-se 7 bam ara isind lathiu-sa indiu."

325 21. In tan ro siacht Cú Chulaind co forcend na buidni co n-accai in diis oc imessorgain ara bélaib 7 cáinte co culluaisc oca. "Is mebol duit," ol indala fer, "a Chú Chulaind, cen etairgaire etruind." La sin tarblaing Cú Chulaind chuccu 7 sreith cechtar de a leth co nderna brosnaig ndiib immon carraic ro boí ina farrad. "In gaí-sin dam-sa, a Chú Chulaind," ol in cáinte. "Tongu-sa a tonges 330 mo thúath ní mó ríchtain a lessa in gaí duit-siu oldaas dam-sa. Cethri chóicid Érend form láim 7 form gail 7 form gaisced do aurscartad di Maig Murthemni isind ló-sa indiu." "Nott-aírub-sa," ol in cáinte. "Ní dlegar dím acht óenáilgis isind ló-sa 7 dano ro íccus do chind m'enig indiu chena." "Aírfat-sa Ultu it chinaid-siu," ol in cáinte. "Níra áertha ém riam," ol sé, "i cin mo díbe-se nách 335 mo dothchernais. A mbec ara-thá didiu dom ṡácgul-sa ní aírfaither issind lathiu-sa indiu." Do-bert Cú Chulaind in gaí dó ar urlaind co ndechaid triana chend 7 coro marb nónbur ris aníar et fethid triasin mbuidin amal at-rubramar remaind.

22. Ro gab Erc mac Cairpri in tres gaí indlithi ro boí oc maccaib Calatín. "Cid 340 bias din gaí-seo, a maccu Calatín?" ar Erc mac Carpri. "Ní andsa. Do-fuit rí din gaí-sin," ar meic Calatín. "Ro chúala lib do-faíthsad din gaí ó chíanaib ro léici Lugaid." "Is fír ón ém," or meic Calatín. "Do-rochair rí arad Érend de .i. ara Con Culaind .i. Láeg mac Riangabra." "Tongu-sa a tonges mo thúath ní tét ar guin ríg rod-mbí." La sin do-lléici Erc in gaí fair conid-ecmaing issin 345 Líath Macha. Gataid Cú Chulaind in ngaí ass et celebrais cách dia chéile díb. La sodain léicthi in Líath Macha 7 leth a chunga fo brágit co ndechaid i lLind Léith i Sliab Fúait. Is ass do-dechaid dochum Con Culaind. Is inti dano do-chuaid íarna guin. Conid de as-bert Cú Chulaind, "Riris dá ech óenchuing sund indiu," ol Cú Chulaind.

gaí] gae L; tongu-sa] tongus L; do-dechaid dochum Con Culaind] dodechaid Con Culaind L; Riris dá ech] rires tech L; riris deach H; óenchuing sund] aencuing sunn H; óenchuing sunda L

350 23. La sain at-aig Cú Chulaind a lethchoiss fo chend inna cunga 7 fethid tresin mbudin in n-innas cétna. Co n-acca in dís ocind immesorgain ara chind 7 cáinte co cullisc ocaib. Ros-etarscar íarum 7 nírbo messu int etarscarad do-rat

forru andaas forsin cethrur n-aile. "In gaí-sin dam-sa, a Chú Chulaind," ol in
cáinte. "Ní mó a ríchtain a lessa duit in gaí andás dam-sa." "Not-aírub-sa," ol
355 in cáinte. "Ro íccus dom inchaib indiu. Ní dlegar dam acht óenálgis isind lóu-
sa." "Aírfat-sa Ultu it chinta." "Ro íccus dia n-inchaib," ol sé. "Aírfat-sa do
chenél," or in cáinte. "Tír ém nád ránac-sa riam ní ricfat scéla m'écnaig
remum úair is bec atá dom sáegul." Do-theilg Cú Chulaind in ngaí dó 7 a
urlond reme co ndechaid triana chend 7 tre trí nónboru aile. "Is rath co feirg,
360 a Chú Chulaind," ar in cánti.

fethid] faidid *L*; n-innas] n-inas *L*

24. Íar sin trá luid Cú Chulaind aridisi tresin mbuidin co forcend. Íar sin dano
ro gab Lugaid in tres gaí indlithi ra boí oc maccaib Calatín. "Cid bias din gaí-
seo, a maccu Calatín?" "Tuitfid rí de," ar meic Calatín. "Ro chúala lib do-
fáethsad din gaí ro léci Erc imbúaruch." "Is fír ón," or sé. "Da-rochair rí ech
365 Érend de .i. in Líath Macha." "Tongu-sa a tonges mo thúath ní taít ar guin ríg
rod-bí." La ssin do-lléci Lugaid in ngaí do Choin Culaind co n-ecmoing ind
co tarlaic an ro buí ina broind co rrabi for fortchi in charpait. La sin do-lluid
in Dub Sainglend úad co lleith a chunga co lluid i lLoch nDub i crích
Muscraige Tíre. Is ass do-dechuid dochum Con Culaind. Is and luid aridisi
370 coro fichi in loch la sodain.

25. Íar sain trá tarrasair in carpat a oínur forsin maig. Íar sin at-bert Cú
Chulaind, "Rop áil dam-sa," ol Cú Chulaind, "dul connici in loch ucut d'ól
digi ass." "Is cet lind," ar iat, "acht co tís chucund aridisi." "For-congér-sa
foruib," or Cú Chulaind, "mani thísiur-sa féin co tístai-si armo chend." Íar sin
375 trá ro theclaim inne a brond ina ucht 7 téit ass dochum ind locha. Amal ro-n-
ánic in loch at-aig a láim sethno a brond co fargab an ro boí do indib ina
broind. Ibid dig íarum 7 fo-thruci ass. Is de atá Loch Lámraith i mMaig
Murthemni. Ainm aile dó dano Loch Tondchuil. Íar sin do-curidar bedg ass 7
for-congair foraib co ndigsitis ara chend.

380 26. Do-dechaid íarum crích mór ónd loch síar. Et rucad a rosc airi. Et téit
dochum coirthi cloiche file isin maig co tarat a choimchriss immi nár ablad na
suidiu nách ina ligu combad ina sessam at-balad. Is íar sin do-dechatar na fir
immacúairt immi 7 níro lámsatar dul a dochum. Andar leo ropo béo. "Is mebol
dúib," ol Erc mac Carpri, "cen chend ind fir do thabairt lib i ndígail chind

385 m'athar-sa rucad leis coro adnacht fri airsce Echdach (Nia Fer)." Rucad a
chend as-saide co fil i Síd Nenta íar n-Usciu.

27. Íar sin trá do-dechaid in Líath Macha co Coin Culaind dia imchomét i céin
ro boí a anim and 7 ro mair in lón láith assa étun. Is íarum birt in Líath Macha
na trí dergrúathra immi 'macúairt co torchratar .l. leis cona fíaclaib 7 .xxx.
390 cach cruí dó. Iss ed ro marb dont ślúag. Conid de atá: "Nít áthe búadrémmend
ind Léith Macha íar marbad Con Culaind." Conid íar sin do-lluid ind ennach
fora gúalaind. "Nírbo gnáth in corthe út fo énaib," ar Erc mac Corpri. Íar sin
trá ra chóraig Lugaid a moing dara aiss 7 benaid a chend de. Íar sin trá do-
rochair a chlaideb a lláim Con Culaind co n-eccmoing a láim doí di Lugaid co
395 rrabi for lár. Benair a lám doí dano di Choin Culaind dia dígail.

28. Do-cumlat ass íarum int ślúaig 7 do-berat leo cend Con Culaind 7 a láim
doí co táncatar Temraig. Conid and atá otharlige a chind 7 a láimc doí 7 lán
lainne a scéith di úir. Conid de as-bert Cend Fáelad mac Ailella i nAidedaib
Ulad:
400 Do-ceir Cú Chulainn, caín tuir,
trénfer i nnAirbiu Rofir.
Reraig buidne—ba mó clith—
for Mac Trí Con, for Lugthig.

Lín tod-forchair—ferda nglé—
405 nírbo thuttim midlaige.

Cethri ochtair, cethri deich,
cethri coícait, caíni in tréith.
Cethri tríchait, tolgda rím,
cethri cethrachait, crúaid gním.

410 Cethri fichit—fríth co feib—
fos-roirtib mac Sualtaim.

Ro gáeta i n-athgubu
trícha ríg di erchoraib.
Im vii. fichtiu anchinne
415 fos-n-ácaib di erbonaib.

Atá cend in chon ar dó,
droneirr i n-óchtor Temro.
Úaigthe íarom a forceth
d'airsciu Cairpri Niod Fer.

420 Atá cend n-Echdach indiu
i sSíd Nenta íar n-Usciu.
Úaigthe cend Corpri, caín rí,
do airsciu Echdach i Tethbai.

caíni in tréith] caín in tréith *L*; ro gáeta] ro gáet *L*; cend in chon] cend chon *L*;
cend n-Echdach] cend Echdach *L*; n-Usciu] Usciu *L*

29. Íar sin do-cumlat int ṡlúaig ass fades co ráncatar abaind Lifi. Amal ráncatar
425 in n-abaind as-bert Lugaid fria araid, "Is trom lim mo chriss lán immum," ol
sé. "Is áil dam mo fothrucud." Do-curedar ass erchomuir int ṡlúaig. Fothraicid
íarum. Do-cumlaiset ass íar suidiu. At-etha íach eter a dá cholptha. Do-
cuiredar súas dia araid. Benaid-side tenid dia urgnum fo chétóir.

30. Is íar sin do-cumlat slúaig Ulad atúaid ó Emuin Macha dochum Sléibe
430 Fúait íar cur a cessa díb. Ro boí cinniud tria chombáig íarum eter Chon
Culaind 7 Conall Cernach .i. ciped chía díb no marbtha ar tús a dígail dia
chéiliu. "Et mad misse marbthair ar tús," ar Cú Chulaind, "cía lúathe nom-
digéla?" "A llá not-géntar," ar Conall Cernach, "do dígail dam-sa resin fescur-
sin. Et mad misse marbthair and," or Conall, "cía lúathe nom-digéla?" "Nípa
435 úar th'fuil-siu lim-sa for talmain," ol Cú Chulaind, "in tan not-digél."

31. In tan íarum do-dechaid Conall Cernach resin slúag ina charput co
comarnic frisin Líath Macha 7 a thóesca fola triit oc dul do Lind Léith. Conid
and as-bert Conall Cernach:
.R. "Ní cumgid cuinge
440 co lLind Léith
co rrega co fuilib fonnaidib
fo chollaib clí
co fuidlechtaib fuili
fir sceo eich
445 im láim doí Lugdach.
Lugaid mac Con Ruí meic Dáre

iss é ro marb

mo chomalt-sa Coin Culaind."

fonnaidib] fonnaide *L*

32. Luid íar sin Conall Cernach 7 in Líath Macha reme coro lá cúairt sinn
450 árbaig. Co n-accatar Coin Culaind immon corthe. Luid dano in Líath Macha
co tarat a chend for brunnib Con Culaind. "Is dethitiu don Líath Macha in corp
út," ar Conall. Téit trá Conall íar tain et at-aig a thraig fri airrbe. "Tongu-sa a
tonges mo thúath," ar sé, " rop airrbe rofir in so." "Ro batsis ainm dond inud,"
ol in druí. "Bid ed ainm in tíri-seo co bráth: Airrbe Rofir."

455 33. To-cumlai íarum i ndegaid int ṡlúaig. Is and ro boí Lugaid oca ḟothrucud.
"Décce dún a mmag," ol Lugaid fria araid, "ná tístar chucund cen aicsin." Do-
féccai secha int ara. "Do-fil óenmarcach sund chucund," or sé, "7 is mór a
gripe 7 a lúas do-thét. Indar lat is feochuine Érend fil úasa. Indar lat it lóa
snechtai breccait a mmag fris anair." "Ní inmain in marcach do-tháet and," ar
460 Lugaid, ".i. Conall Cernach in sin forsin Deirg Drúchtaig. Na héoin at-
chonnarcais úasu na fóit a cruíb ind eich-sin. Na lóa snechtai at-chonnarcais
do breccad in maige friss anair úanbach a bélaib ind eich-sin 7 a gglomraib
int ṡréin. Fég darísse," ar Lugaid, "cisi chonar do-tháet." "Do-tháet dochum
ind átha," ar int ara, ".i. in chonar do-dechaid in slúag." "Do-lléic sechund int
465 ech-sin," ar Lugaid. "Ní áil dún comrac fris."

34. In tan íarum ro siacht Conall Cernach co medón ind átha do-féccai secha.
"Dé de araid sucut," ar sé. Do-féccai secha in tres fecht. "Dé de ríg sút," ar sé.
"Is ferr dam-sa a adall." Ad-ella cuccu. "Is fochen aged ḟécheman," ol Conall
Cernach. "Int-í dano dia ndligi ḟíachu dos-fothlaig fair." "Dligim dít-su," ar
470 Conall Cernach, ".i. marbad mo chomchéili Con Culaind 7 itú ic tríall a acrai
fort." "Ní cóir ón," or Lugaid, "ar ní ármide ar láechdacht duit-siu comrac
frim-sa sund co rrí búaid mo choscair lim tír Muman." "Do-génaind-sa mani
beth techt dún for óenchonair 7 i comlabrai 7 i cotchennas," or Conall
Cernach. "Nípa ansa a mbia di ṡudiu," or Lugaid. "Regat-sa amne for Belach
475 Gabrúain co ndechus for Belach Smechuin. Airg-siu amne for Gabuir for
Mairg Lagen co comairsem i mMaig Argetrois." Lugaid is é céta-ránic. Tánic
a chéile ina diaid .i. Conall Cernach. Tarlaic urchor fair dia ṡlig 7 a choss frisin
coirthe fil i mMaig Argetrois co ndecmaing i lLugaid. Conid de atá Corthe
Lugdach i mMaig Argetrois.

480 35. Luid íarum íarna chétguiniu co mboí oc Fertai Lugdach i nDroictib
Ossairge. Conid and imma-n-arraid dóib. "Rop áil dam-sa," or Lugaid,
"conum-rabad fír fer úait-siu." "Cid ón?" or Conall Cernach. "Connácham-
thísed úait acht óenlám ar ní fil acht óenlám lim." "Rot-bia," or Conall
Cernach. Cengaltar a lám íarum dia thóeb co súanemnaib. Ro bátar indsin eter
485 dá thráth din ló. Et ní fúair nechtar de eill fora chéile. In tan nád fúair Conall
Cernach eill fair do-féccai secha a gabuir .i. in Deirg nDrúchtaig. Cend con
furri-side for-díbad na firu isna cathaib 7 isna irgalaib. La sin do-n-ic in gabuir
chuci co rragaib mír assa thoíb co tarlaic inna raba ina broind co rraba imma
chossa. "Fé amae," or Lugaid. "Ní fír fer aní-sin, a Chonaill Chernaig." "Ní
490 tharddus-sa duit-siu," or Conall Cernach, "acht darmo chend féin. Ní tharddus
immurgu duit dar cend na robb 7 na n-écodnach." "Ro fetur-sa trá," or Lugaid,
"nád raga-su co rruca mo chend-sa latt úair do-fucsam-ni cend Con Culaind.
Co tardda trá," ar sé, "mo chend-sa ardo chend 7 co n-erbara mo rígi-se fordo
ríge et mo gaisced fordo gaisced. Ar is ferr lim-sa combad tú láech bad dech
495 no beth i nÉrind." La ssin benaid Conall Cernach a chend de.

tharddus-sa] tharddusa *L*

36. To-cumlai ass íarum cosin cend leiss co comarnic fri Ulto i rRoirind i tírib
Lagen. Fo-rruimther a cend forsin chloich 7 ro dermatad and. Co rráncatar
Grís. Is andsin im-chóemnacair Conall Cernach, "In tuc nech úaib a cend?" ar
sé. "Ní thucsam," ar cách. Is and as-bert Conall Cernach, "Tongu-sa a tonges
500 mo thúath," or sé, "ní midbine in sin." Is de atá Midbine oc Roirind. Tintaíset
dochum in chind arise. Co n-accas ní ro berbai in cend in cloich co ndechaid
treithe.

37. Níro dámsat Ulaid co mbúaid choscair do Emuin Macha int šechtmain-
sin. Ro dámastar immurgu anim Con Culaind co tarfad don .l. rígan ro
505 šáraigestar a llaa re tuidecht don chath. Co n-accas ní Cú Chulaind ina
šíaburcharpat isind aeór ós Emuin Macha. Conid and ro chan Cú Chulaind
dóib co n-erbairt íarna eistecht:
"Emuin, Emuin,
oll olleith aton-ré.
510 Tálcind trebfait íathu Emna.
Ticfat de Eóraip Elpae.
Di-uiscebthar domun do nim
co slúagaib Succet sáiliu gil.

54

Gigsit co ríg n-ardnime
515 alchél coton- Sion -suidigthe leis.
Raigma do lathiu lánbrátha.
Fer caín con-géba frim
anair isind oínmaig.
Maith (in) sin co comairsem, a Emain."

Emuin] Eomuin *L*; aton-ré] tan ré *L*; Di-uiscebthar domun do nim] di uisciu
ethar domuin dobním *L*

520 38. Síaburchobra Con Culaind i llathiu a eitsechta
"Úaine ortae, a Emuin.
Dítiu ortae, a Emuin.
Ar cleith do-class, a Emuin.
Do-cer i cath, a Emuin.
525 Cíabo óen fri iliu
do lóeg do-fúart firu.
Úaine ortae, a Emuin.
Do-fius mórfer fermart.
For-ríadam réim n-érchian
530 ar ba rom ron-tráethad.
To-rét im gáir ngubae
caínandrae dún subae
sétu finna forcu
Dechtire dúin deme.
535 Dim-emed art úasal
mad arg n-erred -ríssed.
Do-fius márfer fermart.
Mad óen fri óen n-úathad
ad-muindfind mac nEithnend.
540 Cach cruth cach leth -robae.
Ro-fertad fer Aífe.
At-bath Lóeg áirilled
nách bad trummu turbaid.
Tom-… mo chaurchobraid (*Conall*)
545 con-oí luing lúaith ó Ultaib
echraid echlaig Dílind Duib
a mMuig Éo i mMaig Cride. U."

Emuin] Eomuin *L*; dítiu ortae, a Emuin] dítiu ortae Emuin *L*; do-class] do-clast *L*; cíabo óen] cíab óen *L*; Úaine ortae, a Emuin] Úaine ortae Emuin *L*; mórfer fermart] mórfer már fermart *L*; márfer fermart] már fermart *L*; áirilled] iruilled *L*; lúaith] lúath *L*; echraid] echraig *L*

39. Cú Chulaind at-bert: *De adventu Christi*
1. "Críst céta-rét íathu écmacht n-anfót.
550 Frecnairc fallnabthair; ar chenél féchid.
Ar chel cóemrí Coimdiu, ísund úasund,
athardae domuin, doim dún dúin fri nélbruig.

2. Nia doíne ticfa a recht.
Cach leth línfaid; lénfaid do thogaís.
555 Tróethfaid Ísu iffern imergib áil Ádaim
i flaith forbáis fo láim fris mbet formdig ingair,
fris failtniget, fris ráidfet recht nime.

3. Cía rí seo, cía tuili dia n-epérat arbuir?
In rí ro ícc talmain ar flaith fordon-ossa,
560 ar ríchid ná tesbai do foirm nert nime.
La forlínad suide seiss for dindaib flatha
in rí íar mbúaid chatha óenaib, dédaib, trédaib
tria chumachta nát érglond, nád écgut, nád érbur.

4. Dall taidbsiu do doínib robud ría mbás bias:
565 renna nime fo-chroithfet,
grían gel in derg dithistair,
réim nglas rotha resair,
ésce fo- leth -luigther in lúachthaidiu
amser tria torromu.

570 5. Ísu as úaisliu as ísliu
tria erscartad iffirn,
tria ṡuidigud suide,
tria thúaslucud flatha,
tria lánarbur catha,
575 tria lánchumachta nime
im nimib, im doíne, im dúile,

56

i mbethu tria bithu. Críst."

Coimdiu] Comdiu *L*; domuin doim dúin] domoin do imdún dúin *L*; fordon-
ossa] fordonosdá *L*; seiss] séis *L*; écgut] écguth *L*; dithistair] dithsir *L*; ressair]
resair *L*; lánchumachta] lánchumacta *L*

40. Luid in Líath Macha do chelebrad do Emir. Co tarat a chend ina hucht. Et
do-chuaid ina dessel fo thrí 7 desel Dúin Imrid 7 Dúin Delga.
580 Núallguba Emire in so:
1. "A Léith Macha,
mór n-essad,
mór ndirsan,
mór ngalgat,
585 mór mairg
nádat-décai immut-dídnad,
náchit-toisci cotut-eilged,
eirr caín cumachtach cathbúadach úas do chlíu nád chliss
críchmrugib Macha Mo Chaí Nóendromma.

590 2. Nél find fo-retis ríg síde,
séol n-óir úas dindaib ar thúathaib ilib -imgonad,
gein óir úas t'anáil ar fáebraib -féchad
fo-rrúair dubae Delgae dílachtai.

3. To-rreith rígeirr sceo bás rí ech úas echaib.
595 Úas bémmennaib oc búadaib,
oc foromnaib for énaib,
nít-ecmaing flesc ná urlond ná urchor,
nít-ecmaing féin clé con-gaibed ferna aurdlochtai,
nít-ecmoing dess dia mbenad bidbadu.

600 4. Fordom-benad a bunad.
Immum-díched a urúath.
Nam-bíathad a aruit.
Ardum -cétmuinter caín cathbúadach -cíallastar.

5. Íarsin chath chrúaid
605 óenguine ata-mbebai écomlund

57

i cétaíne i cétlathiu ḟogomuir
eirr mroga Murthemni.
Millsit ammaiti—
díchimmidi étain,
610 gránne genite—
crúancern Con Culaind cathbúadaig.

6. Car in méte násad nó míad nó mét
nó gal nó gart no grád nó gním
inid Cú Chulaind cathbúadach oconá ragaib ré?
615 Ro lá ár do Galianaib fri Érnu.
Ros-mbí Éraind arind-mbebsat bás
ar ro fitir eirr caín cumachtach cathbúadach
co ngresse gríssaib cloítis ríana gail.

7. Gabais immi écóir
620 ara torchair a scíath,
ara n-imgaib a ech.
At-cummai a delg.
Dolluid a tollus
ara tethraig a nert
625 nách nderbai dia chéim.
Co farnaic ammaiti
túathcháecha ara chind.
Cú glas fo-noíset
fri tindell a clíu.
630 Do-cossecht foa urṡeilb
óa bund coa mullach
corbo marb a leth.
Láith gaile friasa comarnic
…(?)
635 co torchair a ech. (*ainmem Líath*)
Olc lige
líagair Dub Sainglend.
Adbul slúag do-ceir
cíarbo óenchossid óenlámaid
640 díthrachtai dia óenuch."

tarat] tara *L*; nádat-décai immut-dídnad] nodat décai immuddídnad *L*; náchit-toisci] nachitoisci *L*; caín cumachtach] chaín chumachtach *L*; críchmrugib] críchbrugi *L*; Mo Chaí Nóendromma] meic huí Nendrúaid *L*; -féchad] fechaid *L*; dubae] dubu *L*; flesc] fleisc *L*; clé] clí *L*; aurdlochtai] aurdloctai *L*; cétmuinter] cétmunter *L*; íarsin] íardun *L*; óenguine] n-óenguine *L*; mroga] broga *L*; díchimmidi étain] dichimmid n-etain *L*; arind-mbebsat] arid mbebsat *L*; caín cumachtach cathbuadach] chain chumachtach chathbuadach *L*; ngresse] gressed *L*; at-cummai] athcummai *L*; tollus] dollus *L*; tethraig] thethraig *L*; *Líath*…Sainglend] Líath leggur Dub aiglend olc lige *L*

41. Ro marb Cú Chulaind .uiii. Láith, .uiii. Níaith,.uiii. Féci,.uiii. Óengusa,.uiii. Fíachaig,.uiii. Fergusa, .uiii. Fáelgusa, .x. mBrudi, .x. mBróin, .x. mBrenaind, .x. Corpri, .x. Crimthaind, .x. Conaire, .x. Conaill, .ix. truich, .ix. ndruíd, .ix. nDóelgusa, .ix. Sáergusa, .ix. n-Illaind, .xl. arad, .xl. brolach,
645 .xl. brugad, cét mulach, .c. ndíbergach, .c. sen, .c. n-óc, .c. midaís, .xx. ríg, .xx. colomon, .xx. eirred n-án, .xx. olloman, im ocht cét lám ndess do imdibe, im ocht cét súle do cháechad co fargaib in slúag-sin uile fo anim dia eís issind óenló.

eirred n-án] eirred án *L*

42. 1. "Apraind, a Léith Macha, nábu díb n-echaib cóemaib fo charput bá-so.
650 Dursan nápu díb lámaib comlánaib -comarnic.
Apraind nách Conchobar claidebrúad -comairlestar.
Dursan nád Eirrge Echbél -arnic.
Apraind nách Sencha Sobeóil ro siacht.
Dursan nách Fiacha Foltlebor -fallnastar.
655 Apraind nách Éogain Álaind -acillestar.
Dursan nách Fergna mac Findcháeme -forcmastar.
Apraind nách Fergus mac Lete luid.
Apraind nách Feidlimid Fáeborderg -forcachai.
Dursan nách Munremur mórglonnach -míadaigestar.
660 Apraind nách Amargin -urdaircaigestar.
Dursan nách Rochad Rigderg -ráthaigestar.
Apraind nád bátar errid Ulad uile ocond airm i torchair i n-écomlund ar no réided-som a chorp ngel créchtach ar Ultu fri iltúathu ilairbriu.
Dursan nách Conall Cernach -cobrastar.
665 Apraind nách Celtchar comramach -cúala.

Dursan nách Lóegaire Búadach -báigestar.
Apraind nách Fergus mac Rossa -roacht.
Dursan nád bátar Ulaid uile imme airm i torchair.

2. Dom-chommart a chuma.
670 Cotom-essart a díth.
Rom-díthracht a díbad.
Am dímaín dia éis
ar ním-thá ní íarum.

3. Ba méite cach cride rod-car con-bóssad.
675 Ba méite cech clúas rod-cúala co bráth noco ndermanad.
Ba méite cach dér no cíthe co bráth bad dia bithchoíniud.
Ba méite cach rosc at-connairc no cíad frassaib fola
ar is dered fo dubai in domuin dia éis,
ar níba fri céili aile íarum nom-accfither.
680 Níbat gárechtaig aiscedaig fergnúsi ocom urnaidm
ar ní fugéb céli fri Coin Culaind cosmail."

cóemaib] commaib *L*; créchtach] chréchtach *L*; comramach] comrach *L*; ním-
thá] nimda *L*; bad] ba *L*; domuin] domain *L*

43. 1. "Bit brónaig Delguin dílachtai.
Níbat fáilti búad bantrochta.
Do-beba Mis Gegra gnímrathu
685 ro gní mórdígail.
Ad-rulaid luing Mossad mórgníma
i mMaig Siamrach.
Ro sephaid Conall íar Cormaic comaitecht
co nderaig a daltae dígáirsi.
690 Mórgein ro gabai ar galaib óenfir
íar mbreth ban síde.
Siachtum mórthochmarc meic dea Dechtiri.
Derbad soaltim sainaltram Loga.
Inn-reith frim indretha Scáithchi scélaige—
695 eochair inna n-Ulad n-úath óa n-áthaib.

2. Teist ro fersur ré síabordai

60

ina urchomair sé mbliadna déc.
Dlegmai scur sáetha.
Sechmai mórthúatha alchél:
700 cách úand dia eól
imma-cíam, imma-caínem, imma-n-airchisem.
Is trúag in bith a táthar and
ar ní chomraicfem nach laithiu aile,
a Léith, a Léith."

705 Finit. Amen.

Cormaic] Cormac *L*; inn-reith frim indretha] imréith fri mind rotha *L*; eochair]
eochraide *L*; dlegmai] dlegma *L*

TRANSLATION

1.   "...that I've never suffered the wails of women and children without intervening on their behalf until today." Then the fifty queens marched toward him and bared their breasts to him. It is they who—in the *Boyhood Deeds*—introduced the custom of baring breasts to keep Cú Chulainn in Emain Macha. And the three vats of water were brought to quench his fury. And he wasn't allowed into battle that day.

2.   "I see that you've failed to lure Cú Chulainn today with your baiting trick, sons of Calatín," said Lugaid. "The men from Dún Chermna, Belach Con Glais, Temair Lóchra, and Comar Trí n-Uisce have been waiting a long time here at Béolu Menbolg. Your baiting strategy is terrible. It's taking too long for Cú Chulainn to show up," said Lugaid. "We'll get him to come tomorrow," said the sons of Calatín. They were there until the next day. And the sons of Calatín conjured hosts around Emain Macha so that all of Macha was a burnt-down cloud of smoke. Emain Macha was overthrown by the hosts. Weapons fell from their racks. And the ominous news was brought to Cú Chulainn.

3.   Then Lebarcham said:
"Rise, Cú Chulainn, arise!
Protect Mag Murthemne from the Leinstermen!
Well-reared child of Lug,
turn to your warrior feats.
Cú Chulainn, arise so that claps may resound
at the invasion of Murthemne.
Great are the nobles and warriors going to battle.
Don't let Cormac lull you,
far from Conchobar's kin.
You don't have Conall, Cormac's
kinsman, to protect us.
For it's not through kin-spirit
that Lugaid with his alliance
will slay you to avenge slaughter.
Equip yourself, splendid fighter.

Grandson of Cathbad, arise! Rise!"

4.   Then Cú Chulainn said:
"Leave me alone, girl.
I'm not the only one who enjoys Conchobar's province.
Though the enemy be worrisome, I won't fight alone
because my exertion after exertion is unwise.
I'm not a willing warrior eager for battle today."

5.   Then Níab, Celtchar's daughter and Conall Cernach's wife, said:
"That's proper for you, indeed, Cú Chulainn.
Conall's chariot isn't protecting you.
Isn't he very pure, he who's sacrificed for the Ulstermen?
In muddied fords he was beaten
so that it's lambhead-weapons he invokes
because they don't fight anymore.
Nothing else is a deed
but the great circuit
of Amergin's son."

6.   "Now, woman," said Cú Chulainn,
"Though I may be doomed, I am peerless.
I have preserved my honor.
Valor wasn't stolen from me.
I do not avoid my death."

7.   Then Cú Chulainn leapt to his weapons. And he wrapped a cloak
around himself. But the first fold he wrapped around himself got tangled
so that the brooch fell out of his hand. Then Cú Chulainn said:
"The cloak that warns
is not to blame.
To blame is the brooch
that wounds the skin
so that the spoil-scattering shield
falls through the foot
as the shield's edge splits
from my right hand's fist.

Soon I'll die from an untimely wound
that champions will deal.
There will be lamenting on the great day
south of Mag Murthemne after me."

8.   Then he wrapped his cloak around himself and grabbed his shield
with the engraved edge on it. And he said to Lóeg mac Riangabra,
"Harness the chariot for us, sir Lóeg." "I swear to the god to whom my
people swears," said Lóeg, "that even if all of Conchobar's province were
around Líath Macha, they couldn't bring him to the chariot. He has never
defied you until today. But I couldn't summon his usual splendid spirit. If
you want, come speak to Líath himself."

9.   Cú Chulainn approached the horse. But the horse turned his left
side to him three times. And the Mórrígan had dismantled the chariot the
night before because she didn't want Cú Chulainn to go to battle. She knew
he'd never return to Emain Macha. Then Cú Chulainn said to Líath Macha:
"It's odd for you, Líath,
to show me your left.
Fierce to you the raven
for our deed to seek death.
My mind doesn't yearn
for our plain of long rides.
Long red reins,
splitting of horse and wheel,
of yoke and frame
and familiar seat.
Badb has favored us
in Emain Macha."

10.   Then Líath Macha came and let fall his great swelling tears of
blood on his two feet. Then Cú Chulainn jumped into the chariot and set
out with a leap south along Slige Midlúachra. Then he saw a girl before
him—Lebarcham, daughter of Auae and Adarc, a slave and servant, who
was in Conchobar's house. And Lebarcham said:
"Don't leave us, don't leave us, Cú Chulainn.
Your face is noble.

Your brow is honorable.
Your wound-dealing form
is glowing and fair-faced.
Isn't the fate that has doomed you
a grief we will mourn?
Woe to our women!
Woe to our children!
Woe to our eyes!
Everlasting your grief-filled lament. (*that we will cry*)
You'll march regally to battle,
whereby nobles will die.
There will be lamenting on the great day
of Mag Murthemne after you."

The three fifties of women in Emain Macha spoke as she had in a loud voice.

11.   "It would be better not to leave them," Lóeg said, "for you've never flouted the power of your mother's kin until today."
"No indeed," said Cú Chulainn.
"Accept the law, Lóeg.
A charioteer accepts.
A chariot-fighter protects.
A champion advises.
Men are manly.
Women are fainthearted.
Come before me to battle.
Don't heed unhelpful lamenting."

The chariot turned clockwise. At that the woman-troop cried and wailed and clapped their hands in grief. They knew he'd never return to Emain Macha.

12.   *Cú Chulainn's Living Speech on the Day of His Death*
"The woman-troops are sad
with hosts of tears for my death
from plains on a dark day.

66

Victories will buy the discovered treasure
so that I prevail....
Ever has it grieved you
that worldly rulers crossed
the boundary of life.
A calf of lands
reddens reins.
Witches blind in the left eye
will bring my destruction.
Many Ulstermen will lament me.
They'll bury boons
when generous lords perish,
hindering sureties.
By righteous hands the world will be divided.
Vehemently the single chariot-fighter
will drive three raids
amid covetousness for the kingdom.
He'll bind battles.
Eyes don't weep
for something they don't see.
With sorrowful lament
the belly will waste
for loss of the champion.
Battle honor will be broken—
a single man's spear thrusts,
many unequal combats.
Between two wheels
revenge will directly reach
Líath Macha's trail.
Woe to covetousness in peacetime.
It will yield blood-red wonders
at the time of death.
Strongly I celebrate
a spirited horse
amid very deceptive satirists.
I'll slay them for hostile reproaches.
Reproach will be transcended

on the day of ancestral
Mag Murthemne.
From a gushing, wholesome stream
I'll drink with my…belly's wound.
After rest, a bright,
pleasant cloud
calming my bodily wounds
will cleanse me from vicious battle.
Have I not fought famously?
The slain frame's spoils will be gathered.
The strong earth resounds.
Wise ones will divide
heirs' trifling powers.
In your time will come
destruction of cattle
and sparse protection.
A miser will be born
soon before the world's destruction.
His clientship will be base.
His time will be dark.
He'll deceive a multitude.
He'll lead many astray.
He'll be known
by his lack of truth.
He'll extend falsehood.
He'll destroy truth.
Battles will be fought—
captivity of a leader,
hacking of limbs,
breaking of bones,
cutting of skin,
lancing of eyes,
perverse, proud laws,
gold for homages,
silver on trees,
gems from slopes.
Crystal mountains will

gratify greed.
Hostile the undertaking,
concealment of nobles.
For we'll find him out
at the end of his life.
On the day he will be destroyed,
there will be one who exalts humanity
to save Creation for you.
Adore the Son with his justice.
It is far better for you.
I in my pride have reflected on his law.
I would do better if granted life."

Then the woman-troop raised a crying shout and wailing lamentation because they knew Cú Chulainn wouldn't return to Ulster.

13.   The house of his fostermother who had reared him was before him on the path he used to take on his way south and back. She always had a drink waiting for him. He drank a cup and set out and bade her farewell. He went along Slige Midlúachra past Mag Mogna. Then he saw three witches blind in the left eye before him on the path. They were cooking a dog on rowan spits with poisons and spells. It was one of Cú Chulainn's taboos not to visit a cooking pit to eat. It was also taboo for him to eat his namesake's flesh. He ran to get past them. He knew they weren't there acting in his interest. Then one of the witches said to him, "Come visit, Cú Chulainn." "No," Cú Chulainn replied. "Indeed, the food is just a hound," she said. "If it were a great feast, you would visit. Because it is meager, you don't. He who doesn't endure or accept something small isn't capable of anything great." So then he visited them and the witch offered him half the hound with her left hand. Cú Chulainn took it out of her hand and put it under his left thigh. The hand that accepted it and the thigh under which he placed it seized up from top to bottom so that their strength was gone.

14.   Then he and his charioteer set out along Slige Midlúachra south around Sliab Fúait. Cú Chulainn said to Lóeg, "What do you see for us?" Lóeg answered, "Many doomed men and great spoils."
"Woe indeed!" said Cú Chulainn.

"The sound of battle,
blood-red horses racing,
the left chariot-side
of a chief who dies before his time,
for soon horses will fall among warriors.
Woe! Long have I feared
the men of Ireland's troops."

15.   When Cú Chulainn went southward along Slige Midlúachra, he and the host in Mag Murthemne beheld each other. Then Erc mac Carpri said:
"I see here a fair, perfect, brightly ornamented chariot with a green awning and a trove of weapons for martial feats—a beautifully helmeted feat-performer's beautiful chariot. The chariot is drawn by two horses with small, round heads and pointed snouts—deadly, leaping, broad-chested, broad-bellied horses with flaring nostrils and bulging eyes. Although the two horses are similar and equally swift, they are not of the same color. One of the horses is lynx-grey, bounding, big, spirited, and skittish and performs high, arching thunder-feats. The other is jet black, white-headed, and big-browed with dark black brows. There are two high, golden yokes on them. There is a man with fair, long, curling hair in that chariot with a red, fiery spear in his hand glittering like a red flame. A fluttering bird of valor (i.e., the warrior's light) floats above this chariot champion. His tresses of hair are tricolored: brown hair next to the scalp, blood-red hair in the center, and a crown of gold on top. Fairly arranged is that head of hair with three encircling rows. The sparkle of each lock of that youth's hair is like that of strands of gold thread over an anvil edge worked by a master craftsman or like that of buttercups on which the sun shines on a mid-May summery day."

16.   "His sign is coming toward us. Heed that man, men of Ireland." Then a mound of sods was raised around Erc mac Carpri and an array of shields was made around him, and three fierce troops were made then of the men of Ireland. And Erc said, "Men of Ireland, heed that man Cú Chulainn." And he uttered these words:
"Set out, men of Ireland. Arise. Protecting, victorious, red-sworded Cú Chulainn is here. Prepare, prepare. Cry out. Heads will be lamented on his

70

account. Honor will be insulted. Build a mound over a protective wooden barrier. That is one only, the son of God, the son of humankind. Woe to warriors, woe to battle divisions, woe to battle ranks, woe to benevolent lords. I recognize the heavenly, steadfast, fierce, well-defending Lord who is strong in the face of doom. He lay for nine months in a brave-born maiden's womb. They destroy Emain Macha, whose heavenly hero has been slain. Woe to him who slew him—he's made of the stuff of a blemished leader. Cú Chulainn has fallen. Arise. Arise."

17.   "How can we prepare? How can we resist his feats?" said the men of Ireland. "Easy. Here's my advice to you," said Erc. "Make a single troop of the four provinces assembled here and surround them with a single board of shields. And place three men at every corner—two of the strongest of the host exchanging blows and a satirist with a hazel wand next to them—and let them demand his spear (called Triumph on Triumphs) as well as the spears that are cast at him. It is prophesied of his spear that a king will be killed by it unless it be demanded. And utter a cry and scream. The man won't hold back his fury or the horses' fury. And he won't demand single combat from you as he did at the cattle raid of Cúailnge." They did as Erc said.

18.   Cú Chulainn then approached the troop and performed three thunderfeats on the chariot—that is, the thunderfeat of hundreds, the thunderfeat of three hundreds, and the thunderfeat of thrice nine—to clear away the hosts from Mag Murthemne. Cú Chulainn came to the troop and began a bout of weapon wielding on them. He was plying the spears, the shield, the sword, and the feats in such a way that their cloven heads; skulls; hands; feet; and torn, red bones scattered all over Mag Murthemne were as numerous as the sand of the sea, the stars of Heaven, May dew, snowflakes, hailstones, forest leaves, yellow flowers on the plain of Brega, and grass under horses' feet on a summer day. That field was grey with their brains after that wrathful battle and Cú Chulainn's weapon wielding.

19.   Then Cú Chulainn saw two men exchanging blows but didn't separate them. "Shame on you, Cú Chulainn, for not separating this pair," said the satirist. Then Cú Chulainn leapt toward them and struck each one's head with his fist so that their brains gushed out of their ears and

noses. "You have separated them," said the satirist. "Neither of them can harm the other now." "They wouldn't have shut up if I'd just asked them to," said Cú Chulainn. "Give me that spear, Cú Chulainn," said the satirist. "I swear what my people swears that you need it no more than I do. The men of Ireland are upon me here and I upon them." "I'll satirize you if you don't give it to me," said the satirist. "I've never been satirized for miserliness or bad lordship." With that Cú Chulainn cast the spear at him handle first so that it went through his head and killed nine men behind him.

20.   Cú Chulainn went through the host to the end. Then Lugaid mac Con Roí grasped one of the three spears prepared by the sons of Calatín. "What will fall by this spear, sons of Calatín?" said Lugaid. "A king will fall by that spear," said the sons of Calatín. Then Lugaid cast the spear at the chariot so that it hit Lóeg mac Riangabra and spilled his innards out onto the chariot cushion. Lóeg said, "I've been bitterly wounded." Then Cú Chulainn withdrew the spear and bade Lóeg farewell. And Cú Chulainn said, "I will be a chariot-fighter and a charioteer today."

21.   When Cú Chulainn reached the end of the host, he saw two men exchanging blows before him and a satirist with a hazel wand next to them. "Shame on you," said one of the men, "for not intervening between us." With that Cú Chulainn leapt toward them and threw each of them aside so that they shattered into fragments against the rock that was beside him. "Give me that spear, Cú Chulainn," said the satirist. "I swear what my people swears that you need the spear no more than I do. My prowess, valor, and skill at arms must clear the four provinces from Mag Murthemne today." "I'll satirize you," said the satirist. "Only one demand is due from me today and I've paid for my honor already." "I'll satirize the Ulstermen for your crime," said the satirist. "They've never been satirized for my stinginess or bad lordship. For the little that remains of my life, there will be no satirizing today." Cú Chulainn cast the spear at him by the handle so that it went through his head and killed nine men behind him. And he went through the host as we said above.

22.   Erc grasped one of the spears prepared by the sons of Calatín. "What will come of this spear, sons of Calatín?" he said. "That's easy: a

king will fall by that spear." "I heard from you that a king would fall from the spear that Lugaid cast just now." "That's true," said the sons of Calatín. "The king of charioteers of Ireland has fallen by it—Cú Chulainn's charioteer, Lóeg mac Riangabra." "I swear what my people swears that it won't wound the king who slew him." With that Erc cast the spear at him so that it struck Líath Macha. Cú Chulainn removed the spear and each bade farewell to the other. With half the yoke around his neck, Líath Macha left him and came to Linn Léith in Slíab Fúait. Thence he had come to Cú Chulainn and there he went after being slain. Then Cú Chulainn said, "Half a yoke will drive here today."

23.   Then Cú Chulainn put one of his feet on the end of the yoke and went through the host the same way. He saw two men exchanging blows and a satirist with a hazel wand beside them. He separated the men, and the intervention was no worse than that with the four previous men. "Give me that spear, Cú Chulainn," said the satirist. "You don't need the spear more than I do." "I'll satirize you," said the satirist. "I've paid for my honor today. Only one request is due from me today." "I'll satirize the Ulstermen for your crimes." "I've paid for their honor," he said. "I'll satirize your kindred," said the satirist. "Tidings of my slander will not precede me to the land I haven't reached yet, and little remains of my life." Cú Chulainn cast the spear at him handle first so that it went through his head and through thrice nine other men. "It's an angry gift, Cú Chulainn," said the satirist.

24.   After that Cú Chulainn went again through the host to the end. And Lugaid grasped another of the three spears prepared by the sons of Calatín. "What will come of this spear, sons of Calatín?" "A king will fall by it," said the sons of Calatín. "I heard from you that a king would fall from the spear that Erc cast a little while ago." "That is true," they said. "The king of the horses of Ireland fell by it—Líath Macha." "I swear what my people swears that it won't come at the king who slew him." Then Lugaid cast the spear at Cú Chulainn so that it hit him and the contents of his belly spilled out onto the chariot cushion. Then with half the yoke, Dub Sainglenn left him and went to Loch Dub in Muscraige Tíre. Thence he had come to Cú Chulainn and there he went again so that the lake boiled over from it.

73

25.   Then the chariot stood alone on the plain. After that Cú Chulainn said, "I'd like to go to that lake to have a drink from it." "We allow it," they said, "as long as you return to us." "I'll command you," Cú Chulainn said, "to come get me if I don't come myself." Then he gathered his innards into his belly and went toward the lake. When he reached the lake, he raised his hand across his belly and discarded his innards. He took a drink then and bathed himself in the lake. From that is named Loch Lámraith in Mag Murthemne. Another name for it is Loch Tondchuil. Then he darted away and commanded them to come to him.

26.   He came then to a great territory west of the lake and his vision failed him. He approached a pillar stone on the plain and placed his body-belt around it so that he might not die sitting or lying down but rather die standing. Then the men surrounded him but didn't dare approach him. They thought he was still alive. "Shame on you," said Erc mac Carpri, "for not taking the man's head in revenge for my father's head taken by him and buried next to Echaid's neck." His head had been brought from there to Síd Nenta íar n-Usciu.

27.   Then Líath Macha came to Cú Chulainn to guard him for as long as his soul was in him and the hero's light still emanated from his forehead. Then Líath Macha wrought three bloody attacks around him so that fifty fell by his teeth and thirty by each of his hooves. That's the amount of the host he killed. That's why it is said, "Not keener were the victorious courses of Líath Macha after the killing of Cú Chulainn." Then a scald-crow alit on his shoulder. "It's strange for that pillar stone to have birds perched on it," said Erc mac Carpri. Then Lugaid arranged his hair over his back and struck off his head. Then Cú Chulainn's sword fell from his hand so that it struck Lugaid's arm off so that it was on the ground. Cú Chulainn's arm was then struck off in revenge.

28.   The hosts then set out carrying Cú Chulainn's head and arm and arrived in Tara. There is the burial place of his head and arm and the full cover of his shield of earth. Cenn Faelad mac Ailella said of this in the *Death Tales of the Ulstermen*:

Cú Chulainn, fair hero,
strong warrior, fell in Airbe Rofir.
He subdued troops—great protection!—
against Lugaid mac Con Roí.

The number that fell—a manly conflict.
It was not a cowardly fall.

Thirty-two men, forty men,
two hundred men—fair lords.
One hundred twenty men—a strong number.
One hundred sixty men—a harsh deed.

Eighty men—an excellent gain.
Sualtaim's son destroyed them.

In great lamentation were slain
thirty kings with weapons.
Along with one hundred forty chiefs,
he left them ....

The head of the hound is in two,
firm fighter in Tara's height.
...was joined then
with the neck of Cairpre Nia Fer.

Echaid's head is today
in Síd Nenta íar n-Usciu.
The head of Cairpre, fair king,
was joined with Echaid's neck in Tethbae.

29.   Then the hosts set out southward and reached the River Liffey.
When they reached the river, Lugaid said to his charioteer, "My full belt
feels heavy around me. I'd like to bathe myself." He set out in front of the
host. He bathed then and they set out again afterward. He caught a salmon
between his two shins and tossed it up to his charioteer. The charioteer
kindled a fire to prepare it right away.

30.   Then the Ulstermen set out from the north from Emain Macha toward Slíab Fúait after shaking off their debility. There was a covenant between Cú Chulainn and Conall Cernach that whichever of them would be killed first would be avenged by the other: "If I'm killed first," Cú Chulainn said, "how soon will you avenge me?" "I'll avenge you by the evening of the day you're slain," Conall Cernach said. "And if I'm killed first, how soon will you avenge me?" "I won't allow your blood to have become cold on the ground before I avenge you," Cú Chulainn replied.

31.   When Conall Cernach arrived before the host in his chariot, he met Líath Macha gushing blood as he went to Linn Léith. Conall Cernach said:
"You cannot manage a yoke
to Linn Léith.
You will go with bloody tires,
with bodily injuries,
with gushing wounds
of man and horse
and the arm of Lugaid.
Lugaid mac Con Roí mac Dáre
has slain my fosterbrother Cú Chulainn."

32.   Then Conall Cernach and Líath Macha advanced and visited the battlefield. They saw Cú Chulainn at the pillar stone. Líath Macha placed his head on Cú Chulainn's bosom. "That corpse is troubling to Líath Macha," said Conall. Then Conall went and placed his foot against a hedge. "I swear what my people swears," he said, "that this hedge would be one of a great man." "You have conferred a name on the place," said a druid. "That will be this land's name forever: Airrbe Rofir."

33.   He set out then toward the host. There Lugaid was bathing. "Look out for us over the plain to make sure no one's coming," Lugaid said to his charioteer. The charioteer looked out. "A single rider is coming toward us with great swiftness and speed," he said. "You'd think the ravens of Ireland were above him and that snowflakes speckled the plain in front of him." "The rider approaching is no friend," said Lugaid. "That's Conall Cernach riding Derg Drúchtach. The birds you saw above him are the sods

from that horse's hooves, and the snowflakes you saw speckling the plain in front of him are the foam from that horse's lips and from the bridle's bridle bits. Look again," Lugaid said, "to see which way he's coming." "He's approaching the ford—the path the host has come," said the charioteer. "Let that horse pass us. We don't want to confront it."

34.   When Conall Cernach reached the middle of the ford, he looked out. "That's quite a salmon," he said. He looked again. "That's quite a charioteer," he said. He looked a third time. "That's quite a king. I should visit him." He visited them. "Welcome is a debtor's face," Conall Cernach said. "He from whom you are owed debts, demand them of him." "You owe me for the slaying of my comrade Cú Chulainn, and I'm prosecuting the claim for it upon you." "That's not proper," said Lugaid, "because meeting with me here won't be counted as valor for you until I bring my victory spoils to Munster." "I would do it if we don't travel the same path speaking in company together," said Conall Cernach. "That will be easy," said Lugaid. "I'll go on Belach Gebráin and then go on Belach Smechuin. You go on Gabur in Mairg Lagen and we'll meet in Mag Argetrois." Lugaid got there first. His partner, Conall, arrived after him and cast a shot at him with his spear as his foot was against the pillar stone and hit him in the foot. Thence is named Coirthe Lugdach in Mag Argetrois.

35.   After his first wounding, Lugaid went to Fertae Lugdach in Droichit Ossairge. They met there. Lugaid said, "I'd like to have battle honor from you." "How so?" asked Conall Cernach. "That you fight one-handed because I have only one hand." "Alright," Conall Cernach said, and his hand was tied to his side with cords. They were there for a few hours but neither prevailed. When Conall wasn't winning, he looked to his horse, Derg Drúchtach. She had the head of a hound and used to slay men in battles and contests. The horse came and seized a chunk of flesh from Lugaid's side so that his guts spilled out around his feet. "Woe indeed," said Lugaid. "That's no battle honor, Conall Cernach." "I granted you battle honor only on my own behalf," Conall replied. "I did not grant it to you on behalf of animals and insensible creatures." Lugaid said, "I know you won't leave until you carry my head with you because we've taken Cú Chulainn's head. Take then my head and wield my kingship in addition to your kingship and my weapons in addition to your weapons. I prefer

that you be the best warrior in Ireland." Thereupon Conall Cernach struck off his head.

36.   He set out then with the head and met up with the Ulstermen in Roiriu in the lands of Leinster. The head was placed on a stone and left there. They reached Gris. Then Conall Cernach asked, "Has someone brought the head?" "No," they all said. Then Conall Cernach said, "I swear what my people swears that that is no small crime." Thence is named Midbine at Roiriu. They turned back toward the head again and saw that it had dissolved the stone so that it had gone right through it.

37.   The Ulstermen did not allow themselves to go to Emain Macha with the victory spoils that week. But Cú Chulainn's soul did so that he appeared to the fifty queens he had defied the day before going into battle. They saw Cú Chulainn in his phantom chariot in the sky above Emain Macha. Cú Chulainn chanted to them and said after his death:
"Emain, Emain,
great the mighty Lord who will rise for us.
Priests will dwell in the territories of Emain.
They will come from the Alps of Europe.
The world will be awakened to Heaven
with the hosts of bright Patrick on the sea.
They will pray to the King of High Heaven
that we be settled by Him in Zion.
We will go to Judgment Day.
A fair man will receive me
in the east on the supreme plain.
That is good until we meet, Emain."

38.   *Cú Chulainn's Phantom Speech on His Death Day*
"The little lamb was slain, Emain.
The protector was slain, Emain.
By a spear he was pierced, Emain.
He fell in battle, Emain.
Though one against many,
your calf crushed men.
The little lamb was slain, Emain.

I will avenge great men's slaughter.
We ride a long course
for we were killed too soon.
Amid a fair woman's grieving cries,
Dechtire's darling rides fair paths
for us from darkness to a fort of joy.
A noble lord protected me
if he came to the champion of chariot-fighters.
I will avenge great men's slaughter.
If alone in single combat,
I'd call on Eithne's son.
He was everywhere in every form.
Aífe's son has been buried.
Lóeg has died—the heaviest misfortune.
My warrior-protector (*Conall*) … to me—
he who protects the swift Ulster exile,
with a charioted messenger of Delenn Dub
from Mag Eo in Mag Cride."

39.　　　Cú Chulainn said: *De Adventu Christi*
1. "Christ first rides through the lands of the powerless and the inadvertent
　　　sinners.
He will reign presently; He watches over His kin.
The Lord, the fair king, has died.
Below us, above us, the world's founder,
a home, a fort for us toward Heaven.

2. The law of the Son of humankind will come.
Everywhere it will extend; it will hinder your deception.
Jesus will conquer Hell for Adam's descendants
in an illusory realm, under a hand
toward which there may be envious and sorrowful ones,
at which they will rejoice,
at which they will recite the law of Heaven.

3. What king is this, what flood, of whom hosts will speak?
The king who has saved the world for the realm that awaits us,

for the kingdom that lacks no form of heavenly powers.
After victory in battle our king will rule fully over mighty kingdoms—
as one, as two, as three—
through powers I cannot examine,
I cannot utter, I cannot describe.

4. Dark the vision (that will appear) to people, the warning that will be
        before death:
The stars of Heaven will shake.
The bright sun's redness will be crushed.
The sky's blue course will be overrun.
The moon's light will be concealed
for the time of His mourning.

5. Jesus who is most humble, most noble,
through His harrowing of Hell,
through His establishment of rule,
through His deliverance of kingdoms,
through His mighty battle host,
through His great heavenly power
encompassing the heavens and humankind and Creation,
alive through ages."

40.   Líath Macha went to bid farewell to Emer. He placed his head on her bosom and went clockwise around her three times and clockwise around Dún Imrid and Dún Delgae.
Emer's Lament
1. "Líath Macha,
great sorrow,
great sadness,
great calamity,
great woe
that he who protected you doesn't behold you,
that he who yoked you doesn't support you,
that the fair, powerful, battle-victorious chariot-fighter
doesn't perform feats above you
in the borderlands of Macha and Mo Chae of Nendrum.

2. The bright cloud whom fairy kings aided,
the golden course above peaks who fought for many kingdoms,
the golden being above you who watched for sharp-bladed weapons—
he has caused the grief of bereft Dún Delgae.

3. The king of horses runs to the king of chariot-fighters and to death.
Above victorious blows or bird hunts,
you feel no switch or weapon-handle or shot,
you feel no chariot's left side holding cloven shields,
you feel no chariot's right side from which he'd strike enemies.

4. His ancestry benefited me.
His fearsomeness protected me.
His … supported me.
My fair, battle-victorious husband cared for me.

5. After harsh battle on Wednesday, the first day of autumn,
the chariot-fighter of Murthemne fell by a single wound in unequal
        combat.
Crooked-faced witches—loathsome demons—
destroyed the bloody triumph of battle-victorious Cú Chulainn.

6. Tell me, is fame or honor or greatness
or valor or generosity or rank or achievement likely now
when battle-victorious Cú Chulainn hasn't prevailed?
He slaughtered the Leinstermen when fighting the men of Ireland.
He slew the men of Ireland so that they died.
The fair, powerful, battle-victorious chariot-fighter knew,
with ardor for attack, that they'd be vanquished by his valor.

7. He arrayed himself wrong
so that his shield fell.
His horse avoided him.
His brooch wounded him.
The piercing wound damaged him,
sucking his strength

but not stemming his stride.
He encountered witches
blind in the left eye.
They cooked a grey hound
to ensnare his body.
He was kept under its power
from foot to crown
so that one side of him died.
The warriors he encountered
(…?)
so that his horse fell. (*Líath by name*)
Foully was Dub Sainglenn laid low.
Mighty the host that fell
though he went weakened, one-footed,
and one-handed to his encounter."

41.   Cú Chulainn killed eight Láths, eight Níaths, eight Fécs, eight
Óenguses, eight Fíachachs, eight Ferguses, eight Fáelguses, ten Brudes,
ten Bróns, ten Brenands, ten Corpres, ten Crimthands, ten Conaires, ten
Conalls, nine doomed men, nine druids, nine Dóelguses, nine Sáerguses,
nine Illands, forty charioteers, forty fronts, forty hospitallers, one hundred
crowns, one hundred marauders, one hundred old men, one hundred young
men, one hundred middle-aged men, twenty kings, twenty champions,
twenty splendid chariot-fighters, and twenty master warriors, along with
striking off eight hundred right hands and blinding eight hundred left eyes,
leaving the entire host blemished in one day.

42. 1. "Pity, Líath Macha, that you weren't one of two fine horses at the
          chariot.
Grief that Cú Chulainn didn't meet in combat with two perfect hands.
Pity that red-sworded Conchobar didn't counsel him.
Grief that Eirrge Echbél didn't come to him.
Pity that Sencha Sobeóil didn't reach him.
Grief that Fíacha Foltlebor didn't restrain him.
Pity that Éogain Álaind didn't speak to him.
Grief that Ferga mac Findcháeme didn't guard him.
Pity that Fergus mac Lete didn't go to him.

Pity that Feidlimid Fáeborderg didn't watch over him.
Grief that great, valiant Munremur didn't honor him.
Pity that Amergin didn't praise him.
Grief that Rochad Rigderg didn't guarantee him.
Pity that all Ulster's chariot-fighters weren't there where he fell in unequal
        combat
for his bright, wound-dealing body rode against many kingdoms and many
        hosts for the Ulstermens' sake.
Grief that Conall Cernach didn't help him.
Pity that victorious Celtchar didn't hear him.
Grief that Lóegaire Búadach didn't boast of him.
Pity that Fergus mac Rossa didn't reach him.
Grief that all the Ulstermen weren't around him where he fell.

2. Grief for him has oppressed me.
His loss has crushed me.
His death has weakened me.
I am lost after his death for I have nothing after him.

3. Surely every heart that loved him must burst.
Surely no ear that ever heard him can forget him.
Surely every tear ever shed must constantly lament him.
Surely every eye that has ever seen him must cry with gushing tears of
        blood
for grief after him ends the world,
for I won't be seen with another husband hereafter.
Men's faces won't be merry and generous at my wedding
for I won't find a husband like Cú Chulainn."

43. 1. "The bereft ones of Dún Delgae will be sad.
The best of the woman-troop will not be joyful.
He by whose deeds Mess Gegra died
wrought great vengeance.
The exile of Mag Mossad of great deeds
entered Mag Siamrach.
Conall came after accompanying Cormac
and fiercely avenging his fosterling.

Great being who prevailed
in single combat
after capture by fairy women—
the great courtship of Dechtire's
divine son sought me.
Lug's supreme fosterage
confirms his great rearing.
For me he fought storied Scáthach's fights—
sole guide of the Ulstermen from their fords.

2. I could attest to a bewitched period
of sixteen years in his time.
We deserve an end to troubles.
To provinces we proclaim:
Let each of us who knew him weep for him, lament him, bewail him.
Wretched is the world we are in
for we'll never meet another day, Líath, Líath."

Finit. Amen.

TEXTUAL NOTES

§1. l. 1 **gol ban** For lack of indication of a nasal after the accusative between a liquid and another consonant, see *GOI* §180 (2).

l. 2 **banrígan** Middle Irish genitive plural of feminine ī-stem, for which see *OIGR* 182.

Is accu ro taiscélad with accusative for dative plural of *oc* in Middle Irish agential use and with simple verb *taiscélaid* replacing Old Irish *do-scélai.* For the use of a singular passive verb as an impersonal taking a plural accusative, see Carney (1964: 115, n. 45). See *DIL* D 372.50–54 for translation of *do-scélai* as "makes known the custom of."

l. 5 **a llaa-sin** accusative of point of time, for which see *GOI* §249 (3).

§2. l. 6 **ní thic…úaib** literally "he is not coming from/because of you." For additional examples of this construction, see *DIL* O 74.55–61. For Middle Irish lenition in a main clause after *ní* see *EIV* 173.

l. 7 **tošúigthi** Thurneysen (1918) explains *tošúgud* in this text as a magical skill of attracting or causing someone to appear and discusses the term's use in Cormac's Glossary (Meyer 1912: 55, §676) in reference to the *gilldai,* who sucks learning from his teacher's tongue.

Is cían dond fir fil sund ó… literally "it is long for the man who is here from…." *fir* is for Old Irish *fiur,* translated as plural to convey the distributive sense of the singular in the text.

ll. 7–9 **Dún Chermnai, Belach Con Glais, Temair Lóchra, Combur Trí nUisce** are all Munster placenames.

l. 9 **Is cían cu tic Cú Chulaind** literally "it is long until Cú Chulainn comes."

l. 11 **na slúaig** nominative for accusative plural, for which see *OIGR* 180.

l. 12 **forsna** loss of -*b* in the dative plural of the article through replacement by the accusative plural form, for which see *OIGR* 183. Also note the use of *for* for *ar.*

§3. l. 15 **At-raí, a Chú Chulaind, comérig** The vocative phrase in this line stands outside the metrical pattern.

l. 17 **firu Galeoin** The genitive singular of the o-stem plural Gaileoin where one might expect a genitive plural *Galion* appears also in the Irish version of Nennius's Historia Brittonum—for example, *Fir Gaileoin* (Todd 1848: 44) and *Clanda Gaileoin* (ibid.: 48)—and in the Leinster genealogical poems by Find macc Rossa Rúaid edited in *Corpus Genealogiarum Hiberniae*: "lāithe Gailēoin"; "slōg Galiain" (O'Brien 1962: 1); "tuath Galēoin" (ibid.: 3).

l. 18 **soalta** Meyer (1916: 9–11) suggests that the name of Cú Chulainn's human father, Sualtaim, with the variants Sualtach, Soalta, and Soailte (the latter two forms appearing in *Serglige Con Culaind, Aided Óenfer Aífe,* and *Síaburcharpat Con Culaind*) originated in a misinterpretation of this adjective, the form Sualtaim having developed from the superlative of *su-alta* (see further §43, l. 693). Thurneysen (1921: 90–91), however, casts doubt on this suggestion.

l. 21 **co mbúretar basa** literally "so that palms may strike (loudly)." The line is either too short or too long by one syllable.

l. 23 **airdi óic do níth** literally "nobles and warriors to battle." *Airdi* could also be taken as nominative plural of *airde* "sign, portent"; the line could then be translated "great are the signs, warriors (going) to battle."

l. 24 **cotalgad** ipv. 3 sg. of *com-to-ad-luig*; perhaps originally *innád ...cotalgad* ("Wasn't Cormac lulled?"), with pret. pass. sg. of the verb (?).

l. 25 **admuintire i céin Chonchobuir** (= *i céin admuintire Chonchobuir*). The line is a syllable long (assuming elision between *admuintire* and *i*). Perhaps the original reading was *muintire i céin Chonchobuir*, the first syllable of *admuintire* arising through dittography. The essential meaning would be the same (although *admuinter* in the sense of "former kin" may imply a shift in Cormac's kin loyalties through his exile). The line would then appear to lack linking alliteration with the preceding line; however, it may have been considered permissible to skip a word in the long alliterative chain, perhaps especially in the context of interlaced alliteration (see metrical analysis of this passage in the Introduction). Carney notes that "in archaic verse an alliterating series of three or more words may be broken by a non-alliterating word" (1981: 259).

l. 26 **nít-tá** This reading is supported by Níab's poem in the following section, in which she points out that Conall Cernach is not available to protect Cú Chulainn (§5, l. 42).

ll. 26–27 **comnesam/Cormaic** See Breatnach (2016b), where definiteness is identified as a common characteristic of enjambment with genitive phrases. See also §5, ll. 48–49 and §38, ll. 531–532 and ll. 533–534.

l. 27 **arndin-nderóemad** augmented past subjunctive 3 sg. of *do-eim* with conjunction *ar* and 1 pl. infixed pronoun; literally "so that he may protect us."

ll. 29–30 **cot-gní...gním** literally "Lugaid (with his) full alliance together carries out your slaying, which will avenge a deed." As *con-gní* in the meaning "assists" is used with a preposition—usually *fri* or *la* (for the latter see Corthals 1989b: 48)—and as the sense of the passage suggests it, the verb is here interpreted as "acts or carries out together," with the infixed pronoun expressing the object of the verbal noun *goin* in the following line. For additional examples of the genitive use of the infixed pronoun, see O'Brien (1938), *SnaG* 26, and O'Rahilly (1976: 3, l. 91). The line as written in *L* (with *cotob-gní*) is a syllable long; emending to the 2 sg. class B infixed pronoun (see *GOI* 259) yields a heptasyllabic line that is consistent with the use of the 2 sg. in the rest of the poem without changing the meaning.

l. 29 **lánchlemnas** dative of accompanying circumstance (*GOI* §251, 3), referring to Lugaid's alliance of avengers from the provinces of Ireland against Cú Chulainn.

l. 30 **fris-gegna** The form *-gegna*, for *-géna*, appears in the YBL version of *Táin Bó Regamna*. Pedersen considers this an earlier form, as Corthals notes in his edition (1987: 45–46). With Thurneysen (*GOI* 651), however, Corthals interprets it as a later form, possibly a later spelling for /ge:na/. McCone (1991: 160–162) considers *-gign(e)a* the original future form of *-goin*, replaced in Middle Irish by a form in the productive *é*-future, instancing the appearance of *not-gignether* in *Cath Maige Mucrama*. The form *fris-gegna* is here taken as the future 3 sg. of a compound verb with verbal noun *frithguin* ("counter-wounding or slaying," *DIL* F 440.45), with the meaning "will slay in return for" (i.e., "avenge").

l. 31 **ándrennuig** vocative sg. of *án* + *drennach*; literally "splendid and combative one."

§4 l. 34 **An dím** literally "desist from me."

l. 35 **Ní mm'óenur do-miul-sa** literally "not alone do I enjoy."

l. 36 **Cíabo bidbu imnedach** literally "though it may be a worrisome enemy."

l. 37 **ar is díairle íarna scís mo scís** literally "my fatigue after its fatigue is ill advised," taking *díairle* as an adjectival compound of *di-* with *airle* (vn. of *airlithir*) (compare *díárim*).

l. 38 **Nídam** Middle Irish form of present indicative 1 sg. of the copula, for which see *EIV* 231.

§5. l. 43 **Cain róg renar ar Ultaib?** literally "Isn't the one who is sacrificed for the Ulstermen very pure?" For *cain* in this position, see Corthals (1989: 49, note to line 6a). The word might also be taken as written in *L* (*caín*), with the translation "fair." The former interpretation is chosen here on the strength of the appearance of a parallel use of *cain* in l. 104 (see note) and the text's frequent use of rhetorical questions in verse passages. For discussion of the shift in l. 43 from second- to third-person singular as a poetic feature, see Ó Baoill (1990) and Sims-Williams (2005).

l. 44 **-bíth** preterite passive singular of *benaid* in final-verb construction.

ll. 45–46 **conid úanchend airm inid accid/ar ní imgonat na aill** Literally *inid accid* translates as "that he invokes for it." *airm* may be genitive sg. of apposition or nominative pl. in a compound (reading *condat* for *conid*, which may have been influenced by the following *úanchend*). The reading of *airm*, "weapons/weaponry," as a metonym for Cú Chulainn and as subject of *imgonat* is supported by the similar metonymic use of *carpat* for Conall earlier in the passage. Alternatively, the phrase may be read "lambhead of the army," with an early use of *arm* in this meaning. The neuter *na aill* is taken in the current reading as adverbial. Alternatively, the text may have read *na haili* (referring to the other Ulstermen), yielding the translation "because the others don't fight," in accordance with Cú Chulainn's above-expressed reluctance to fight alone. For *úanchend* see §38, l. 521 and Nad Crantail's remark to Cú Chulainn in TBC I: *noco rucaim-se cind úain bic don dúnud, ní bér do chend ngillai n-amulaig* (O'Rahilly 1976: 45, ll. 1449–1450).

l. 49 **meic Amairgin** The line break as analyzed involves enjambment of a definite genitive phrase (see Breatnach 2016b).

§6. l. 51 **Cíabam trú-sa ním-tharraid cubés** literally "Though I may be a doomed person, a peer does not reach me."

l. 52 **con-róetar** deponent augmented preterite 1 sg. to *con-oí* (suppletive preterite with *con-eim*), for which see *GOI* §684.

l. 53 **Ním- ág -archelad** The line could also be translated as "my valor was not stolen." *-archelad* is preterite passive sg. of *ar-cela.*

l. 54 **Ní mmo guin -immgabaim** This sentence and the preceding are examples of Greene's category of Tmesis II (Greene 1977). The position of the verbs perhaps serves a poetic function, as it yields parallel sentences in Tmesis II with trisyllabic cadences.

§7. l. 55 **ro ling** Middle Irish s-preterite replacing Old Irish reduplicated *leblaing.*

l. 56 **ro meth fair** literally "fumbled on him." The *H* reading likely preserves the earlier form and fits Cú Chulainn's following reference to culpability (*bidba*). *Ro maid*, with its use of the s-preterite for earlier *memaid*, is likely a later reading.

ll. 58–59 **Ní bidba bratt beres robud** literally "the cloak that brings a warning is not a culprit."

l. 61 **ad-chumben** Restoration of this form provides alliteration with following *chness*. Note appearance of the preterite form *at-cummai* in §40, l. 622, narrating the same incident.

chness For lenition of the object after a verbal form see *GOI* §233, 2.

l. 63 **for scánfaiter** See *GOI* 313 for elision of the relative particle (*a* or *sa*) in poetry. Contrast §9, l. 90.

ll. 64–65 **scarad fáebuir/fri** literally "by separation of [the shield's] edge."

l. 65 **fri desláim mo duirn** literally "from the right hand of my fist," with *dorn* in genitive of apposition, for which see *GOI* §250, 1(a).

l. 66 **n-anabaid** emended to reflect accusative treatment of cause of death (see Breatnach 2021).

l. 67 **créchtnaigfit** future 3 pl. relative with loss of deponent inflection and Middle Irish absolute for Old Irish relative ending, for which see *EIV* 182.

l. 68 **airchisfither** For confusion of palatal and nonpalatal *-r* in passive/impersonal endings see *EIV* 228.

día *día* may also be the nominative sg. of *día* "a god or supernatural being."

ll. 68–69 **día mór/des…** The phrase is partially echoed by the final lines of Lebarcham's speech in §10. See note to ll. 112–113.

89

§8. l. 72 **Tongu do día a tonges mo thúath** Ó hUiginn (1989) argues that this sentence combines the phrase *Tongu a tonges mo thúath* ("I swear that which my tribe swears") with the Christian expression *Tongu do día* ("I swear to God") and reflects an earlier stage in the development of the common formula *Tongu do día tonges mo thúath* (through elision of the unstressed particle). Watkins (1990) argues, however, that the latter phrase reflects an inherited Indo-European formulaic oath, adducing Russian and Greek parallels. Ó hUiginn (1992: 56–57) does not accept this case for the expression's antiquity but does not deny the possibility that the oath "represents an archaic pre-Christian survival" (1989: 340).

l. 73 **nís-tibritis** use of 3 sg. feminine/3 pl. -s- for masculine 3 sg. infixed pronoun, for which see *EIV* 171.

l. 74 **In menma nom-airfitiged do grés ní hé dom-riacht** literally "the spirit that always used to delight me is not what has come forth to me."

§9. l. 77 **remi** Old Irish *riam.*

l. 80 **Níbu gnáth** literally "it was not customary." Note use of the modal preterite of the copula, for which see Quin (1974).

l. 81 **leithe for clé frim** literally "side to the left against me." For this by-form of *leth* in the meaning "side" see *DIL* (L 124.11–15).

l. 82 **Fechuir fiach fondat-gaib** literally "fiercely the raven encounters you."

l. 83 **im gním do-tluchemar éc** literally "concerning an action (i.e., going to battle) by which we seek death." *do-tluchemar* is 1 pl. present indicative of *do-tluchethar* in a nasalizing indirect relative construction. Restoration of this form is supported by the stronger linking alliteration it provides with the following line. Perhaps *do-tluchethar éc* may be considered a semantic unit, like those detailed by Carney (1981: 260), allowing the alliteration to skip over *éc.*

l. 84 **ní thintlaig** present indicative 3 sg. of *to-in-tluch.* This reading is supported by the preceding line's use of a form of the same verb, supplying verbal echo (see Carney 1981: 258). Alternatively, David Stifter suggests, *thintla* may represent *thintoí*, present indicative 3 sg. of *do-intoí.*

ll. 85–86 **i mmuige mag diandot-imrédinn cíana** literally "into the plain of plains through which I used to ride you for long distances."

l. 89 **creta cungai fortche** taken as genitive forms dependent (like *eich* and *ruith*) on *scarad.* Though one might expect *creitte* as genitive singular for *crett* (an earlier form according to *DIL* C 523 l. 74), reading *creta* as a plural form would yield little sense unless the word were interpreted to refer to single ribs of the chariot frame, in which case one might expect *asnai creite* (see Greene 1972: 69). See also *cretta* (taken as genitive singular) in §12, l. 184.

l. 90 **forsa suidmis suide** Note use of figura etymologica. Contrast the form of the preposition with relative in l. 63; perhaps the relative particle is maintained here without elision because of its contribution to the alliterative pattern.

ll. 91–92 **Suilig rodon-baí Badb** literally "Badb has been favorable/agreeable to us."

§10. l. 93 **bolgdéra móra fola** See §42, l. 677 for another reference to tears of blood. For further instances of this motif in the literature see Hull (1954).

l. 94 **do-curidar bedg** literally "casts a leap."

l. 98 **Nán** Old Irish *nachan.*

l. 104 **cain in tocad** The length-mark in *caín* (*L*) is taken as an error facilitated by the closely preceding *caíngnúis.* The reading as the negative interrogative *cain* (*cani*) is supported by the sense and by its yielding of a two-stress line in keeping with the rest of the passage. For *cain* in this position see Corthals (1989: 49, note to line 6a) and §5, l. 43 above.

ardo díth literally "for your destruction."

l. 110 **Cichsi dano céim rígairech** literally "you'll step then a regal step to the battle." For *cichsi* see *GOI* §666. Note use of figura etymologica with *céim.*

dano This adverb may be a later scribal addition as it yields a four-stress line and interrupts the line-internal alliteration.

ll. 112–113 **Airchisfither** It is tentatively suggested that l. 112 began with *airchisfither*, echoing ll. 68–69 more completely and supplying stronger linking alliteration with the preceding line.

díe Cormac's Glossary defines this word as "lament": "die dano.i. caoine" (Stokes 1862: 15). Mac Eoin (1977) considers this interpretation to have arisen from a misunderstanding of *día*, a word for "day," the view followed here. A passage in §12 (ll. 173–174), *lathe Maige Murthemni atharda*, perhaps parallel to the recurring phrase *díe mór Maige Murthemni*, may support this interpretation.

l. 114 **as-rubairt-si** Old Irish *as-rubart*; for palatalization see *EIV* 240.

§11 l. 116 **ná fácbaitis** literally "that they not be left."
sáraigis Old Irish deponent *sáraigser*.
l. 119 **Geib leic** This phrase may contain the imperative 2 sg. of *gaibid* with object *leig* (Latin *lex*), for which see also l. 225, or the imperatives 2 sg. of *gaibid* and *léicid*, with unclear meaning.
ll. 120–124 **La araid...mifre** Literally the phrases mean "with a charioteer, acceptance; with a chariot-fighter, protection" and so on.
l. 126 **nachit-chobradar** literally "that does not help you."
l. 127 **To-ssuíther** literally "is turned."
ll. 127–128 **do-beir in banchuire gáir guil 7 golgaire 7 bosschaire** literally "the woman-troop brings a lamenting cry, a wailing shout, and a clapping of hands."
nícon ricfed literally "he would not come."

§12. l. 130 **It brónaig...** Note the echo of this passage at the outset of §43.
l. 132 **diar n-apthaib** *apthaib* perhaps represents a short dative singular *apthae* influenced by the following dative plural *maigib* or by the analogy of *écaib* used to denote individual deaths.
l. 133 **dall** This word is used in the sense of "dark, gloomy" also in §39, l. 564 (*dall taidbsiu do doínib*).
ll. 134–135 **fríth fo-n-úair/fas-cíurat ceirn** *DIL* (F 432.53) lists for *fríth* a meaning of "lucky find, a treasure-trove, an unexpected gain." *fo-n-úair* may be an impersonal preterite active (literally "it found"); alternatively, it might be emended to the preterite 1 sg. *fo-n-úar*. *fas-cíugrat* (*L*) would seem to be future 3 pl. of *fo-ceird* with 3 pl. or fem. 3 sg. infixed pronoun; the meaning is difficult to interpret, however, although *DIL* (F 191.28–30) lists a reflexive use of the verb with the meaning "form ranks," for which *ceirn*, for *ceirm* (*L*), nominative pl. of *cern*, might serve as a subject if understood as meaning "victorious warriors." The speculative reading offered here emends *ceirm* (*L*) to *ceirn*, taken as nominative pl. of *cern* in the meaning "battle victories," and *fas-cíugrat* to *fas-cíurat*, future 3 pl. of *fo-cren* (influenced by the future form of *fo-ceird*) with a Middle Irish 3 sg. feminine infixed pronoun serving for a masculine infixed pronoun (referring to *fríth*), for which see *EIV* 171 and note to l. 73. Translated as "victories will buy the discovered treasure (or the treasure I found)," the

passage perhaps refers to the Biblical Parable of the Hidden Treasure, in which one sells all one has for the treasure of the Kingdom of Heaven (Suggs et al.: 1282). That is, in keeping with the rest of the text, the passage may suggest that Cú Chulainn is exchanging his battle victories for Christian salvation.

l. 136 **co for-cingiu dinn drisib** taking *co* as 1. co (*GOI* §896). The meaning of *for-cing* (literally "steps on or over") is uncertain. Possibilities may include "ascend" or "prevail," intensifying the meaning of the simplex *cingid* as either "steps, proceeds" (*DIL* C 192.54) or "overcomes, surpasses, excels" (*DIL* C 193.23). If the verb is taken to mean "ascend," *dinn* may represent the accusative sg. ("to a height"); if taken to mean "prevail," *dinn* may represent the dative sg. ("as a peak or high one)." *drisib* is (independent) dative pl. of *dris* ("among (or from among) briars"). The passage might thus continue the possible allusion to Biblical parable begun in the previous line. The word *dris* also appears, however, in *Bretha Nemed* (Breatnach 1987: 21), where Breatnach suggests it may be a mistake for *drisiuc* (ibid.: 25), a grade of satirist. If the word is taken here as a form of *drisiuc*, the passage might be interpreted as referring to the satirists mentioned in 1. 170 (*dulu*) and in §17 and thereafter (*cáinte*), yielding a translation of "among (or from among) satirists." Note also the etymological glosses in *Uraicecht na Ríar* §19 (Breatnach 1987: 113) and notes (ibid.: 134), relating the *drisiuc* to *dris* ("briar") and *cú* ("hound").

l. 137 **rot-bith-mairg** See *GOI* §384 for adverbal prefixes.

ll. 137–138 **ro fáthatar/flathi fer** *ro fáthatar* is augmented preterite 3 pl. of *fethid* (see *GOI* §692).

l. 139 **mbuntáib bethad** *buntáib* is taken as a compound of *bun* and *táeb* tentatively understood as "fundamental side" or "fundamental boundary," with the phrase thus meaning "boundary of life (i.e., death)."

l. 145 **con-cechalsat búada** *con-cechalsat* is future 3 pl. of *con-claid*. The word *búada* is understood here in the sense of "advantage, profit," referring to the protections and favors that will be lost when generous lords perish.

l. 146 **a n-at-mbélat** The emendation assumes loss of the particle *a* or *i* (see Murphy 1956: 279) in the meaning "when."

l. 147 **a baccaib ráth** literally "from/out of hindrances of sureties." The sentence in ll. 145–147 is more easily understood in English if translated with a different ordering of phrases: "They will bury advantages because of hindrances of sureties when generous lords perish." Alternatively, *ráth* may represent *rath* ("gifts"). In the first edition (Kimpton 2009: 38), this phrase is taken to mean "from corners of forts."

ll. 149–152 **díchra aige...forránu** Note the adverbial use of figura etymologica with dual accusative (see Ó hUiginn 1983).

l. 156 **Aithguba sírechtach** The phrase is taken as in the independent dative.

l. 159 **fír fer** literally "truth of men," often translated as "fair play."

ll. 160–161 **forgoba óenfir/écomluind ili** Alternatively, one might emend to *for-géba óenfer écomlund iliu*, retaining the *L* reading *óenfer*, to yield the meaning "one man will attack many in unequal combat" (taking *écomlund* as an independent dative).

l. 165 **i ssídib** The passage can also be read as "in fairy mounds," with a possible play on words (see Ó Cathasaigh 1977–1978).

l. 166 **sies** for *siais*, future 3 sg. of *saigid*.

l. 167 **úane** genitive of time of *úain* (see *GOI* §250, 4).

l. 168 **nós níbu thais** literally "in a manner that was not weak" (see *GOI* §505).

l. 169 **arcu** This word appearing without *fuin* is glossed, as David Stifter points out, using forms of *ad-tluchethar*. The translation aims to convey the senses of "gives thanks" and "rejoices at" at the time of Líath Macha's death.

l. 170 **dílúba** This word is tentatively taken as accusative plural of *dílúib* (*dílúbai*), an i-stem adjectival formation with *lúb* (in the sense of "deceit, subterfuge") plus the intensive prefix *dí-* (see *GOI* §345). A spelling with *p* for unvoiced /b/ might be expected; however, the text elsewhere shows such a spelling (*anabaid*, l. 66). See also *GOI* §31 for such spelling fluctuations. If this reading is correct, the form would be an early example of the use of *lúb* in this sense. The word might also be taken as *di-lúba* (for *lúbaid* used intransitively to describe the action of fighting, see *DIL* L 229.2–8), in which case the translation might be "who contends with satirists."

l. 171 **écraitiu aithber** *aithber* is in genitive of apposition ("hostilities of reproaches").

l. 172 **díthide** This word is tentatively taken as a past participle in future sense (for which see Quin 1974) or verbal of necessity of *di-fen* with a meaning of "releases" or "transcends."

94

ll. 175–178 **íba…** The following description of the aftermath of Cú
Chulainn's wounding (from *íba* to *tormaid*) seems to resemble the
narration of the Crucifixion as seen, for example, in Blathmac's poems
(parting drink: l. 233; Christ crying out to His father in momentary despair:
ll. 239–240; the elements responding to Christ's death: §§61, 62, 65; the
division of spoils (*noíbfodb*): ll. 215–216).

ll. 175–176 **srúaim sruthbarr slán** The phrase is taken as in the
independent dative, with *sruthbarr* understood as a compound of *sruth* and
barr ("streaming excessively").

l. 177 **brond** (*broind L*) preposed genitive dependent on *crú* (dependent
on *lam*, "with my"), acquiring in *L* syntactic dependence on the latter
word's governing preposition *la* (see Corthals 1996: 27 and note below on
ría ndomuin díth, l. 194).

begdolb This word is unclear. Possibly *d* and *g* were transposed. One
could read *bedgaib* in independent dative use; a meaning of "jumping out"
may yield an apt description of Cú Chulainn's wound, which causes his
innards to leave his belly. Alternatively, if *g* was written for *c* (see *GOI*
§31), the word might be taken as an adjectival compound of *bec* and *dolb*.
Carney analyzed the latter word appearing in Blathmac's poems as
"substantival, related to *dolbaid*" (1964: 123), translating it as
"deception." The verb *dolbaid* appears in §2, l. 10, where it has the
meaning "fashions, (magically) conjures." A speculative meaning of the
compound might then be something like "characterized by petty sorcery."

l. 178 **-fothraicfe** Middle Irish simple verb *fothraicid*, as below in l. 426,
in contrast with Old Irish *fo-thruci* in l. 377.

l. 179 **níth nemnech** The phrase is taken as in the independent dative. See
also Cormac's Glossary (Stokes 1862: 32) "níth .i. guin duine."

ll. 181–182 **sémite fuile form chuirp crí** literally "by which wounds on
the flesh of my body calm." *sémite* (*sémide L*) is taken as present indicative
relative 3 pl. of *sémid* used intransitively. Alternatively, reading *sémide*,
the word may be taken as an adjective (with the meaning "smooth")
describing *nél*, with *fuile* representing *file*, present indicative relative of
the substantive verb.

l. 183 **clú im cathu canis-n-immarburt?** literally "Have I not wielded
fame concerning battles?" This line appears in *L* somewhat later in the
section (between *comdetae* and *gand*, ll. 191–192), where it interrupts the
narrative sense and does not provide linking alliteration with the following

line (although there is internal alliteration in the following line). It may have been placed there mistakenly—an error perhaps encouraged by the alliteration between *comdetae* and *clú*. Moving this line up to its current position in the text resolves several issues. First, it restores sense, as Cú Chulainn's despairing cry over his wound—in apparent momentary doubt about his fame in battle, perhaps in parallel to Christ crying out to God on the Cross—comes right after the narration of his wounding. Second, in combination with the emendation of the difficult *cribsaite* (see note below), it provides linking alliteration both before and after the line. Third, removing the line from its original position in *L* restores linking alliteration and narrative sense in that section of the poem.

l. 184 **bibsaitir cretta fuidbechta** literally "the frame's fragments will be distributed," with the future passive plural of *boingid* and substantivized participle of *fo-di-boing* and with *crett* used in the sense of "trunk" or "body."

l. 189 **Bérthair** literally "will be brought."

ll. 190–191 **díth slabrae slab comdetae** This passage is quoted in O'Mulconry's Glossary (429) as "díth slabrae slabir coindith" (Stokes 1898: 255). *Comdetae* is perhaps genitive sg. of *coimded* "security, protection." Perhaps *slab* is a substantive form; if so, the syntax here would parallel that of the previous line.

l. 194 **ría ndomuin díth** In *L* the dative form of the governing word spread to the preposed genitive.

l. 197 **Togáethfaid** Middle Irish simple verb replacing *do-gáetha*.

l. 200 **i mbo cen athfír** literally "when he may be without great truth." *athfír* is taken as the intensive prefix *ath-* with *fír*.

l. 203 **fessair cathu** See note on *is accu ro taiscélad* in §1, l. 2 for the use of a singular passive verb as an impersonal taking a plural accusative.

l. 208 **todlach** See Binchy (1966: 38–39, §27), where *todlach*, referring to a wound, is identified as from *to-uss-dloing*. The word also occurs in *Félire Óengusso*, where it is translated as "affliction" (Stokes 1905: 216). A meaning of "cuts away, rends" fits the context.

ll. 216–217 **sáer díamlad. Ar...** Alternatively, perhaps read *sáer -díamlathar*, with the present indicative 3 sg. of *di-samlathar* in final-verb construction: "that conceals (i.e., causes concealment of) a noble."

ll. 219–220 **lathe dia mbáidfider bith móras doíne** an instance of the use of *dia* in the meaning "when" with a tense other than the narrative preterite, for which see Breatnach (1989b: 39–40) and, as there noted, Binchy (1966b). Perhaps read *mórad* (the verbal noun) (?). Alternatively, read as in the first edition (Kimpton 2009: 38) "…on the day when the world will be extinguished through one who…." Perhaps, alternatively, the text read *bith mór do-indnastar* ("great the one who will be delivered") (?).

l. 223 **ferr dúib co fa šecht** literally "better for you by seven."

l. 227 **a ro mbeth mad cet bith** literally "if I had permission to be." The verbal noun would be expected to appear in the genitive.

l. 229 **nách ricfad** literally "would not come."

§13 l. 232 **in tan na théiged** Middle Irish use of *in tan* with leniting rather than nasalizing relative, for which see *EIV* 180.

l. 234 **Co n-accai ní na téora** literally "He saw something: the three…."

l. 238 **ro bass** For the s-variant of the preterite passive, see *EIV* 232.

l. 241 **Ní túalaing mór nád fulaing nó nád geib in mbec.** See the Introduction for discussion of this (perhaps proverbial) phrase's appearance in the writings of Columbanus (*cui pauca non sufficiunt, plura non proderunt*, "The man to whom little is not enough will not benefit from more," Sermon III.4, Walker 1957: 78–79) (Stancliffe 1997: 98–99).

l. 243 **rod-n-gab** *rod-gab* (*L*) could also be taken as an example of Middle Irish relative use of infixed *-d-*, for which see *EIV* 175.

l. 244 **ro gabtha** literally "were seized."

conná rabi a nnert cétna indib literally "so that the (or their) same strength was not in them."

§14. l. 245 **Do-cumlat** literally "they set out."

l. 246 **facca** Old Irish *-accai*. For Middle Irish prosthetic *f*, see *EIV* 200.

l. 250 **dubderga** literally "dark red." Note Middle Irish masculine plural ending, for which see *OIGR* 184, and the compound alliteration, for which see Stifter 2016.

comrethi attributive genitive singular of *comrith*.

l. 251 **clár clé cleithe** For the use of *clár* to indicate the side-piece of a chariot, see Greene (1972). For the figurative meaning of *cleth* as "warrior, chief," see *DIL* (C 233.72).

l. 253 **fochluib** For the meaning of *fochla* in the figurative sense of "champion," see *DIL* (F 196.15).

§15. ll. 258–272 **at-chíu-sa…ind óclaig-sin** Thurneysen (1912–1913: 18–19) notes that this description of Cú Chulainn and his chariot, which closely resembles those in other texts, replaces an earlier *retoiric*. The excerpt from this passage in *H* suggests that it may have been structured in stressed alliterative lines.

l. 259 **-saide** See Watkins (1979) for etymology.

colgatchaín *DIL* (C 326.9) considers *colgat* equivalent to *clocat*.

ll. 259–260 **Is amlaid** *amlaid* for earlier *samlaid*.

l. 260 **dá n-echaib** accusative for dative *díb*, continuing nasalization of latter form, for which see *SnaG* 260.

cendbeca cruindbeca corrbeca loss of *-b* in the dative plural of the adjective, for which see *SnaG* 252.

corrbeca *DIL* (C 483.78–79) translates as "small-nuzzled," reading *corr* as a substantive referring to the horse's snout; it may also be considered a dvandva compound and translated as "pointed and small." Note C. O'Rahilly's reference (1976: 279, note to line 2951) to *corrderga* in *Togail Bruidne Da Derga*.

l. 261 **crúeich** For this meaning of *crú* in a compound, see *DIL* C 554.15–35.

Cidat Old Irish *cetu*.

l. 263 **maignech** *DIL* (M 33.34) identifies this term as a "frequent epithet of horses" and suggests it to be a derivative of *maigne* ("big, great").

focursid *DIL* identifies *fochorsid* as an "epithet of a horse." See also LU 6490.

l. 264 **duba dorchaide** See note to l. 260.

l. 266 **énblaith** Similar passages in *Fled Bricrenn* (Henderson 1899: §§4 and 47) read *anblúth n-én*. *DIL* (E 123–124) defines *én gaile* as a "bird of valour, a phenomenon supposed to accompany the martial fury of heroes," comparable to the *lúan/lón láith* defined as a "radiance, light" that appears "above the head of a warrior in battle" (*DIL* L 224.33–37).

erra alternatively for dative plural of *err*, "point, sharp edge" (of a chariot).

l. 268 **ra tuigedar** see *EIV* 197 for replacement by *ro-* (*ra-*) of *no-* with infixed pronoun.

l. 269 **téora** If *imṡrotha* is taken as *imm + sruth* (see following note) this would be an instance of use of *téora* with a masculine noun, for which see *SnaG* 261.

imṡrotha analyzed in *DIL* (I 176.4) as *imm* + *sruth* and translated as "encircling streams." In a similar passage, *Fled Bricrenn* has *imrotha* (Henderson 1899: 56), translated in *DIL* (I 178.12) as "circles." C. Ó'Rahilly (1976: 280, note to line 2962) suggests reading *imsretha* ("encircling rows") in accordance with a passage in Recension II.

ll. 269–271 **comba samalta ra tétaib...taídlech cecha fadmainni** literally "the sparkle of each lock...was like strands...." For other examples of ellipsis of this kind, see ll. 9–10 of *The Poems of Blathmac* (*estu cech ingir/Críst cháid*, Carney 1964: 2, 113), ll. 3–4 of a poem by Colmán mac Lénéni (*drecha ban n-athech/oc ródaib rígnaib*, MacCotter 2004: 129), and Havers (1956: 260), referenced in Carney (1964).

l. 269 **ra tétaib** substitution of dative for accusative.

l. 270 **saincherda** genitive singular of agent noun in apposition to *suad.*

§16. Some words in this passage appear in the *H* excerpt from the replaced passage in §15 (Thurneysen 1912–1913: 17).

l. 273 **In fer-sin...no frithalid** nominativus pendens construction with analeptic 3 sg. masculine infixed pronoun; for Middle Irish confusion of *no-/na-*, see *EIV* 169.

l. 274 **do-ringintea** Middle Irish augmented preterite passive 3 sg. of *do-gní*, for which see *SnaG* 306–308 and *EIV* 232–234.

ll. 277–284 **Comérgid...** Some words of this passage appear in the *H* excerpt from the replaced *retoiric* above in §15.

ll. 279–280 **óenní...duini** See also ll. 562–563 and accompanying notes.

l. 279 **amáin** Old Irish *nammá.*

ll. 280–281 **aid-gén** preterite 3 sg. of *ad-gnin* with present meaning.

l. 281 **fírchlich** The meaning of this word is unclear.

l. 282 **ingeni détlai bunaid** literally "of a maiden of brave stock."

l. 283 **imma- nár néoil -slecht** literally "the champion of a cloud (i.e., cloudlike champion) has been slain," with preterite passive sg. of *imm-slig* in tmesis.

ll. 283–284 **Bud adbur anmich airchind dia-n-tic** literally "that from which he comes would be the stuff of a blemished leader."

§17. l. 285 **fuirechlem, aurisfemmar** deuterotonic *fo-roichlem*, *ar-sissfemmar*; for the use of prototonic forms of compound verbs in a relative clause, see *GOI* §493.6.

99

l. 286 **chúicid** Old Irish *cóiced*; see *SnaG* 233 for change of *ó* to *ú* after initial *c-* and before a slender consonant.

Filet plural form of the relative of the substantive verb, an example of development of inflected forms of the Old Irish impersonal, for which see *SnaG* 323.

l. 287 **dona scíathaib** loss of *-b* in the dative plural of the article through replacement by the accusative plural form, for which see *OIGR* 183.

l. 288 **tabraid** For the nonpalatal final consonant in the present stem, see *EIV* 212 and l. 299.

l. 289 **tressiu** Middle Irish use of comparative for superlative, for which see *SnaG* 257 and note to l. 570.

cáinte See Breatnach (1983) for analysis of *cáinte* as an agent noun with suffix *-e* added to the verbal noun *cáiniud.*

l. 290 **accu** accusative for earlier dative *occaib.*

l. 294 **Do-gníther aní-sin** literally "that is done."

§18. l. 299 **gabaid** See note to l. 288.

no imbred Middle Irish simple verb of *imm-beir.*

l. 303 **íarna n-esrédiud** literally "after their being scattered."

§19. l. 306 **co n-acca** literally "he saw."

l. 309 **tánic** literally "came."

da-rónais an example of skew between active and passive preterite forms of *do-gní*, for which see *EIV* 234; *da-* reflects either Middle Irish spelling variation between *o* and *a* (*EIV* 169) or a proleptic infixed pronoun.

l. 310 **drónand** present indicative 3 sg. Middle Irish ending *-ann* with potential augment (Old Irish deuterotonic *do-rónai*, prototonic *-dernai*).

ll. 310–311 **Ní betis na tost tria impide forru** literally "they wouldn't have been silent through asking it of them."

l. 314 **mani thuca** literally "if you don't give it."

§20 l. 320 **ro theilg** Middle Irish simple verb replacing earlier compound; note also Middle Irish lenition.

l. 321 **a mbuí do innib ina medón co rrabi** literally "what was of innards in his abdomen so that it was."

§21. l. 328 **co nderna brosnaig ndiib** literally "he made fragments of them."

l. 330 **ríchtain** accusative for nominative.

cethri accusative for nominative, for which see *SnaG* 261.

l. 333 **Aírfat-sa** Middle Irish 1 sg. future ending.

l. 334 **cin** short accusative, for which see McCone (1978) and §32, l. 452.

l. 337 **fethid** See Schaffner (2004), where this passage is quoted, for the etymology of *fethid* from IE **wete-ti*. Given the earliness of the forms in the surrounding portion of text (e.g., *sreith, cin*) the instance of the verb may be considered further evidence for its early spelling as *fethid* and its proposed derivation. The augmented preterite 3 pl. *ro fáthatar* appears in §12, l. 137.

at-rubramar See *EIV* 240–241 for Middle Irish combined s-/suffixless ending with a former t-preterite.

§22. l. 340 **bias** literally "will be."

Do-fuit rí literally "a king falls."

ll. 348–349 **riris dá ech…** *H* provides a superior reading.

§23 l. 358 **do-theilg** *do-* for *ro-* or repetition of preverb, for which see *EIV* 194–196.

§24. l. 363 **Tuitfid** Middle Irish simple verb with f-future, in contrast with closely following Old Irish future *do-fáeth* and secondary future *do-fáethsad* in ll. 318 and 319 and ll. 363–364.

§25. l. 374 **thísiur-sa** Note Middle Irish 1 sg. present subjunctive ending, for which see *EIV* 217 and 219.

ll. 375–376 **amal ro-n-ánic** Note preservation of nasalizing relative clause.

l. 378 **ainm aile** Use of masculine *aile* and lack of nasalization indicate that the Old Irish neuter noun *ainm* is treated here as masculine (earlier *ainm n-aill*).

§26. l. 380 **crích mór** *DIL* suggests "distance" as a translation of *crích* in this passage.

l. 383 **níro lámsatar** See *EIV* 238 for hybrid s-/suffixless 3 pl. preterite ending *-satar*.

l. 385 **Nia Fer** Thurneysen (1921: 54, note 1) observes that this is a mistake for *Eochaid Airem*.

§27. l. 388 **ro mair** literally "remained."

l. 390 **nít áthe** Stokes (1877: 182) reads *nitat áithiu* ("no keener"). Other examples of *nit* for usual *nitat* are as follows: Ml. 128d1 (Stokes and Strachan 1901: 437), *Félire Óengusso* Mar. 1 and Sept. 8 (Stokes 1905: 80, 193). See McCone (2006: 234–235) for the argument for *nit* as the original 3 pl. form.

l. 394 **láim doí** *DIL* (D 243.44–47) suggests that this may originally have been a compound *lámdoe*.

§28. l. 396 **do-berat** literally "they carry."

l. 411 **fos-roirtib** For confusion of *fo-* and *for-*, see *EIV* 140.

l. 414 **fichtiu** The form shows either confusion of final unstressed vowels or the use in consonant stems of the masculine accusative plural ending in *-iu*, for which see *SnaG* 249.

l. 415 **erbonaib** This word is unclear.

l. 418 **forceth** *DIL* (F 320.67–68) suggests that this word refers to a part of the head.

§30 l. 432 **marbthair** For Middle Irish confusion of relative and nonrelative endings, see *EIV* 228.

ll. 432–433 **nom-digéla** Middle Irish simple verb *díglaid* based on verbal noun replacing Old Irish *do-fich*, for which see *EIV* 193, and with Middle Irish é-future, for which see *EIV* 222.

l. 435 **in tan not-digél** literally "when I will avenge you."

§31. l. 441 **co fuilib fonnaidib** The reading assumes scribal omission of the dative plural ending of *fonnaide* through confusion with preceding *fuilib*. The phrase is a hendiadys with the literal translation of "with blood [and] with tires" and meaning "with bloody tires" (the chariot tires are bloody from riding on the battle-plain). See *DIL* (F 470.69–76) for the use of *fuil* in the plural to mean "blood of more than one individual."

l. 442 **fo chollaib clí** literally "under injuries of bodies" with *clí* in genitive (plural) of apposition.

l. 443 **co fuidlechtaib fuili** literally "with gushes of wounds."

§32. ll. 449–450 **sinn árbaig** an example of the infrequent confusion of *-nn* and *-nd* in spelling of the article, for which see *SnaG* 29, and an early example of confusion of lenited *m* and *b*.

l. 452 **thraig** short accusative singular; see note on *cin* in §21, l. 334.

§33. l. 459 **breccait** Old Irish *brectae*. For Middle Irish use of absolute rather than relative endings, see *EIV* 182–183.

ll. 460–461 **at-chonnarcais** Old Irish *at-chonnarc*; an example of the spread of the s-preterite ending to the 2 sg., for which see *EIV* 237.

ll. 464–465 **Do-lléic…int ech-sin** Middle Irish *do-* for *da-*, for which see *EIV* 169, and nominative for accusative of the article.

§34. ll. 466–467 Following Thurneysen (1912–1913 and 1921: 555), missing lines of the manuscript are supplied in the translation.

l. 477 **šlig** an instance of *i* in the ā-stem dative singular, for which see Breatnach (1997: 51–52).

§35. Thurneysen (1921: 549) states that the scene of Mess Gegra's slaying in *Talland Étair* is modeled on that of Lugaid's slaying in the present text.

l. 480 **chétguiniu** Compounds of *guin* form neuter io-stems (*GOI* §254).

ll. 482–483 **Connácham-thísed úait acht óenlám** literally "that only one hand should come to me from you."

l. 483 **Rot-bia** literally "you'll have it" (i.e., "it will be to you").

l. 484 **Cengaltar** for *cengaltair*. For confusion of palatal and nonpalatal endings, see *EIV* 228.

l. 485 **eter dá thráth din ló** literally "between two canonical hours of the day."

ní fúair nechtar de eill fora chéile literally "neither got an advantage over the other."

nád fúair replacement of nasalizing by leniting relative, for which see *EIV* 180.

l. 487 **for-díbad** past subjunctive 3 sg. of *for-díben* expressing hypothetical state or supposition.

do-n-ic Old Irish *da-n-icc.* For confusion of *do-* and *da-*, see *EIV* 169.

l. 488 **co rragaib** For palatal final in the preterite, see *EIV* 212.

ll. 488–489 **co tarlaic inna raba ina broind co rraba imma chossa** literally "so that it spilled what was in his belly so that it was around his feet."

§36. l. 497 **forsin chloich** literally "on the stone."

l. 498 **im-chóemnacair** Old Irish *im-comarcair.*

§37. ll. 503, 504 **-dámsat, -dámastar** For the Middle Irish hybrid preterite with strong stem preserved and s-preterite endings, see *EIV* 213–214. For the Middle Irish spread of 3 sg. ending *-astar*, see *EIV* 216–217.

l. 507 **n-erbairt** For palatal 3 sg. t-preterite ending, see *EIV* 240 and l. 114.

l. 509 **olleith** This word is taken as a compound of *oll + flaith*, as suggested by Kim McCone.

aton-ré future 3 sg. relative of *at-reig* with 1 pl. infixed pronoun.

l. 512 **di-uiscebthar domun do nim** This tentative emendation to the future passive sg. of *do-fiuschi* aligns with the sense of the surrounding lines. Alternatively, the first three words may be read as *di- uisciu -ethar*, present indicative sg. impersonal passive of *di-etha* in tmesis, with the translation "they come by water from Heaven to the land." A further possibility is to read *di uisciu ethar domun do nim* "from water, air, land, and Heaven" (i.e., "from every place") with *ethar* taken as dative sg. of *ethiar* ("air, ether").

l. 513 **gil** *gil* is defined in O'Clery's Glossary as "uisge" (Miller 1881–1883: 3). It is here taken as genitive singular of *gel*, modifying *Succet*. It could also be taken as dative singular, modifying *sáiliu* (see Carney 1964: 114, note to line 43).

l. 515 **alchél** This word is taken as a compound of *al/ol* ("beyond") and *cél*. Carney (1964: 141, note to line 598), understanding *célmaine* as a compound of *cél + maine*, translates this word as "mystic utterance" (see further Barrett 2019). See also §43, l. 699, where the context suggests a meaning of "declaration" or "exhortation." A meaning of "transcendent utterance" is suggested for *alchél*, understood as a "prayer" in Cú Chulainn's poem here and as a "proclamation" (to multiple provinces) in Emer's poem in §43, expressing the contrast between the sacred and the secular in their parallel uses of the word. Literally *Gigsit…alchél* translates as "They will pray…a transcendent utterance."

§38. ll. 525–526 **Cíabo óen fri iliu do lóeg do-fúart firu** literally "though your calf was one against many, he crushed men."

l. 528 **do-fius márfer fermart** The phrase appears in *L* as *mórfer már fermart* and then is repeated a few lines later as *már fermart*. The tentative emendation of adjusting both lines to *márfer fermart* enables the phrase to align with the six-syllable line pattern.

l. 531 **to-rét** Linking alliteration secures early Old Irish pretonic *to-*.

ll. 531–532 **ngubae caínandrae** If the proposed line division is correct, the line break would involve enjambment of an indefinite genitive. However, perhaps the identification of the "fair woman" as Emer (Cú Chulainn's wife) would have been assumed, making the construction definite (see Breatnach 2016b).

ll. 533–534 **forcu/Dechtire** The line break as analyzed involves enjambment of a definite genitive phrase (see Breatnach 2016b). Dechtire is Cú Chulainn's human mother.

l. 534 **deme** taken as an independent dative.

l. 535 **dim-emed** Linking alliteration secures early Old Irish pretonic *di-*.

art Cormac's Glossary (Stokes 1862: 2) quotes from this passage, defining *art* as *día*: "'Domemaid art ūasal' .i. dīa ūasal." The word is defined in O'Mulconry's Glossary (Stokes 1898: §55) as "potens." Thurneysen (1937: 302) further discusses the use of a word *art* in the sense of "head of a sept," equivalent to *áge fine* or *flaith fine*.

l. 539 **mac nEithnend** Cú Chulainn's divine father, Lug.

ll. 542–543 **áirilled nách bad trummu turbaid** literally "incurment than which there would be no heavier misfortune."

l. 544 **Tom-** Linking alliteration with the preceding line secures early Old Irish pretonic *to-*. It seems likely that *tom-* represents preverbal *do-* plus the 1 sg. infixed pronoun and that the rest of a verb is missing.

chaurchobraid taken here as an agent noun from *cobraithir*. Note the compound alliteration, for which see Stifter 2016.

Conall It is possible that Conall's name was added later as a gloss to clarify the identity of *chaurchobraid*, which the following line explains. (See also §43, l. 688.) If so, the line's syllable count aligns with that of either the preceding lines or the following three lines. In §§3 and 43 we are told that Conall Cernach is away accompanying Cormac.

l. 545 **luing** Appearing again in §43, l. 686 with a verbal form related to that accompanying it here (*con-oí; comaitecht*) and therefore unlikely to have arisen through error, this word presents difficulties. It is taken here tentatively as referring to an individual (Cormac Conn Loinges) embodying the concept *luinges* (see Breatnach 2016a). Unlike the examples adduced in Breatnach's article, however, this usage (if correctly interpreted) appears to be a back formation (from *luinges*) analogous to the relationship between, for example, *lánamain* and *lánamnas*.

§39. l. 549 **céta-rét** See *GOI* §384 for similar adverbial prefixes.
n-anfót literally "of inadvertent ones."
l. 550 **frecnairc** literally "present" (i.e., in the flesh).
l. 553 **nia doíne ticfa** This passage is quoted in Cormac's Glossary (Stokes 1862: 31). See also *Echtrae Chonnlai* §11: *mo-tub-ticfa a recht* (McCone 2000: 122).
l. 559 **fordon-ossa** for *ardon-ossa*. In the first edition (Kimpton 2009: 46), this verb is taken as *fordon-osna* ("who illumines us").
l. 560 **nert nime** For the sense of *nert* as moral strength, virtue, or gift of the spirit, see *DIL* N 35.34–42.
l. 561 **La forlínad suide seiss** literally "He will sit with fullness/abundance of seats."
for dindaib flatha literally "over heights of kingdoms."
ll. 562–563 **óenaib…érbur** Note the expression of the Trinity and of apophatic theology. Compare Columbanus's first sermon on the Trinity: *Deum unum ac trinum… totus invisibilis, incomprehensibilis, ineffabilis…investigabilia* "God, one and three…wholly invisible, inconceivable, unspeakable…unsearchable" (Walker 1957: 60–61). (See discussion in Introduction.) The *Sermons* repeatedly emphasize God's inexpressibility. For an example of apophatic theology from the Church Fathers, see Gregory of Nyssa's *The Life of Moses*, especially the second theophany on the ascent of Mt. Sinai: "the divine is by nature something above all knowledge and comprehension" (Malherbe and Ferguson 2006: 81). Gregory of Nyssa particularly viewed the "hypostases of the Father, Son, and Holy Spirit as being constitutionally revelatory of the unknowable divine essence" (Beeley 2008: 308). Perhaps this theological perspective contributed to the poetic use and valuing of "dark speech" (see Carey 1996, Fogarty 2016, and Stacey 2007).

l. 563 **nát erglond nád écgut nád érbur** augmented present potential indicatives 1 sg. of *as-gleinn*, *ad-fét*, and *as-beir*, respectively, as noted by Bergin (1938).

ll. 565–568 **renna...lúachthaidiu** This passage resembles descriptions of the portents of the coming of the Son of Man (e.g., Matthew 24.29: "The sun will be darkened, the moon will not give her light, the stars will fall from the sky, the celestial powers will be shaken," Suggs et al.: 1296) and Old Testament precedents (e.g., Isaiah 13.10, ibid.: 717). See also Carney (1964: §§61, 62, 65) for a description of darkness and disturbance of the cosmos and earth at the time of the Crucifixion.

l. 566 **grían gel in derg** literally "the bright sun, the red one (or the redness)."

dithistair future passive sg. of *dingid* (see Carney 1964: 972: *didistair in díumusach*).

l. 567 **réim nglas rotha resair** literally "the blue course of the sphere/firmament will be overrun," with *resair* taken as future passive sg. of *reithid* in the transitive sense (*DIL* R 39.61–67). *resair* might additionally be taken in a causative sense ("causes to run or move," ibid.: l. 61). The line is perhaps based on a passage in Revelation: "The sun turned black as a funeral pall...the stars in the sky fell to the earth...the sky vanished like a scroll being rolled up" (Suggs et al., 1562). If so, the line might be translated as "the sky's blue course will roll up."

l. 568 **fo- leth -luigther in luachthaidiu**, with *fo- leth -luigther* as present subjunctive passive sg. of *fo-lugi* with *leth* interposed in tmesis. Given the context, it should perhaps be emended to the future form. However, see McQuillan (2002: 35) for use of the subjunctive in a future sense. This reading would continue the sense of the preceding lines and resemble the passage from Matthew quoted above: "the moon will not give her light." Alternatively, perhaps read *folethnaigthir in luachthaidiu* (literally "the light is extended") and compare the absence of night for the duration of St. Patrick's mourning in Muirchú's *Life of St. Patrick* (Bieler 1979: 119).

l. 569 **amser** nominative for accusative, for which see *SnaG* 243.

l. 570 **as úasliu as ísliu** Middle Irish use of comparative for superlative (*SnaG* 257). See also *tressiu* above (§17, l. 289). For the frequent appearance of this usage already in the poems of Blathmac, see Stifter (2015: 84).

l. 576 **im nimib** According to *DIL* (I 102.4–7), "In late Old Irish and Middle Irish *imm* sometimes governs the dative in plural."

§40. l. 579 **dúin** Note eighth-century declension of *dún* as an o-stem; according to *GOI* §280.5, *dún* changes to s-stem inflection toward the end of the eighth century.

l. 582 **n-essad** Stifter (2015: 96) suggests that *essad* may be an adjective used substantivally.

l. 586 **nádat-décai** Thurneysen (*GOI* §419) and Ó hUiginn (1987) note the occasional use of *nád* rather than *nách* with the infixed pronoun.

immut-dídnad For the meaning "protects," see Carney (1964: 117–118, note to line 88). If not an indication of mutual familiarity between this text and the poems of Blathmac, the common usage may perhaps indicate a shared place of origin.

l. 587 **cotut-eilged** imperfect indicative 3 sg. of *con-ellaing.*

l. 589 **críchmrugib** Restoration of earlier *mrugib* and *mroga* (l. 607) is justified by alliteration (with *Macha* and *Murthemni*, respectively).

Mo Chaí Nóendromma Nendrum monastery, founded by Mo Chae, was the primary episcopal church of the Ulstermen in the seventh century (Charles-Edwards 2000: 260) and was associated with St. Patrick (ibid.: 27–28).

l. 590 **fo-retis** *fo-rethitis* with syncope and delenition.

ll. 597–599 **nít-ecmaing flesc**… literally "no…reaches you."

l. 600 **fordom-benad a bunad** literally "his origin/ancestry was on me." *fordom-benad* is imperfect 3 sg. of *for-tá* through assimilation with *for-ben* (see *GOI* §783).

l. 602 **aruit** This word is unclear. Perhaps it is to be taken as opposite of *díuit* ("simple-minded, foolish, timid").

l. 603 **cétmuinter** See Breatnach (2016a) for the meaning of *cétmuinter* as "spouse."

l. 605 **ata-mbebai** The pronoun may represent a reflexive Middle Irish 3 sg. masculine infixed pronoun or treatment of the preceding *óenguine* (a neuter io-stem), indicating the cause of death, as masculine (see Breatnach 2021 for use of the accusative to indicate cause of death).

l. 609 **díchimmidi** intensive prefix *dí-* to a noun form from *camm* ("crooked, bent") with the suffix *-id* (see *GOI* §267, where an example is given of a similar formation from an adjective: *cotarsnid* "adversary" from *cotarsnae*). See also l. 639 (*óenchossid óenlámaid*).

l. 612 **car** Lat. *quare*

in méte See Bergin (1920) for the meaning "it were likely" and the use of the phrase with the subjunctive or accusative.

l. 616 **arind-mbebsat bás** with 3 sg. masculine infixed pronoun referring to Cú Chulainn as cause of death (see Breatnach 2021).

l. 618 **cloítis** For omission of *no-* see Corthals (1989: 48, note to line 3a).

l. 621 **n-imgaib** See *EIV* 212 for palatal 3 sg. s-preterite ending.

ll. 623–625 **Dolluid a tollus…dia chéim** literally "that which pierced was a damage so that it caused his strength to ebb while it did not hinder him from his stepping [forth]." *Dolluid* might also be taken as preterite 3 sg. of *do-tét*, yielding a translation of "he came to that which pierced (him)."

l. 624 **ara tethraig** Breatnach (2005: 143) demonstrates *tráigid* "ebbs, recedes" to be a strong verb in Old Irish, citing this passage as an instance of the reduplicated preterite 3 sg.

l. 625 **nách nderbai dia chéim** See Breatnach (1980) for the adverbial use of the nasalizing relative clause in a temporal sense.

l. 628 **cú glas** This term denotes a "stranger, castaway," a "man without legal status except through his wife" (*DIL* C 566.85–567.13).

l. 632 **corbo marb** See MacCana (1997–1998).

l. 633 **láith gaile friasa comarnic** It is possible that a portion of text was omitted; the previous line (*corbo marb a leth*) would appear to conclude a sentence, and *láith gaile friasa comarnic* would appear to be an unrelated relative clause introducing another sentence. If not, the passage may be taken to mean "one side of his warrior body that it contacted died." *Co torchair a ech* could conclude a sentence after the (hypothetical) missing portion or stand on its own.

l. 635 **ainmem Líath** This appears to be a later gloss (like that in §38, l. 544) identifying the horse by name (see following note).

ll. 636–637 **olc lige…Sainglend** literally "bad the lying that Dub Sainglend lay." It is possible that words were transposed to provide alliteration between *Líath* (introduced by the later gloss) and the following line (*líagair*). The emendation supplies linking alliteration throughout the passage as well as word order parallel to that of another figura etymologica in the text (§12, ll. 149–150: *díchra aige/eblas eirr*). The linking alliteration between ll. 636 and 637 and between ll. 637 and 638 as

109

emended provides complex linking alliteration as well as continuation of an interlaced alliterative pattern, presenting more sophisticated links (*Olc lige/líagair Dub Sainglend/adbul slúag*; see metrical analysis), in keeping with the rest of this poem and other poems in the text, as can be seen in the immediately following line with complex linking alliteration (*do-cer/cíarbo*).

l. 637 **líagair** This form may represent the preterite 3 sg. of *laigid*, parallel to *siasair*, the preterite 3 sg. of *saidid*. The two verbs have parallel perfect forms (*dessid, dellig*) (see *GOI* §690). The appearance of the verbal noun (*lige*) here in an adverbial figural etymologica construction may support this analysis of the form.

l. 639 **cíarbo** literally "though he (i.e., Cú Chulainn) was."

óenchossid óenlámaid agent noun formations with suffix *-id* (see *GOI* §267).

§41. l. 646 **olloman** According to *DIL* (O 139.5–9), *ollam* is used of warriors in early poetry; an example is there given from Meyer (1913–1914: ii 7, §4): *mandrais arma athar ollam*.

§42. l. 649 **cóemaib** The *H* reading is superior.

l. 653 **ro siacht** Compare with the prototonic form *-roacht* in l. 667. The contrast indicates the influence of metrical considerations on the use of final-verb constructions. Here the deuterotonic form allows alliteration with preceding *Sobeóil*, whereas the prototonic form in l. 667 allows alliteration with preceding *Rossa*.

l. 663 **iltúathu** The spelling is influenced by the following *ilairbriu*.

ll. 674–677 **Ba méite…** See Bergin (1920) for the meaning "it were likely" and the use of the phrase with the subjunctive or accusative. Compare §§132–133 in Carney (1964: 44–46), where the responsibility to lament Christ is expressed in similar terms: *Ba méte no bed co bráth/tar cech ngruaid hi cech óentráth/tromdér folo, loim cró/oc coíniud in chimbetho....cith cách ro-choalae a chlú/forda-tá a bithchoíniu.*

l. 678 **is dered fo dubai in domuin dia éis** literally "it is the end of the world under grief after him."

l. 679 **nom-accfither** Note f-future form for Old Irish *-accigestar*.

§43. l. 684 **do-beba…gnímrathu** The reading, suggested by Kim McCone, takes *do-beba* as a genitive relative construction and assumes elision of the masculine 3 sg. possessive pronoun before *gnímrathu*. Accusative plural *gnimrathu* indicates the cause of death (see Breatnach 2021). Alternatively, read "he who will die of Mess Gegra's deeds wreaks great vengeance," taking *do-beba* as future 3 sg.

l. 685 **ro gní** taking *ro* as representing *do* (see *EIV* 189–191 and Uhlich 2018: 234–235) and the form as in the historical present. The form may also be read as "can wreak" with *ro* in potential sense.

l. 686 **luing** See note to §38, l. 545.

Mossad Mag Mossad is identified in Hogan (1910) as near Cashel.

l. 688 **ro sephaid** The reduplicated preterite form of *séitid* is also attested with suffixed pronoun in the seventh-century poem in praise of Colm Cille *Fo réir Choluimb* (Kelly 1973: 17, l. 14b).

l. 689 **co nderaig** literally "so that he avenged."

a daltae referring to Cormac, Conall Cernach's fosterling.

dígáirsi taken as an independent dative.

l. 690 **ro gabai** For the Middle Irish 3 sg. conjunct s-preterite ending in *-a(i)* see *EIV* 236.

l. 691 **íar mbreth ban síde** literally "after being taken by fairy women."

l. 692 **meic dea Dechtiri** literally "of the son of a god and Dechtire."

l. 693 **derbad soaltim** literally "confirmation of the best-reared one." This passage perhaps lends support to Meyer's suggestion that Sualtaim's name derives from a misinterpretation of the superlative of *soalta* (see note to §3, l. 18).

l. 695 **eochair** tentative emendation supported by use of *eochair* to refer to warrior heroes (*DIL* E 146.35).

n-úath taken as an independent dative.

l. 696 **ro fersur** Middle Irish augmented present subjunctive 1 sg. of *feraid*.

l. 697 **sé mbliadna déc** See Hull (1949: 48, ll. 201–203), a passage from *Longes mac n-Uislenn* referring to duration of hardship and exile.

l. 699 **sechmai** *sechid* used with accusative of both the utterance and the addressee.

mórthúatha perhaps with the meaning of "province" (see McCone 1990: 9).

alchél See note to §37, l. 515. Literally *Sechmai...alchél* translates as "We declare...a transcendent utterance."

GLOSSARY

a (n-) neuter of article used as demonstrative before relative clause *a*

a (possessive pronoun) 3 sg. masc. *a*; 3 pl. *a*

a (vocative particle) *a*

a (prep. + dat.) "from, out of" *a*; 3 sg. masc. *ass*; 3 sg. masc. poss. *asa, assa*; 3 sg. fem. poss. *assa*

ab (f., -n-) "river" as. *abaind, n-abaind*

acallam (f., -a-, vn. of *ad-gládathar*) "act of addressing, conversing" ds. *acallaim*

acc "no" *acc*

accobrach "desirous of, interested in" ns. *accobrach*

acht (prep. + acc.) "except for, but" *acht*

acht (conjunction) "but"

acrae (n., -io-, vn. of *ad-gair*) "act of prosecuting, pursuing a claim" gs. *acrai*

ad-ágathar "fears" augm. pret. 1 pl. *ad-ráigsemar*

ad-aig "raises, puts forth (a cry)" pres. ind. 3 sg. *at-aig*

adaig (f., -i-) "night" ds. *aidchi*

adall (-o-, vn. of *ad-ella*) "act of visiting, approaching" ns. *adall*; as. *adall*

ad-anaig "buries" augm. pret. pass. sg. *coro adnacht*

adbal "mighty, vast" ns. *adbul*

adbar (n., -o-) "makings of, cause, reason" ns. *adbur*

ad-caíni "laments, bewails" fut. 3 pl. *atom-chuínfet*

ad-cí "sees" pres. ind. 1 sg. *at-chíu, at-chíu-sa*; pres. ind. 2 sg. *-facca*; pres. ind. 3 pl. *-aiccet*; fut. pass. sg. *nom-accfither*; augm. pret. 2 sg. *at-chonnarcais*; augm. pret. 3 sg. *at-connairc*; pret. 3 sg. *co n-accai, co n-acca*; pret. 3 pl. *co n-accatar*; pret. pass. sg. *co n-accas*

ad-cuimben (ath-com-ben) "strikes, cuts, wounds" pres. ind. 3 sg. *ad-chumben*; pret. 3 sg. *at-cummai*

ad-cumaing (in-com-icc) "strikes" pres. ind. 3 sg. *-ecmaing, n-ecmoing, n-eccmoing, -ndecmoing*

ad-cumaing (ad-com-icc) "reaches, extends to" pres. ind. 3 sg. *-ecmaing, -ecmoing*

adderg (*ath-* + *derg*) "very red" apl. *adderga*

ad-ella "visits, approaches" pres. ind. 1 sg. *-adliub*; pres. ind. 3 sg. *ata-ella-som, ad-ella*; augm. past subj. 2 sg. *ro adelta*

ad-etha "takes, seizes" pres. ind. 3 sg. *ad-etha, at-etha*

ad-fét "tells, relates" augm. (potential) pres. ind. 1 sg. *-écgut*

ad-gládathar "addresses, speaks to" pret. 3 sg. *-acillestar*

ad-gnin "recognizes" pret. 1 sg. *aid-gén*

ad-guid "pledges, invokes surety" pres. ind. 3 sg. *-accid*

admat (m., -o-) "material, device" gs. *n-admait*

ad-muinethar "calls on, invokes" sec. fut. 1 sg. *ad-muindfind*

adraid "adores, worships" ipv. 2 pl. *adraid*

ad-ranna "distributes, apportions" fut. 3 pl. *ad-rainnfet*

aer (m., -o-) "air, atmosphere, sky" ds. *aeór*

áeraid "satirizes" fut. 1 sg. *not-aíriub-sa, nott-aíriub-sa, aírfat-sa*; fut. pass. sg. *aírfaither*; augm. pret. pass. sg. *nírom-áerad-sa*; augm. pret. pass. pl. *ro áertha, níra áertha*

afrithissi see **frithissi**

ág (m., -u/o-) "valor, prowess" ns. *ág*

aicille (f., -ia-, vn. of *ad-gíallna*) "clientship" ns. *acille*

aicsiu (f., -n-, vn. of *ad-cí*) "act of seeing" as. *aicsin*

aidlenn (f,. -a-) "hook or rack for holding weapons" dpl. *adlennaib*

aig (-i-) "ice" gs. *ega*

aige (vn. of *aigid*) "act of driving" ns. *aige*

aiged (f.) "face, honor" ns. *aged*; npl. *aichthi*

aigid "drives, carries out" fut. rel. 3 sg. *eblas*

aignech "spirited, swift" as. *n-aignech*

áil (-i-, used impersonally with copula and *do*) "wish, request" ns. *áil*

aile "other" ns. *aile*; as. *aile, n-aile*; ds. *aile*; npl. *aill* (see notes); apl. *aile*

áilges (f., -a-) "demand, request" as. *álgis*

ailid "rears" augm. pret. 3 sg. *rod-n-alt-som*

ailid "insults; strikes" fut. pass. pl. *ailfitir*

aimser (f., -a-) "period of time" as. *amser*

aimserad "period of time" dpl. *amserdaib*

ainching "great hero, champion" gpl. *anchinne*

ainech, enech (n., -o-) "honor" ns. *ainech*; as. *n-ainech*; gs. *enig*; dpl. *inchaib, n-inchaib*

ainim (f., -a-) "blemish" ds. *anim*

ainimm (f., -n-) "soul" ns. *anim*

ainmech "blemished, maimed, indicating a blemish" gs. *anmich*

ainmm (n., -n-) "name" ns. *ainm*; as. *ainm*; ds. *ainmem*

114

airbe "hedge, fence" ns. *airrbe*; as. *airrbe*

airchenn as subst. "leader, chief" gs. *airchind*

airchían "very long" ns. *n-érchian*

airchisid (earlier *ar-ceissi*) "pities, has compassion for" fut. pass. sg. *airchisfither*

airchissecht (f., -a-, vn. of *ar-ceissi*) "pity, compassion, lamenting" as. *n-airchisecht*

airchomair "contemporary with, in preparation for in front of" ds. *erchomuir, urchomair*

airchor (m., vn. of *ar-cuirethar*) "cast, shot, weapon" ns. *urchor*; as. *urchor*; dpl. *erchoraib*

aird (f.) "peak, point, corner" gs. *arda*

airde (f., -ia-) "height, noble person" npl. *airdde, airdi* (see notes)

airdircigidir "praises, celebrates, makes renowned" pret. 3 sg. *-urdaircaigestar*

airdlochtae (part. of *ar-dloing*) "split, cleft" apl. *aurdlochtai*

airfitigid (Middle Irish denominative from *airfitiud*, vn. of *ar-peiti*) "delights, satisfies" ipf. 3 sg. *nom-airfitiged*

airgal (f., -a-, vn. of *ar-fich*) "act of fighting, battle" dpl. *irgalaib*

áirilliud (m., -u-, vn. of *ad-roilli*) "act of deserving, incurment" ns. *áirilliud*

airitiud (f., vn. of *ar-eim*) "act of receiving, accepting" ns. *airitiud*

airlann (-o-) "weapon handle" ns. *urlond*; ds. *urlaind*

airm (f.) "place" ds. *airm*; *airm i n-* "where"

airmedón (m., -o-) "middle, center" ds. *n-irmedón*

áirmidi (vbl. of necessity of *ad-rími*) "to be reckoned, counted as" ns. *ármide*

airnaidm (n., -n-, vn. of *ar-naisc*) "betrothal, marriage" ds. *urnaidm*

airscartad (m., -u-, vn. of *ar-scarta*) "act of clearing away, expelling an enemy" as. *erscartad*; ds. *urscartad, aurscartad*

airsce (-io-) "stump of neck" as. *airsce*; ds. *airsciu*

airselb (f., -a-) "possession, power" ds. *urṡeilb*

airúath "great fearsomeness" ns. *urúath*

ais "back" as. *aiss*

aiscedach "generous" npl. *aiscedaig*

áith "sharp, keen" cpv. *áthe*

aithber (m., -o-) "rebuke, reproach, retribution" ns. *aithber*; gpl. *aithber* (see notes)

ál (-o-) "offspring" gs. *áil*

alchél "transcendent, solemn utterance; prayer, proclamation" as. *alchél*

Alpae (f., -ia-) "the Alps" dat. *Elpae*

amach "out from" *immach*

amae "indeed" *amae*

amáin "only, alone" *amáin*

amal "like, as; when" *amal*

amlaid "thus, so" (adv. use of 3 sg. neuter of prep. *amal*) *amlaid*

ammait (f., -i-) "witch" ns. *ammait*; npl. *ammiti, ammaiti*; apl. *ammaiti*

amne "thus" *amne*

án "fiery, bright, splendid, glorious" gpl. *n-án*

anapaig "premature" as. *n-anabaid*

anaid ~ *di* "desists from" ipv. 2 sg. *an*

anair *fri* X *anair* "before, in front of X" *anair*

anál "breath" ds. *anáil*

anall *fri* X ~ "beyond, past" *anall*

and "there" see **i**

andaas, andás see **oldaas**

ándrennach (*án* + *drennach*) "splendid and combative" as subst.: vs. *ándrennuig*

aness "from the south" *aness*

anfót (m., -o-) "inadvertence, negligence" gpl. *n-anfót*

aníar *fri* X ~ "behind X" *aníar*

ansae "difficult" *andsa, ansa*

anúas "above, down from above" *anúas*

aprainn "alas" *apraind*

apthu (n., vn. of *at-baill/ad-bath*) "death" dpl. *n-apthaib*

ar (prep. + dat. and acc.) "on, from, by, as, for the sake of, to, for" *ar*; 3 sg. masc. acc. *airi*; 1 sg. poss. *armo*; 2 sg. poss. *ardo*; 3 sg. masc. poss. *ara*

ar conjunction "because, for, so that" *ar*; with rel. part. *ara, arind*

ar (n-) "our" *ar*

ar see **ol**

ár (-o-) "slaughter, defeat, destruction" as. *ár*

arae (m., -t-) "charioteer" ns. *ara;* as. *araid*; ds. *araid*; gpl. *arad*

arbar (m., -o-) "host, army" npl. *arbuir*; *lán*~ "great army" as. *lánarbur*

ar-beir "wields" pres. subj. 2 sg. *n-erbara*; ~ *fri* "opposes" pret. 3 sg. *-erbart*

ar-cela "takes away, steals" pret. pass. sg. *-archelad*

ar-cíallathar "cares for" pret. 3 sg. *ardum-...-cíallastar*

arcu "beseeches, thanks, rejoices at" pres. ind. 1 sg. *arcu*

ard "high, tall" npl. *ardda*

ardnem (n., -s-) "high Heaven" gs. *n-ardnime*

ar-éigi "cries out" ipv. 2 pl. *airégid*

ar-foíchlea "prepares against, takes heed" ipv. 2 pl. *iraichlid, eraichlid*; pres. ind. 1 pl. *-fuirechlem*

arg (m., -o-) "champion, hero" as. *arg*

argat (n., -o-) "silver" ns. *arget*

aridisi see **frithissi**

ar-icc "comes upon, meets, finds" pret. 3 sg. *-arnic*

arm (n., -o-) "battle equipment, weapons; army" gs. *airm*; npl.? *airm* (see notes); gpl. *arm*

ármag (n., -s-) "battlefield, field of slaughter" ds. *árbaig*

arnabárach "the next day" *arnabárach*

ar-ossa "awaits" pres. ind. 3 sg. *fordon-ossa*

ar-sissedar "stands fast against, resists, endures" fut. 1 pl. *-aurisfemmar*

art "lord, god" ns. *art* (see notes)

ar-tá "remains" pres. ind. 3 sg. *ara-thá*

as-beir "says" augm. (potential) pres. ind. 1 sg. *-érbur*; fut. 3 pl. *n-epérat*; pret. 3 sg. *as-bert, at-bert*; pret. 3 pl. *as-bertatar*; augm. pret. 3 sg. *as-rubairt-si, -erbairt*; augm. pret. 1 pl. *at-rubramar*

as-ben "smites, slays" fut. 1 sg. *ata-bíu-sa*

as-gleinn "investigates, examines" augm. (potential) pres. ind. 1 sg. *-érglond*

astud (m., -u-, vn. of *ad-suidi*) "act of detaining, keeping in place" ds. *fastud*

atá (substantive verb) pres. ind. 1 sg. *atú, itú*; pres. ind. 3 sg. *-thá, -tá, -fil, atá, fuil, fil, do-fil*; pres. ind. 3 pl. *ataat*; rel. sg. *fil, file*; rel. pl. *filet*; rel. impersonal pass. sg. *-táthar*; pres. subj. 3 pl. *-mbet*; past subj. 3 sg. *no beth, bad*; augm. past subj. 3 sg. *ro mbeth, -rabad*; fut. 3 sg. *mbia, rot-bia*; fut. sg. rel. *bias*; sec. fut. 3 pl. *-betis*; pret. 2 sg. *bá-so*; pret. 3 sg. *baí, boí, mbuí*; pret. 3 pl. *bátar*; augm. pret. 3 sg. *ro boí, rodon-baí, -rabi, -rrabi, -robae,*

-raba, -rraba; augm. pret. 3 pl. *ro bátar*; augm. pret. impersonal sg. *ro bass*

at-bá "dies" pret. 3 sg. *ata-mbeba*

at-baill "dies" past subj. sg. *-ablad, at-balad*; fut. 3 pl. *at-mbélat*; pret. 3 sg. *at-bath*

até "indeed, truly" *até*

áth (m., -u-) "ford" gs. *átha*; dpl. *n-áthaib*

athair (m., -r-) "father" gs. *athar*

athardae "ancestor; ancestral" ns. *athardae*; gs. *athardae*

athfír (n.) "great truth" as. *athfír*

athguba (m., -io-) "great grief, lamentation" ds. *aithguba, n-athgubu*

athmuinter (f., -a-) "kin, descendants; second kin" gs. *admuintire* (see notes)

at-reig "rises" ipv. 2 sg. *at-raí*; ipv. 2 pl. *at-raígid*; fut. 3 sg. *aton-ré*

atúaid "from the north" *atúaid*

aurgnam (m., -u-, vn. of *ar-fogni*) "act of preparing food" ds. *urgnum*

bacc (n., -o-) "hindrance" dpl. *baccaib*

baid "dies" pres. ind. 1 sg. with prefix *mos-* "soon" *mos-baim*; fut. 3 pl. *-mbebat*; pret. 3 pl. *-mbebsat*

báidid "extinguishes, destroys, obliterates" fut. pass. sg *-mbáidfider*

báigid "boasts of, contends with" pret. 3 sg. *báigestar*

baitsid "baptizes, names" augm. pret. 2 sg. *ro batsis*

ball (m., -o-) "limb, organ" gpl. *ball*

banchuire (n., -io-) "troop, host of women" ns. *banchuire*; gs. *banchuire*; npl. *banchuiri*

banrígain (f., -a-) "queen" gpl. *banrígan*

bantrocht "company of women" gs. *bantrochta*

bas (f., -a-) "palm of hand" npl. *basa*

bás (n., -o-) "death" as. *mbás, bás*

becc "small, little" ns. *bec, mbec*; as. *mbec*; apl. *beca*

bedg (m., -o-) "leap, bound, rapid dash" as. *bedg*

bedgach "springing, leaping, shocking" npl. *bedgaich*

béimm (n., -n-, vn. of *benaid*) "blow, stroke" dpl. *bémmennaib*

beirid "brings" pres. ind. rel. sg. *beres*; augm. pres. subj. 2 sg. *-rruca*; fut. pass. sg. *bérthair*; pret. 3 sg. *birt*; augm. pret. pass. sg. *rucad*

beith (vn. of substantive verb) *bith*

bél (m., -o-) "lip, mouth" dpl. *bélaib*

ben (f., -a-) "woman; wife" ns. *ben*; vs. *ben*; apl. *mná*; gpl. *ban*

benaid "strikes, slays" pres. ind. 3 sg. *benaid*; ipf. 3 sg. *-mbenad*; augm. pret. 3 sg. *ros-mbí, rod-mbí, rod-bí*; pret. pass. sg. *-bíth*

béo "alive" ns. *béo*

béochobra (f.) "living speech" *béochobra*

beos "regularly; in addition" *beos, beus*

berbaid "melts, dissolves" augm. pret. 3 sg. *ro berbai*

bethu (m., -t-) "life, existence" ds. *mbethu*; gs. *bethad*

biad (n./m., -o-) "food" ns. *biad*

bíathaid "feeds, nourishes, supports" ipf. 3 sg. *-biathad*

bidbu (m., -d-) "enemy, culprit" ns. *bidbu, bidba*; apl. *bidbadu*

bir (n., -u-) "spit" dpl. *beraib*

bith (m., -t-) "age, period" apl. *bithu*

bithchaíned "perpetual lamenting" ds. *bithchoíniud*

bliadain (f., -i-) "year" gpl. *mbliadna*

bó (f.) "ox, cow" gs. *bó*

boimm (n., -n-) "piece, fragment" apl. *bommand*

boingid "reaps, plucks, gathers" fut. pass. pl. *bibsaitir* (see notes)

bolgdér (n., -o-) "swelling tear" apl. *bolgdéra*

bolgrosc "with bulging eyes" npl. *bolgroisc*

bolgsrón "with flaring nostrils" npl. *bolgsróin*

bonn (m., -o-) "sole of foot" ds. *bund*

bosschaire "clapping of hands in grief" as. *bosschaire*

brága (f., -t-) "throat, neck" ds. *brágit*

bráth (m., -u- and -o-) "Judgment Day" as. *co ~* "forever" *bráth*

bratt (m., -o-) "cloak, mantle" ns. *bratt*

breccad (m., -u-, vn. of *breccaid*) "bespeckling, bespattering" ds. *breccad*

breccaid "bespeckles, bespatters" pres. ind. 3 pl. *breccait*

breth (f., -a-, vn. of *beirid*) "birth; act of taking away" ds. *mbreth*

bríathair (f., -a-) "word" apl. *bríathra*

briugu (m., -d-) "hospitaller" gpl. *brugad*

brisiud (m., -u-, vn. of *brisid*) "act of breaking" ns. *brisiud*

brollach (n., -o-) "chest, bosom" gpl. *brolach*

brónach "sad" npl. *brónaig*

bronnlethan "broad-bellied" npl. *brondlethnai*

brosnach (f.) "heap of fragments" as. *brosnaig*

brú (f., -n-) "belly, womb" ns. *brú*; gs. *brond*; ds. *broind*; dpl. *brunnib*

brú "brow" dpl. *mbrúaib*

brúmár "big-browed" ns. *brúmár*

bruth (m., -u-) "raging fury, fervor" gs. *brotha*; ds. *bruth*

búadarthae "disturbed, troubled" dpl. *búaderthaib*

búadréimm (n., -n-) "victorious course" ds. *búadrémmend*

búaid (n., -i-) "victory, triumph; virtue; benefit, advantage; the best" ns. *búad, búaid*; as. *mbúaid*; ds. *mbúaid*; npl. *búada*; apl. *búada*; dpl. *búadaib*

buide (f., -ia-) "something yellow" as. *budi*

buiden (f., -a-) "group, troop, host" as. *mbuidin, mbudin*; gs. *buidni*; apl. *buidne*; dpl. *buidnib*

buiderad "buttercups" as. *buiderad*

buille (f., -ia-) "blow, stroke" as. *buille*

búirithir "roar, strike loudly" pres. subj. 3 pl. *mbúretar*

bunad (-o-) "stock, ancestry, foundation" ns. *bunad*; gs. *bunaid*

buntáeb see notes ds. *mbuntáib*

cách "everyone, each one" ns. *cách*; as. *cách*

cach "every, each" gs. *cecha, cacha*; ds. *cach*

cáechad (m., -u-, vn. of *cáechaid*) "act of blinding an eye" ds. *cháechad*

cáerthann (m., -o-) "rowan tree" gs. *cáirthind*

caín "fair, beautiful" ns. *caín*; ds. *chain*; npl *caíni*

caínainder (f.) "fair woman" gs. *cáinandrae*

caíngnúis "fair-faced" ns. *caíngnúis*

cáinte (m., -o-) "satirist" ns. *cáinte, cánti*; as. *cáinte*

cair (Lat. *quare*; precedes a question) *car*

caithem (f., -a-) "act of consuming, eating" ds. *chathim*

caithid "casts, carries out" augm. pret. 3 sg. *ro chaith*

canaid "sings, recites, chants" augm. pret. 3 sg. *ro chan*

cani (neg. interrogative particle) *cain, cani*

caraid "loves" augm. pret. 3 sg. *rod-car*

carcair (f.) "captivity, bondage" ns. *carcair*

carna "flesh, meat" ns. *carna*

carpat (m., -o-) "chariot" ns. *carpat*; as. *carpat*; gs. *charpuit, charpait*; ds. *charput, carput*

carrac (f., -a-) "stone, rock" as. *carraic*

cath (m., -u-) "battle, fight" gs. *chatha*; ds. *cath, chath*; apl. *cathu*; dpl. *cathaib*; "troop" npl. *catha*

cathbúadach "battle-victorious" ns. *cathbúadach*; gs. *cathbúadaig*

cathchles (m., -o-) "performance of battle feats" apl. *cathchlessu*

caur (m., -d-) "warrior, hero" gs. *churad*

caurchobraid (m., -i-) "warrior protector" ns. *chaurchobraid*

cechtar "each" as. *cechtar*; gs. *chechtar*

céile (m., -io-) "companion" as. *céili, céli, chéile*; ds. *chéiliu*

céimm (n., -o-) "step" as. *céim*; ds. *chéim*

cel "extinction, death" *téit ar ~* "dies" *chel*

celebrad (m., -u-, vn. of *celebraid*) "act of bidding farewell" ds. *chelebrad*

celebraid "bids farewell" pres. ind. 3 sg. *celebraid*; pret. 3 sg. *celebrais*

celg (f., -a-) "stratagem" ns. *chelg*

cen (prep. + acc.) "without" *cen*; 3 sg. neut. *chenae, chena*; 3 pl. poss. *cena*

cenae (adverbial formation from the preposition *cen* with 3 sg. neut. pron.) "without this, apart from this; already" *chenae, cena*

cenann "white-headed" ns. *cennand*

cenél (n., -o-) "race, tribe" as. *chenél*; gs. *ceniúil*; ds. *chenél*

cenglaid "binds, ties, fastens" pres. ind. pass. sg. *cengaltar*

cenn (n., -o-) "head" ns. *chend, cend*; as. *chind, chend, cend*; gs. *cind, chind*; ds. *chind*; npl. *cind*

cennach (-o-) "redeem, purchase" ds. *cennach*

cennbecc "small-headed" dpl. *cendbeca*

cerd (f., -a-) "trick, craft" as. *ceird*

cern (m., -o-) "victory, triumph" npl. *ceirn* (see notes)

ces "debility" gs. *cessa*

cet "permission" ns. *cet*

cét (n., -o-) "one hundred" *cét*

cétaíne "Wednesday" ds. *cétaíne*

cétamuin "Maytime" gs. *cétamuin*

cétguine (n., -io-) "first wounding" ds. *chétguiniu*

cethair "four" *cethri*

cethracha (m., -nt-) "forty" npl. *cethrachait*

cethrar "four people" as. *cethrur*

cétlathe (n., -io-) "first day" ds. *cétlathiu*

cétmuinter (f,. -a-) "spouse" ns. *chétmuinter*

cétnae "first, same" ns. *cétna*

cétóir *fo chétóir* "at once, immediately" *fo chétóir*

cía "what, who" *cía, cid, cisi*; *ciped chía* "whoever"

cía "though" *cía*

cían "far, long" ns. *cían*; ds. *céin*; as subst.: apl. *cíana*; dpl. *chíanaib*

cích (f., -i-) "breast" apl. *cíche, cíchi*

cíid "weeps for, bewails" pres. ind. 3 pl. *-cíat*; pres. subj. 3 sg. *no cíad*; past. subj. pass. sg. *no cíthe*; fut. 3 pl. *cíchme*

cin (m., -t-) "guilt, fault, crime" as. *cinaid, chinaid, cin*; apl. *chinta*

cindas "how" *cinnas*

cingid "steps, marches, advances" fut. 2 sg. *cichsi*

cinniud (m., -u-) "decision, agreement" ns. *cinniud*

círdub "jet black" ns. *círdub*

claideb (m., -o-) "sword" ns. *chlaideb*; as. *claideb*

claidebderg "red-sworded" as. *claidiubderg*

claidebrúad "red-sworded" ns. *claidebrúad*

clann (f., -a-) "children, descendants" ns. *clann*

clár (n./m., -o-) "board, plank, chariot side-piece" ns. *clár* (see notes)

clé "left side" ns. *clé*; as. *clé, chlé*; ds. *clí, chlí*

cles (m., -o-) "feat, feat-performance; weapons used for martial feats" gs. *cliss*; apl. *clessu, clessa*; dpl. *chlessaib*

clesamain (m., -i-) "feat performer" gs. *chlessamna*

cleth (f., -a-, vn. of *ceilid*) "concealment, protection" ds. *chleith*

cleth (f., -a-) "spear; warrior, chief" gs. *cleithe*; ds. *cleith*

clisid "performs feats, leaps, springs" pres. ind. 3 sg. *-chliss*

clith "protection" *clith*

clíu "body" gs. *clíu*; ds. *chlíu*; gpl. *clí*

cloch (f., -a-) "stone" as. *cloich*; gs. *cloiche*; ds. *chloich*

cloid "overthrows, vanquishes, destroys; turns, leads astray" past subj. pass. pl. *-cloítis*; fut. 3 sg. *cloífid*

clú "fame" ns. *clú*

clúas (f., -a-) "ear" ns. *clúas*; dpl. *clúasaib*

cnáim (m., -i-) "bone" npl. *cnáma*; gpl. *cnáma*

cnedach "wounded, wound-dealing" ns. *cnedach*

cnes (m., -o-) "skin, flesh" as. *chness*

co (prep. + acc.) "to" *co*; 3 sg. *chuci*; 1 pl. *chucund*; 2 pl. *chucaib*; 3 pl. *chucu, chuccu, cuccu*; 3 sg. masc. poss. *coa*; with masc. sg. art. *cusin*

co (prep. + dat.) "with" *co*; 3 sg. masc. poss. *cona*; with masc. sg. art. *cosin*

co "until, so that" *co, cu*

cobraithir "protects, saves" pres. ind. 3 sg. *-chobradar*; ipv. 2 sg. *cobairthe*; pret. 3 sg. *-cobrastar*

cocarus (m., -u-) "proper arrangement" ns. *cocarus*

cóem "fair" as. *cóem*; dpl. *cóemaib*

cóemrí (m., -g-) "fair king" ns. *cóemrí*

coibéis "equal amount, peer" ns. *cubés*

coíca (m., -nt-) "fifty" npl. *coícait*

cóiced (m., -o-) "province" ns. *cóiced*; as. *cóiced*; npl. *chúicid, chóicid*; dpl. *chóicedaib*

coimchriss (m., -u-) "body-belt" as. *choimchriss*

coimded "security, protection" gs. *comdetae* (see notes)

coimdiu (m., -t-) "lord" ns. *Coimdiu*

cóir "proper" ns. *cóir*

coirthe (m., -io-) "pillar, standing stone" ns. *corthe*; as. *coirthi, corthe, coirthe*

coitchennas (m., -u-) "company" ds. *cotchennas*

colcatchaín "beautifully helmeted, beautifully covered" gs. *colgatchaín*

coll (n., -o-) "destruction, injury" dpl. *chollaib*

coloma (f., -n-) "champion, defender" gpl. *colomon*

colpthae (m., -io-) "calf, shin" apl. *cholptha*

comainm (n., -n-) "namesake" gs. *chomanma*

comairle (f., -ia-) "advice, counsel, admonition" ns. *chomairli, comairle*

comaitecht (f., -a-, vn. of *con-éitet*) "act of accompanying, protecting" ds. *comaitecht*

comalta (m., -io-) "fosterbrother" as. *chomalt*

comarbae (m., -io-) "heir, successor" gpl. *comarbae*

combág "rivalry" as. *chombáig*

comchéile (m., -io-) "comrade" gs. *chomchéili*

comchóir "equally fitting, well proportioned" npl. *comchóire*

comdath "the same color" gs. *comdatha*

comlabrae (f., -ia-) "dialogue, act of conversing" ds. *comlabrai*

comlán "complete, perfect" dpl. *comlánaib*

comlann (n., -o-) "single combat" as. *comlund*

comnesam (-o-) "relative, kinsman" ns. *comnesam*

comrac (-o-, vn. of *con-ricc*) "act of meeting, encounter" ns. *comrac*

comramach "victorious, triumphant" ns. *comramach*

comrith (m., -u-, vn. of *con-reith*) "act of running together, racing" gs. *comrethi*

comríata "equally swift" npl. *comríata*

comscaílte "torn apart" npl. *comscaílte*

con-airlethar "advises" pret. 3 sg. *comairlestar*

conar (f., -a-) "way, path" ns. *chonar*

con-boing "breaks" past subj. 3 sg. *con-bóssad*

con-claid "buries" fut. 3 pl. *con-cechalsat*

con-coilli "damages, violates, destroys" fut. pass. sg. *con-coillfither*

condúalae "ornamented, engraved" ds. *chondúala*

con-éirig "arises, sets out to attack" ipv. 2 sg. *comérig*; ipv. 2 pl. *comérgid*

con-ellaing (com-in-loing) "joins together, yokes" ipf. 3 sg. *cotut-eilged*

con-essoirg "crushes, kills" pret. 3 sg. *cotom-essart*

con-gaib "settles, establishes; holds, gathers together" fut. 3 sg. *con-géba*; ipf. 3 sg. *con-gaibed*

con-gní "acts together" pres. ind. 3 sg. *cot-gní* (see notes)

con-icc "is able" pres. ind. 2 pl. *-cumgid*

conicci "as far as, up to" *connici*

conn (m., -o-) "top" ds. *chund*

con-oí "protects, guards, preserves" pres. ind. 3 sg. *-comathar, con-oí*; augm. pret. 1 sg. *con-róetar*

con-ricc "meets, encounters, joins" pres. subj. 1 pl. *-comairsem*; fut. 1 pl. *-chomraicfem*; pret. 3 sg. *-comarnic*

con-táilgi (com-to-ad-luig) "lulls" ipv. 3 sg. *-cotalgad* (see notes)

córaigid "arranges" augm. pret. 3 sg. *ra chóraig*

cor (m., -o-) "act of putting, throwing" ds. *cur*

corp (m., -o-) "body" ns. *chorp, corp*; gs. *chuirp*

corrbecc "pointed and small" dpl. *corrbeca*

cos (f., -a-) "foot" ns. *choss*; apl. *chossa*; dpl. *chossaib*

cosc (n., -o-, vn. of *con-secha*) "act of preventing, hindering; hindrance" ns. *cosc*

coscar (m., -o-, vn. of *con-scara*) "spoils" gs. *choscair*; npl. *mórchoscuir* "great spoils"

coscarach "victorious" as. *coscarach*

cosindiu "until today"

cosmail "like" ns. *cosmail*

costudach "supporting, protecting" as. *costodach*

crann (m., -o-) "tree" dpl. *crannaib*

créchtach "wounded, wound-inflicting" ns. *créchtach*

créchtnaigid "wounds" fut. 3 pl. rel. *créchtnaigfit*

124

crét "what" *cráet*

crett (f., -a-) "frame, body, trunk" gs. *creta, cretta*

crí (f.) "flesh, body" ds. *crí*

crích (f., -a-) "territory, land" as. *crích*; ds. *crích*

crichid "perfect" as. *crichid*

críchmruig (m., -i-) "borderland" dpl. *críchmrugib*

cride (n., -io-) "heart" ns. *cride*

criss (m., -u-) "body-belt" ns. *chriss*

cró (m., -io-) "hoof" gs. *cruí*; dpl. *cruíb*

cródae "fierce, brave" npl. *cróda*

cróderg "blood-red" ns. *cróderg*

crú (n., -u-) "wound" as. *crú*

crúaid "hard, harsh" ns. *crúaid*; ds. *chrúaid*

crúancern (m., -o-) "bloody victory" as. *crúancern*

crúech (m., -o-) "deadly horse" npl. *crúeich*

cruinnbecc "round, compact, and small" dpl. *cruindbeca*

cruth (m., -u-) "form, shape, appearance" ds. *cruth*

cú (m., -n-) "dog, hound" ns. *cú*; gs. *chon, con*

cúairt (m., -i-) "circuit, visit" as. *cúairt*

cubaid "harmonious, in accord" npl. *cuibdi*

cuillesc "hazel wand" ds. *culluaisc, cullisc*

cuing (f.) "yoke" ns. *chuing*; gs. *cungai, chunga*; ds. *cuing*; as. *cuinge*

cuingid (m., -i-) "champion, warrior, hero" as. *cunnid*

cuinnid (earlier *con-dieig*) "asks demands" fut. 3 sg. *-chunnécha*; augm. pret. 3 sg. *ro chunnig*

cuma (f., -t-) "grief, sorrow" ns. *chuma*

cumachtach "powerful" ns. *cumachtach*

cumachtae (n., -io-) "power" apl. *cumachta, chumachta*; *lán~* "great power" apl. *lánchumachta*

cumal (f., -a-) "female slave" ns. *cumal*

cummae (n., -io-, vn. of *con-ben*) "the same, like; act of cutting, hacking, destroying" ns. *cumma*

cumtachglan "brightly covered" as. *cumtachglan*

dá "two" nom. *dá*; acc. *dá*; dat. *dá, dó, díb*

dáer "base, unfree" ns. *dáer*

dabach (f., -a-) "large vat or tub with two ears" npl. *dabcha*

daigerdae "fiery, fierce" ns. *daigerda*

dáil (f., -a-) "circumstance, condition, affair" gs. *dála*

daimid "endures, allows" augm. pret. 3 sg. *ro dámastar*; augm. pret. 3 pl. *níro damsat*

dall "dark, gloomy" ns. *dall*; as. *dall*

daltae (m., -io-) "fosterling" as. *daltae*

dano "then" *dano*

dar ~ *la* X "X thought" *andar, indar*

dath (m., -u-) "color" gpl. *ndatha*

de, di (prep. + dat.) "from, of" *de, di, do, d'*; 1 sg. *dím*; 2 sg. *dít*; 3 sg. *de*; 3 pl. *díb, ndiib*; 1 sg. poss. *dim, dom*; 2 sg. poss. *dit*; 3 sg. masc. poss. *dia*; 1 pl. poss. *diar*; 3 pl. poss. *dia*; with rel. part. *dia*; with ds. art. *dont, don, din*; with dpl. art. *dona*

dé "enough, what a" *dé*

dead (f., -a-) "after" ds. *diaid*

déc "ten" *déc*

degaid (m., -i-, old vn. of *do-saig*) "after, to" *ndegaid*

deich "ten" *deich*

déide (-io-, -ia-) "two things, pair of things" dpl. *dédaib*

déidenach "last, final" gs. *dédenaig*

deime (f., -ia-) "darkness" ds. *deme*

deired (n., -o-) "end" ns. *dered*

deithbir "reasonable, fitting" ns. *deithbir*

delg (n., -s-) "pin, brooch (fastening mantle)" ns. *delg*

dénum (m., -u-, vn. of *do-gní*) ds. *dénam*

deog (f., -a-) "drink" as. *dig*; gs. *digi*; ds. *ndig*

dér (n., -o-) "tear" ns. *dér*; gpl. *dér*

derbad (m., -u-, vn. of *derbaid*) "act of confirming, establishing" ns. *derbad*

derg "red" ns. *derg*; npl. *derga*; as subst.: *derg*

derglassad *ar* ~ "glittering like a red flame" *derglassad*

dergrúathar (m., -o-) "bloody attack" apl. *dergrúathra*

des "right (side); south" ns. *dess, des*; gpl. *ndess*

desel (n., -o-) "right side, righthandwise" as. *desel, dessel*

deslám (f., -a-) "right hand; just hand" as. *desláim, deslám*; dpl. *deslámaib*

dethitiu (f., -n-) "concern, trouble" ns. *deithitiu*

détlae "brave-tempered" gs. *détlai*

Día "God" gs. *Dé*

día "supernatural being, god" gs. *dea*; ds. *día*

día "day" as. *díe, día*

dia "if, when" *dia*

díairle "ill advised" ns. *díairle*

díamlad (m., -u-, vn. of *di-samlathar*) "act of hiding, concealing, ignoring" ns. *díamlad*

díanechtair "on the outside" *díanechtair*

días (f., -a-) "two people" ns. *días*; as. *dís, diis*; gs. *déssi*

díbad (m., -o-) "destruction, death" ns. *díbad*

díbairgid (earlier *do-bidci*) "casts, hurls" *ro díbairg*

díbdud (m., -u-, vn. of *do-bádi*) "extinguishing, quenching" ds. *díbdud*

díchimmid (-i-) "crooked, bent one" npl. *díchimmidi*

díbe (n., -io-, vn. of *do-ben*) "denying, refusal, stinginess" gs. *díbe*

díberg (f., -a-) "vengeance, wrath" gs. *díberge*

díbergach (m., -o-) "marauder, bandit" gpl. *ndíbergach*

díchra "zealous, vehement" ns. *díchra*

didiu "indeed" *didiu*

dígáirse (f., -ia-) "promptness, zeal" ds. *dígáirsi*

dígal (f., -a-, vn. of *do-fich*) "revenge, vengeance" ns. *dígal, dígail*; as. *ndígail, mórdígail* "great vengeance"

díglaid (earlier *do-fich*) "avenges" fut. 1 sg. *not-digél*; fut. 2 sg. *nom-digéla*

dílechtae "bereft" gs. *dílachtai*; npl. *dílachtai*

dílúib "very deceptive" apl. *dílúbai*

dímaín "lost, useless" ns. *dímaín*

dind (n., -u-) "height, peak" ds. or as. *dinn* (see notes); dpl. *dindaib*

dingid "crushes, quells" fut. pass. sg. *dithistair* (see notes)

díriuch "straight, direct" ns. *díriuch*

dirsan "sad, calamitous" as subst.: *ndirsan*; as interjection: *dursan*

díth (n.) "loss destruction, absence" ns. *díth*; ds. *díth*

díthrachtae "weak, without strength" ns. *díthrachtai*

díthrachtaid "weakens, impairs" augm. pret. 3 sg. *rom-díthracht*

dítiu (f., -n-) "shelter, protection" ns. *dítiu*; gs. *dítniu*

dligid "deserves, is owed" pres. ind. 1 sg. *dligim*; pres. ind. 2 sg. *-ndligi*; pres. ind. 1 pl. *dlegmai*; pres. ind. pass. sg. *dlegar*

do "your" *do*; *th'*

do (prep. + dat.) "to, for" *do, d'*; 1 sg. *dam-sa*; 2 sg. *duit-siu, duit-seo, duit*; 3 sg. masc. *dó*; 3 sg. poss. *dia, da*; 3 pl. poss. *dia*; 1 pl. *dúin, dún*; 2 pl. *dúib*; 3 pl. *dóib*; with art. *don, dond*; with rel. part. *dia*

do-adbat "shows, displays" augm. pret. pass. sg. *-tarfad*

do-aidlea "visits, approaches, frequents" pres. ind. 2 sg. *-thaidle*; ipf. 3 sg. *taidled-som*; ipv. 2 sg. *tadall*

do-áirci "causes, brings about" fut. 3 pl. *táircébat*

do-airissedar "remains, stands, stays" pret. 3 sg. *tarrasair*

do-airret "catches, seizes, reaches" pres. ind. 3 sg. *-tharraid*

do-aitni "shines" pres. ind. 3 sg. *-taitni*

do-ba "dies" pret. 3 sg. *do-beba* (see notes)

do-beir "brings" pres. ind. 3 sg. *do-beir, da-mbeir*; pres. ind. 3 pl. *do-berat*; pret. pass. sg. *do-breth*; pret. pass. pl. *do-bretha*; augm. pres. subj. 2 sg. *-thuca, -tardda*; sec. fut. 3 pl. *-tibritis*; augm. pret. 1 sg. *-tharddus-sa, -tharddus*; augm. pret. 3 sg. *do-rat, -tarat, -tuc*; augm. pret. 1 pl. *do-fucsam-ni, -thucsam*; ipv. 2 pl. *tabraid*; pret. 3 sg. *do-bert*

dochum (prep. + gen.) "to, toward" *dochum*

do-cing "steps forward, advances" pres. ind. 3 sg. *do-cing*

do-claid "constructs; pierces" pret. pass. sg. *do-class*; ipv. 2 pl. *taclaid*

do-coissig "keeps, preserves, sets apart" pret. pass. sg. *do-cossecht*

do-cuirethar "throws, casts" pres. ind. 3 sg. *do-curidar, do-curedar, do-cuiredar*; augm. pret. 3 sg. *-tarlai*

do-cumlai "sets out, proceeds" pres. ind. 3 sg. *do-cumlai, to-cumlai*; pres. ind. 3 pl. *do-cumlat*; pret. 3 pl. *do-cumlaiset*

doé (f., -nt-) "arm" gs. *doí*

do-éccai "beholds, sees" pres. ind. 3 sg. *-décai, do-féccai*; ipv. 2 sg. *décce, fég*

do-eim "protects" ipf. 3 sg. *dim-emed*; augm. past subj. 3 sg. *-nderóemad*

do-esta "is lacking" pres. ind. 3 sg. *-tesbai*

do-fen "transcends, releases" (modal) pret. pass. sg. *díthide* (see notes)

do-fich "avenges" fut. 1 sg. *do-fius*; augm. pret. 3 sg. *-nderaig*

do-fiuschi (di-uss-sech) "awakens, calls up, resuscitates" fut. pass. sg. *di-uiscebthar*

do-foscai "supports, preserves" pres. ind. 3 sg. *-toisci*

do-fothlaig see **do-tluchethar**

do-fúairc "crushes, beats" pret. 3 sg. *do-fúart*

do-furgaib "raises, sets up" pret. pass. sg. *turgabad*; "utters, raises (the voice)" pret. ind. 3 pl. *túargabtar*

do-gní "does, makes" augm. pres. ind. 3 sg. *-drónand; ro-gní*; pres. ind. pass. sg. *do-gníther*; ipv. 2 pl. *denid*; sec. fut. 1 sg. *do-génaind, do-génaind-sa*; augm. pret. 3 sg. *-nderna*; augm. pret. pass. sg. *do-ringintea*; augm. pret. pass. pl. *do-rónta*; augm. pret. 2 sg. *da-rónais*

do-icc "comes" pres. ind. 3 sg. *-thic, -tic, do-n-ic*; ipv. 2 sg. *tair*; pres. subj. 1 sg. *-thísiur*; pres. subj. 2 sg. *-tís*; pres. subj. pass. sg. *tístar*; pres. subj. 2 pl. *-tístai-si*; pres. subj. 3 pl. *-ndigsitis*; past subj. 3 sg. *-thísed*; fut. 3 sg. *ticfa*; fut. 3 pl. *ticfat*; pret. 3 sg. *tánic*; pret. 3 pl. *-táncatar*

do-immoirg "oppresses" augm. pret. 3 sg. *dom-chommart*

do-indnaig "bestows, gives" pres. ind. 3 sg. *to-n-indnaig*

do-intaí "turns back, returns" pret. 3 pl. *tintaíset*

do-intlaig "desires, craves" pres. ind. 3 sg. *-thintlaig*

dolbid "conjures, shapes" pres. ind. 3 pl. *dolbit*

do-léici "lets go; throws casts, hurls" pres. ind. 3 sg. *do-lléici*; ipv. 2 sg. with 3 sg. masc. inf. pron. *do-lléic*; pres. subj. pass. *do-lléicter*; augm. pret. 3 sg. *-tarlaic, tarlaic*; augm. pret. pass. sg. *-tarlaiced*; as Mid. Ir. simple verb *teilcid*: augm. pret. 3 sg. *ro theilg, do-theilg*

do-ling "leaps, springs, bounds" augm. pret. 3 sg. *tarblaing*

dolud (m., -i/o-) "distress, loss, damage" ns. *dolluid*

dom (m., -u-, later -i-) "house, home" ds. *doim*

do-meil "enjoys, partakes of" pres. ind. 1 sg. *do-miul-sa*

domun (m., -o-) "the world" ns. *domun*; as. *domun*; gs. *domuin, ndomuin*

donn "light brown" ns. *dond*

dorchae "dark" ns. *dorcha*

dorchaide "dark" dpl. *dorchaide*

do-reith "rides, drives" pres. ind. 3 sg. *to-rét, to-rreith*

dorn (m., -o-) "fist" gs. *duirn*; ds. *durn*

do-rorban "prevents, hinders" pret. 3 sg. *-nderbai*

do-ruimnethar "forgets" past subj. 3 sg. *-ndermanad*; augm. pret. pass. sg. *ro dermatad*

do-saig "approaches, comes" augm. pret. 3 sg. *dom-riacht*

do-soí "turns" pres. ind. pass. sg. *to-ssuíther*

dothchernas (m., -o-) "miserliness, churlishness" gs. *dothchernais*

do-tét "comes" pres. ind. 3 sg. *do-tháet, do-thét*; pret. 3 sg. *do-lluid*; augm. pret. 3 sg. *do-dechaid, do-dechuid*; augm. pret. 3 pl. *do-dechatar*

do-tluchethar "desires, demands, asks, seeks" pres. ind. 1 pl. *do-tluchemar* (see notes); ipv. 2 sg. *dos-fothlaig*

do-tuit "falls" pres. ind. 3 sg. *tuit, tuitt, do-fuit*; pres. ind. 3 pl. *mo-thuittet*; fut. 3 sg. *do-fáeth, tuitfid*; sec. fut. 3 sg. *do-faíthsad, do-fáethsad*; pret. 3 sg. *do-cer, do-ceir*; augm. pret. 3 sg. *-torchair, do-rochair, da-rochair, tod-forchair*; augm. pret. 3 pl. *torchratar*

dris (f., -i-) "briar, bramble" (or form of *drisiuc* "satirist"?) dpl. *drisib* (see notes)

drochthindnacol (n., -o-, vn. of *do-indnaig*) "miserliness" gs. *droch-thidnacuil*

droneirr (m., -d-) "firm chariot-fighter" ns. *droneirr*

drúcht (m., -u-) "dew" as. *drúcht*

druí (m., -d-) "druid" ns. *druí*; gpl. *ndruíd*

dúalach "having locks or tresses" ns. *dúalach*

dub "black" dpl. *duba*

dubae (n., -io-) "grief, gloom, mourning" ns. *dubae*; as. *dubae*; ds. *dubai*

dubderg "dark red" npl. *dubderga*

dúil (f., -i-) in pl. "Creation" npl. *dúile*; apl. *dúile*

duille (f., -ia-) "foliage, leaves" apl. *dulli*

duine (m., -io-) "human being" gs. *duini*; apl. *doíne*; gpl. *doíni*; dpl. *doínib*

dul (vn. of *téit*) ns. *dul*; ds. *dul*

dul "satirist" apl. *dulu*

dún (n., -o-, later -s-) "fort" ns. *dún*; as. *dún* (see notes)

dúnad (n., -u-) "encamping army, host" ns. *ndúnad*

é "he, it" *hé*

éc "death" as. *éc*

éccodnach "insensible, legally irresponsible" gpl. *n-écodnach*

éccraite (f., -ia-) "hostility, enmity" apl. *écraitiu*

ech (m., -o-) "horse" ns. *ech*; as. *ech*; gs. *eich*; npl. *eich*; gpl. *ech, n-ech*; dpl. *echaib, n-echaib*

echlach (f., -a-) "messenger, attendant" ds. *echlaig*

echrad (f.) "pair of two horses" in pl. "chariot-riding host" ns. *echrad*; ds. *echraid*; gpl. *echraide*

écmacht "powerless" gpl. *écmacht*

ecnaide "wise, learned person" npl. *ecnaithi*

écndach (n., -o-) "slandering, defaming" gs. *écnaig*

écóir "improperly" *écóir*

écomlann (-o-) "unequal force, unequal combat" npl. *écomluind* (see notes); ds. *écomlund*

ed neuter pron. *ed*

éigme "cry, scream" as. *éigmi*

éim "indeed" *ém*

eirr (m., -d-) "chariot-fighter, champion, warrior" ns. *eirr*; as. *errid*; ds. *erra*; npl. *errid*; gpl. *erred, eirred*

éis "trace, track" *di* ~ "after, in the absence of" ds. *éis, és*

éissi "reins" npl. *éssi*

ell "advantage" as. *eill*

én (m., -o-) "bird" npl. *héoin*; dpl. *énaib*

énblaith see notes

ennach (f.) "scald-crow" ns. *ennach*

eochair (-i-) "key, guide" ns. *eochair*

eól (m., -o-) "knowledge, acquaintance" ds. *eól*

Eóraip "Europe" gs. *Eóraip*

epaid (f., -a-) "spell, charm" dpl. *epthaib*

érimm (n., -n-) "course, journey" as. *érim*

éscae (n., -io-) "the moon" ns. *ésce*

eslabrae (f., -ia-) "generous person" npl. *eslabrai*

esréidiud (vn. of *esrédid*) "act of scattering, dispersing" ds. *n-esrédiud*

essad "affliction, sorrow" gpl. *n-essad*

estecht (vn. of *as-tét*) "departure, death" gs. *eitsechta*; ds. *eistecht*

ét (m., -o-) "zeal, jealousy" as. *ét*; ds. *ét*

étan (m., -o-) "brow, forehead" gs. *étain*; ds. *étun*

etargaire (n., -io-) "intervening, separating" as. *etargaire, n-etargaire, etairgaire*

etarlúamnach "fluttering, hovering" ns. *etarlúamnach*

etarscarad (m., -u-, vn. of *etar-scara*) "act of separating" ns. *etarscarad*; as. *n-etarscarad*

etarscaraid (earlier *etar-scara*) "separates" augm. pret. 3 sg. *ros-etarscar*

eter (prep. + acc.) "between" *eter*; 1 pl. *etruind*

etráin (f.) "intervention on someone's behalf" as. *etráin*

fáebar (m., -o-) "sharp blade of sword, sharp-bladed weapon" gs. *fáebuir*; ds. *fáebur*; dpl. *fáebraib*

fáilid "glad, cheerful, joyful" npl. *fáilti*

failtnigid ~ *fri* "rejoices at, welcomes" pres. subj. 3 pl. *failtniget*

farrad *i* ~ "beside, close to" ds. *farrad*

fastud see **astud**

fathi "cloak; fold of a garment" ns. *fathi*; as. *fathi*

fathmann (f., -a-) "lock, strand of hair" gs. *fadmainni*

fé "woe, alas" *fé*

feb (f., -a-) "excellence, distinction" ds. *feib*

féchaid "looks over, heeds, keeps a lookout" pres. ind. 3 sg. *féchid*; ipf. 3 sg. *-féchad*

féchem (m., -n-) "debtor" gs. *fécheman*

fecht (m.) "time, occasion" as. *fecht*

féin "self" 2 sg. *féin*; 3 sg. *fadessin*

feis (f., vn. of *foaid*) "sleep, rest, repast" ds. *feis*

fén (m., -o-) "cart" gs. *féin*

feochair "fierce, stern, severe" ns. *fechuir*

feochaine (f., -ia-) "ravens, flock of birds" ns. *feochuine*

fer (m., -o-) "man" ns. *fer*; as. *fer*; gs. *fir*, "great man" *rofir*; ds. *fir*; npl. *fir, firu*; vpl. *firu*; apl. *firu*; gpl. *fer*; dpl. *feraib*

fér (n., -o-) "grass" as. *fér*

feraid "supply" augm. pres. subj. 1 sg. *ro fersur* (see notes)

feramail "manly" as. *feromail*

ferda "manly" ns. *ferda*

ferdacht (f., -a-) "manliness" ns. *ferdacht*

fergnúis see **gnúis**

fermart (m., -o-) "slaughter, massacre" as. *fermart*

fern (f., -a-) "shield" apl. *ferna*

fert (m./n., -o-) "mound" ns. *fert*; as. *fert*

fertaid "buries" augm. pret. pass. sg. *ro fertad*

fescor (m., -o-) "evening" ds. *fescur*

fethid "goes" pres. ind. 3 sg. *fethid, faidid*; augm. pret. 3 pl. *ro fáthatar*

fíacail (m., -i-) "tooth" dpl. *fíaclaib*

fiach (m., -o-) "raven" ns. *fiach*

fíach (m., -o-) "debt, obligation" apl. *fiachu*

fíal "honorable, noble" ns. *fíal*

fichdae "fierce, furious" as. *fichda*

fiche (m., -nt-) "twenty" npl. *fichit*; apl. *fichtiu*

fichid "boils" augm. pret. 3 sg. *ro fichi*

fichid "fights" fut. pass. sg. *fessair*

fidbad (f., -a-) "forest" ds. *fidbaid*

finn "fair, white; bright, blessed; just, true" ns. *find*; apl. *finna*

findchass "with fair, curling hair" as. *findchass*

findnélach "of white clouds" as. *findnélach*

fír (-n-) "truth" ns. *fír*; as. *fír*

fírchlich see notes

fithis (f.) "circuit" as. *fithis*

flaith (f./m., -i-) "ruler, lord; kingdom, realm" as. *flaith*; ds. *flaith*; npl. *flathi*; gpl. *flatha*

flesc (f., -a-) "switch, rod" ns. *flesc*

fo (prep. + dat.) "under" *fa, fo*; 3 sg. masc. poss. *foa*; with elided rel. part. *fo*

fo-ácaib "leaves" ipv. 2 sg. *-fácaib*; past subj. pass. pl. *-fácbaitis*; pret. 3 sg. *fos-n-ácaib*; augm. pret. 3 sg. *-fargaib, fargab*

fo-ceird "puts; casts down, overthrows" augm. pret. 3 sg. *ro lá*; augm. pret. pass. *ro cuired*; as Mid. Ir. *cuirid*: pres. ind. 3 sg. *-cuirend*

fochen "welcome" *fochen*

fochla (n., -io-) "champion-seat, champion" dpl. *fochluib*

fo-cren "buys, gives an equivalent for something" fut. 3 pl. *fas-cíurat* (see notes)

fo-crotha "shakes, quivers" fut. 3 pl. *fo-croichfet*

focursid see notes

fo-daim "suffers, endures" augmented pret. 1 sg. *-fordámar-sa*

fodb (m., -o-) "spoils; warrior" npl. *fuidb*

fodes "southward" *fodes, fades, fodess*

fo-fera "causes, produces" augm. pret. 3 sg. *fo-rrúair*

fo-gaib "finds, meets with" pres. ind. 3 sg. *fondat-gaib*; fut. 3 sg. *-fugéb*; pret. 3 sg. *-fúair, fúair, fo-n-úair*

fogamar (m., -o-) "autumn" gs. *fogomuir*

foirm (f.) "form, way, manner" ds. *foirm*

follnathir "rules, reigns, governs" fut. 3 sg. *fallnabthair*; pret. 3 sg. *-fallnastar*

fo-loing "tolerates, bears" pres. ind. 3 sg. *-fulaing*

folt (m., -o-) "hair of head" ns. *folt*; gs. *fuilt*; ds. *fuilt*

foltlebor "long-haired" as. *foltlebor*

fo-luigi "conceals" pres. subj. pass. sg. *fo-...-luigther*

fo-naisc "binds, imposes an obligation" fut. 3 sg. *fo-nena*

133

fonn (m., -o-) "bottom" as. *fond*

fonnad "tire" dpl. *fonnaidib*

fo-noí "cooks, roasts" pret. 3 pl. *fo-noíset*

for (prep. + dat. and acc.) "on" *for*; 1 sg. *form*; 2 sg. *fort*; 3 sg. masc. *fair*; 3 sg. fem. *furri-side*; 2 pl. *foruib*; 3 pl. acc. *forru, forro*; 3 pl. dat. *foraib*; 1 sg. poss. *form*; 2 sg. poss. *fordo*; 3 sg. masc. poss. *for a*; with sg. art. *forint, forna, forsin*; with pl. art. *forsna*; with rel. part. *for, forsa*

foramm (n., -n-) "birdhunting" dpl. *foromnaib*

forbás (m., -o-) "illusion, transient nature" gs. *forbáis*

forbruth (m., -u-) "great fury" ds. *forbruth*

forcenn (n., -o-) "end" ds. *forciund*; as. *forcend*

for-cí "watches, looks over" pret. 3 sg. *-forcachai*

for-cing "marches forth, ascends, overcomes, prevails" pres. ind. 1 sg. *for-cingiu* (see notes)

for-comai "preserves, retains" pret. 3 g. *-forcmastar*

for-congair "commands" fut. 1 sg. *for-congér-sa*; pres. ind. 3 sg. *for-congair*

forcu "choice, darling" ns. *forcu*

for-díben "slays, destroys" augm. pret. 3 sg. *fos-roirtib*; past subj. 3 sg. *for-díbad*

fordon-ossa see **ar-ossa**

fo-reith "helps" ipf. 3 pl. *fo-retis*

forgab (m., -u-) "spear thrust" npl. *forgoba* (see notes)

fo-ricc "comes across, finds" pret. 3 sg. *-farnaic*

forlínad (m., -u-) "filling up, completing; abundance" as. *forlínad*

forloiscthe (part. of *for-loisci*) "burnt (maliciously)" ns. *forloiscthe*

formnae (m., -io-) "choice, the best" npl. *formnai*

formtech "envious" npl. *formdig*

fornélach "of high clouds" as. *fornélach*

forórda "golden" npl. *forórda*

forrán (f.) "violent aggression, attack, raid" apl. *forránu*

for-rét "rides, proceeds" pres. ind. 1 pl. *for-ríadam*

for-tá "is on, upon" ipf. 3 sg. *fordom-benad*

fortche (f., -ia-) "chariot cushion" gs. *fortche*; ds. *fortchi*

fo-ruimi "sets, places" pres. pass. sg. *fo-rruimther*

fossad "steadfast, firm" as. *fossad*

fót (m., -o-) "sod of earth" npl. *fóit*

fótbach (n., -o-) "cut sods" gs. *fótbaig*

fothraicid (earlier *fo-truici*) "bathes" pres. ind. 3 sg. *fothraicid*; fut. 3 sg. *nom-fothraicfe*

fothrucud (m., -u-) "bathing" ns. *fothrucud*

fótmar "nervous, skittish" ns. *fótmar*

fo-truici "bathes" (later as simple verb *fothraicid*) pres. ind. 3 sg. *fo-thruci*

fras (f., -a-) "gush, stream" dpl. *frassaib*

frecnairc "present, in evidence" *frecnairc*

fri (prep. + acc.) "toward, to, against, at, with" *fri, ra*; 1 sg. *frim*; 2 sg. *frit*; 3 sg. masc. *friss, fris, ris*; 2 sg. poss. *frit*; 3 sg. masc. poss. *ria*; with masc. art. *frisin*; with rel. part. *fris, friasa, ris*

fris-áilethar "expects, receives" ipv. 2 sg. *fritháil*; ipv. 2 pl. *frithalid*

fris-goin "slays in vengeance; avenges" fut. 3 sg. *fris-gegna*

fríth (m.) "find, gift, treasure" ns. *fríth*

frithissi "again, back" *afrithisi, aridisi, aridisi, darisse, aríse*

fuidbechta (substantivized part. from fo-di-boing) "fragments; broken, crushed things" npl. *fuidbechta*

fuidlechtae (substantivized part. from *fo-dloing*) "gushes" dpl. *fuidlechtaib*

fúaim (n., -n-) "sound, noise" ns. *fúaim*

fuil (f., -i-) "blood, wound" ns. *fuil*; gs. *fola*; as. *fuil*; npl. *fuile*; gpl. *fuili*; dpl. *fuilib*

fulacht (m., -u-) "cooking pit, cooked food" ns. *fulocht*; gs. *fulachta*

gabor (f.) "horse" ns. *gabuir*; as. *gabuir*

gae (m.) "spear" ns. *gaí*; as. *ngaí, gae*; ds. *gaí*; dpl. *gaíb*; apl. *gaí*

gaibid "takes, holds sway, sides with, accepts, holds back, (with *imm*) dresses, arrays oneself" pres. ind. 3 sg. *-geib, gabaid*; ipv. 2 sg. *gaib, geib* (see notes); augm. past subj. 3 pl. *-rragbat*; pres. subj. pass. *gabthar*; fut. 3 sg. *géba*; pret. 3 sg. *gabais*; augm. pret. 3 sg. *ro gab, rod-n-gab, -ragab, -rragaib, ro gabai*; augm. pret. pass. pl. *ro gabtha*

gainem (m., -o-) "sand" as. *gainem*

gainithir "is born" fut. 3 sg. rel. *gignithar*

gair "a short time" ds. *gair*

gáir (n., -i-) "shout cry" as. *gáir*

gaire see **goire**

gáirechtach "laughing, merry" npl. *gárechtaig*

gaisced (m., -o-) "weapons" as. *gaisced*; gs. *gaiscid*; ds. *gaisced*; npl. *gascid*

gal (f., -a-) "warlike ardor, fury, valor" ns. *gal*; gs. *gaile*; ds. *gail*; dpl. *galaib*

galgat (f,. -a-) "calamity, crime, outrage" gpl. *ngalgat*

gamain (m., -i-) "yearling calf" ns. *gamain*

gand "mean, miserly" ns. *gand*

gart "generosity, honorable behavior" ns. *gart*

gartach "generous, noble" ns. *gartach*

gataid "removes" pres. ind. 3 sg. *gataid*

gáu (f., -a-) "falsehood" as. *goí*

gein (n., -n-, vn. of *gainithir*) "person, being" ns. *gein*; vs. *gein*; ns. *mórgein* "great being"

geis (f.) "taboo, prohibition" ns. *geiss*; dpl. *gessib*

gel "bright" ns. *gel, ngel*; gs. *gil*

gemma (Latin *gemma*) "gem, precious stone" npl. *gemma*

genit (f., -i-) "malevolent female supernatural being" npl. *genite*

glainithe "made of glass or crystal, clear" npl. *glainithe*

glas "blue, grey" ns. *glas, nglas*

glé "dispute" *nglé*

glés "bout, spell" as. *glés*

glomar (m., -o-) "bridle bit" dpl. *gglomraib*

gnáth "customary, usual" ns. *gnáth*

gníid "does" pres. 3 sg. *ro gní* (see notes)

gním (m., -u-) "act, deed, act of slaughter" ns. *gním*; as. *gním*; gpl. *mórgníma* "great deeds"

gnímrad (f., -a-) "deeds, acts, feats" apl. *gnímrathu*

gnúis (f., -i-) "face, countenance" ns. *gnúis*; npl. *fergnúsi* "men's faces"

goire (f., -ia-) "piety, familial affection" as. *gairi*

goirt "keenly, sharply" *goirt*

goirthech "glowing" ns. *goirthech*

gol (n., -o-) "cry" as. *gol*; gs. *goil, guil*

golgaire (n., -io-) "wailing lamentation" as. *golgaire*

gonaid "slays" fut. pass. sg. *not-géntar*; augm. pret. pass. sg. *rom-gáet*; augm. pret. pass. pl. *ro gáeta*

grád (n., -o-) "grade, rank" ns. *grád*

graig (n., -i-) "horses" gs. *grega*

gránda "horrible, ugly, hateful" npl. *gránne*

grés *do* ~ "always" *grés*

gress (f., -a-) "attack" gs. *ngresse*

gressach "hostile, insulting" ns. *gressach*

grían (f., -a-) "sun" ns. *grían*

gripe (f., -ia-) "swiftness" ns. *gripe*

grís (f., -a-) "glow, ardor, valor" dpl. *gríssaib*

gruad (n., -s-) "cheek; honor, brow" ns. *gruad*

gúala (f., -n-) "shoulder" as. *gúalaind*

gubae (n., -io-) "mourning, lamenting" ns. *guba*; gs. *ngubae*

guidid "prays" fut. 3 pl. *gigsit*

guin (n., -i-, vn. of *gonaid*) "act of slaying" as. *goin, guin*; ds. *guin*

guth (m., -u-) "voice" ds. *guth*

i (prep. + dat. and acc.) "in" *i*; with rel. *a*; with 3 sg. neut. dat. pron. "there, then" *and, indsin andsin*; 3 sg. fem. acc. *inti*; 3 sg. masc. acc. *ind*; 3 pl. *indib*; 1 sg. poss. *im*; 2 sg. poss. *it*; 3 sg. poss. *na, ina*; 3 pl. poss. *na*; with ds. art. *isind, issind, issin*; with dpl. art. *isna*; "when" *i*; with pres. ind. 3 sg. cop. *inid*

í (deictic particle) *int-í, aní-sin*

íach (m., -o-) "salmon" as. *íach*

íachtaid "cries out, laments" fut. pass. pl. *íachtbatir*

íar (prep. + dat.) "after, along, across" *íar*; 3 sg. masc. poss. *íarna*; 3 pl. poss. *íarna*; with dat. art. *íarsin*

íarum (*íar* + 3 sg. neuter pron.) "then; now, hereafter" *íarum*

iat 3 pl. pron. "they" *iat*

íath (n., -u- later m., -o-) "land, territory" apl. *íathu*; gpl. *íath*

ibid "drinks" pres. ind. 3 sg. *ibid*; fut. 1 sg. *íba*

íccaid "atones for, saves, redeems, heals" augm. pret. 1 sg. *ro íccus*; augm. pret. 3 sg. *ro ícc*

ifern (n./m., -o-) "Hell" as. *iffern*; gs. *iffirn*

il (f.) "many, a multitude" npl. *ili* (see notes); apl. *iliu*; dpl. *ilib*; equative *lir*

ilarbuir "many hosts" apl. *ilairbriu*

iltúatha "many kingdoms" apl. *iltúathu*

imbárach "tomorrow" *imbárach*

imbert (f., -a-, vn. of *imm-beir*) "weapon plying" gs. *n-immberta, imberta*

imbúarach "a short time ago" *imbúaruch*

imchían "very long" npl. *imchíana*

imchomét (m., -u-) "act of guarding, watching over" ds. *imchomét*

imdae "many, numerous" npl. *imda*

imdegail (f., -a-, vn. of *imm-dích*) "act of protecting, defending" ns. *imdegail*

imdibe (n., -io-, vn. of *imm-díben*) "cutting off" ns. *imdibe*; ds. *imdibe*

imguin (-i-, vn. of *imm-goin*) "act of slaughtering, battle" gs. *imgona*

imm (prep. + acc.) "around, on account of, along with" *im*; 1 sg. *immum*; 2 sg. *immut*; 3 sg. masc. *imme, immi, imbe*; 3 sg. masc. poss. *immi, immo*; with art. *immon*

immacúairt "around" *immacúairt, 'macúairt*

imm-airchisi "pities, laments, has compassion on" pres. subj. 1 pl. *imma-n-airchisem*

immairecc (m., -o-, vn. of *imm-airicc*) gs. *immairic*

imma-n-aicci "sees each other" pret. 3 sg. *imma-n-acci*

imma-n-airret "meets together" pret. 3 sg. *imma-n-arraid*

imm-beir "practices, inflicts, causes" augmented pret. 1 sg. *n-immarburt*; ipf. 3 sg. *no imbred*

imm-caíni "laments, bewails" pres. subj. 1 pl. *imma-caínem*

imm-cí "weeps for" pres. subj. 1 pl. *imma-cíam*

imm-comairc "asks" pret. 3 sg. *im-chóemnacair*

imm-derga "reddens" pres. ind. 3 sg. *imm-derga*

imm-dích "protects, saves, defends" ipf. 3 sg. *immum-díched*

imm-dítnathar "protects" ipf. 3 sg. *immut-dídnad*

immesorcun (f., -a-, vn. of *imm-essoirg*) "act of exchanging blows" ds. *imessarcain, imessorgain, immessorgain, immesorgain*

imm-gaib "avoids" pres. ind. 1 sg. *-immgabaim*; pret. 3 sg. *n-imgab*

imm-goin "wages war, fights" pres. ind. 3 pl. *-imgonat*; fut. 1 sg. *-imgén*

immirge (f,. -ia-) "migrating tribe" dpl. *imergib*

imm-rádi "reflects on, thinks about" augm. pret. 1 sg. *imma-rordus*

imm-réid "rides (a horse)" ipf. 1 sg. *-imrédinn*

imm-slig "slays" pret. pass. sg. *imma-...-slecht*

imm-soí "turns" augm. pret. 3 sg. *ro impa*

immurgu "however, on the other hand" *immurgu*

imnedach "troublesome, worrisome" ns. *imnedach*

impide (f.) "entreaty" as. *impide*

imṡrotha see notes

imtholtanach "eager, willing" ns. *imtholtanach*

in (definite article) neuter ns. *a*; neuter as. *a*; masc. ns. *in, int*; masc. gs. *in, ind*; masc. as. *in*; fem. ns. *in, ind, inn*; fem. gs. *na, inna*; fem. npl. *na*; masc. npl. *na, int*; masc. gpl. *inna, na*; masc. apl. *na*

in (interrogative particle) *in*

inad (m., -o-) "place" ds. *inud*

inchinn "brain" npl. *n-inchind*; dpl. *n-inchinnib*

indala "one of two" *indala*

indas (n./m., -u-) "way" as. *n-innas*

indeóin (f.) "anvil" gs. *n-indeóna*

indiu "today" *indiu*

indlid "harnesses, yokes (a chariot)" ipv. 2 sg. *innill*

indlide "prepared for battle" as. *n-indlithe, indlithi*; dpl. *indlithib*

indred (n., -o-, vn. of *ind-reith*) "incursion, act of invading; fighting" as. *indrid*; apl. *indretha*

ind-reith "invades, fights successfully" pres. ind. 3 sg. *inn-reith*; pres. subj. 3 pl. *-innriset*

ingar "grievous, bitter, sorrowful" npl. *ingair*

ingen (f., -a-) "girl, maiden" ns. *ingen*; as. *n-ingin*; vs. *ingen*; gs. *ingeni*

ingnas (f., -a-) "absence, loss" dpl. *ingnasaib*

ingnath (n., -o-) "a strange, wondrous thing; a marvel" apl. *ingantu*

inmain "dear" ns. *inmain*

inne (f., -ia-) "innards, guts" as. *inne*; dpl. *innib, indib*

in-otat "enters" augm. pret. 3 sg. *ad-rulaid*

is (copula) pres. ind. 1 sg. *am*; pres. ind. 1 sg. with neg. *nídam*; pres. ind. 3 sg. *is, iss*; pres. ind. 3 pl. *it*; pres. ind. 3 pl. neg. *nídat*; pres. ind. 3 pl. with *cía*: *cidat*; pres. ind. rel. *as*; pres. ind. 3 sg. with *co*: *conid*; with pres. ind. 3 sg. with *ma*: *maso*; neg. *mani*; pres. subj. 3 sg. *ba, mbo*; pres. subj. 3 sg. with *cía*: *cíabo*; pres. subj. 3 sg. with *ma*: *mad*; pres. subj. 1 sg. with *cía*: *cíabam*; pres. subj. 3 pl. *mbet*; augm. pres. sub. 3 sg. *rop*; fut. 1 sg. *bam*; fut. 3 sg. *bith, bid, -mbo*; fut. 3 sg. with neg. part. *níba*; fut. 3 pl. with neg. part. *níbat*; past subj. 3 sg. *bad, bud*; past subj. 3 sg. with *dia*: *diambad*; pret. 2 sg. *ba-so*; pret. 3 sg. *ba*; pret. 3 sg. with *co*: *comba, combo*; pret. 3 sg. with neg. part.: *níbu*; pret. 3 sg. with neg. rel. part. *nabu, napu*; pret. 3 sg. with *co*: *comba*; augm. pret. 3 sg. *nírbo, ropo*; augm. pret. 3 sg. with *co*: *corbo*; pret. 3 sg. with *cía*: *cíab*; augm. pret. 3 sg. with *cía*: *cíarbo*; pret. 3 pl. with *co*: *comtar*

ís "below, under" 1 pl. *ísund*

ísel "lowly, humble" comparative (for superlative) *ísliu*

ithe (f., -ia-, vn. of *ithid*) "act of eating" ds. *ithi*

la (prep.+ acc.) "with, amid, by the agency of" *la*; 1 sg. *lim, lim-sa*; 2 sg. *lat, latt*; 3 sg. masc. *leis, leiss*; 3 sg. fem. *lé, lee-si*; 1 pl. *lind*; 2 pl. *lib*; 3 pl. *leo*; 1 sg. poss. *lam*; 3 sg. neuter poss. *lia*

laa (n.) "day" as. *llaa-sin, llá, llaa*; ds. *laa, ló, lóu*; ds. *óenló* "single day"

láech (m., -o-) "warrior" ns. *láech*

láechdacht (f., -a-) "valor, chivalry" ds. *láechdacht*

laigid "lies (down)" pret. 3 sg. *líagair* (see notes)

lám (f., -a-) "hand" ns. *lám*; as. *láim*; gs. *láime*; ds. *láim, lláim*; gpl. *lám*; dpl. *lámaib*

lán "full, whole" ns. *lán*; as subst. ns. *lán*

lánbráth (m., -u-) "full Judgment" gs. *lánbrátha*

lánchlemnas "full alliance" ds. *lánchlemnas*

lann (f., -a-) "panel, cover" gs. *lainne*

lár (n., -o-) "ground" ds. *lár*

láth (m., -i/o-) "warrior" gs. *láith*; npl. *láith* (?) see notes)

lathe (n., -io-) "day" as. *lathe*; ds. *lathiu, llathi*

léibenn (m., -o-) "platform, protective array" ns. *lébend*

lecc (f., -a-) "flat slab of rock" dpl. *leccaib*

léicid "leaves; throws, hurls" pres. ind. 3 sg. with 3 sg. masc./neut. suff. pron. *léicthi*; augm. pret. 3 sg. *ro léici, ro léci*

leig (Lat. *lex*) "law" as. *leic*

léimnech "leaping, agile" ns. *lémnech*

leithe (n., -s-) "side" ns. *leithe*; as. *leithi*

lénaid "impairs, injures, hinders" fut. 3 sg. *lénfaid*

less (m., -u-) "interest, benefit" gs. *lessa*

lestar (n., -o-) "vessel, container (for drink)" ns. *lestar*

leth (n., -s-) "side, half" ns. *leth*; as. *leth*; ds. *leth, lleith*

lethchenn (n., -o-) "cloven head" npl. *lleithchind*

lethchloicenn (f., -a-) "cloven skull" npl. *llethchloicne*

lethchos (f., -a-) "cloven foot; single foot" as. *lethchoiss*; npl. *llethchossa*

lethlám (f., -a-) "cloven hand" npl. *llethláma*

líath "grey" ns. *líath*

lige (n., -io-, vn. of *laigid*) "act of lying down" ns. *lige*; ds. *ligu*

lín (n., -u-) "full number, amount" ns. *lín*

línaid "fills" fut. 3 sg. *línfaid*; fut. 3 pl. *línfait*

lingid "leaps, jumps" augm. pret. 3 sg. *ro ling*

ló "snowflake" npl. *lóa*; apl. *lóa*

loch (m., -u-) "lake" ns. *loch*; as. *loch*; gs. *locha*

lóeg (m., -o-) "calf, favorite, darling" ns. *lóeg*

lón ~ *gaile* "warrior's light" ns. *lón* (see notes)

lorg (m., -o-) "track, trail, path" as. *lorg*

lúachthide (n., -io-) subst. adj. "brightness" ns. *lúachthaidiu*

lúaithe (f., -ia-) "swiftness, speed" ns. *lúathe*

lúas (m., -u/o-) "speed" ns. *lúas*

lúath "swift" as. *lúaith*

luglíath "lynx-grey" ns. *luglíath*

luinech "lance" ns. *luinech*

luing "exiled person" ns. *luing*; as. *luing*

ma "if" with neg. part. *mani*

macc (m., -o-) "son" as. *mac*; gs. *meic*; npl. *meic*; vpl. *maccu*; apl. *maccu*; gpl. *mac*; dpl. *maccaib*

macgnímrad (f., -a- or m., -o-) "boyhood deed" dpl. *Macgnímradaib*

machaid "slaughters, destroys" pres. ind. 3 pl. *machait*

mag (n., -s-) "plain" ns. *mag*; as. *mag, mmag*; ds. *maig*; gs. *maige*; gpl. *mmuige*; dpl. *maigib*

maignech "big, great" ns. *maignech*

mai "May" gs. *maí*

mairg "woe" *mairg, mairgg*

mairgid "grieves (trans. and intrans.), mourns" fut. 1 pl. *-mairgfem*; perf. 3 sg. *rot-...-mairg*

mairid "remains, endures" augm. pret. 3 sg. *ro mair*

maith "good" *maith*; cpv. *ferr, fherr*; spv. *dech*

marb "dead" ns. *marb*

marbad (m., -u-, vn. of *marbaid*) ds. *marbad*

marbaid "kills, slays" pres. subj. pass. sg. *marbthair*; past subj. pass. sg. *no marbtha*; augm. pret. 3 sg. *ro marb*

marcach (m., -o-) "rider" ns. *marcach*

márfer (m., -o-) "great man" gpl. *márfer, mórfer*

máthair (f., -r-) gs. *máthar*

mé "I, me" *mé*; emph. *misse*

mebal (f., -a-) "cause of shame, disgrace" ns. *mebol*

141

medón (m., -o-) "middle; abdomen" as. *medón*; ds. *mmedón, medón*

méit (f., -a-) "amount, magnitude, greatness" ns. *mét*; gs. (after copula) *méite* "likely"

menmae (m., -n-) "feelings, spirit, attention" ns. *menma*

meschuire (m., -io-) "band of followers" apl. *messchuiru*

methaid "fails, comes short" augm. pret. 3 sg. *ro meth*

mí (m.) "month" gs. *mís*; apl. *mís*

míad (n., -o-) "honor, dignity, status" ns. *míad*

míadaigid "honors" pret. 3 sg. *-míadaigestar*

midaís "middle age" gpl. *midaís*

midbine "small offence" ns. *midbine*

midlach (f., -a-) "weakling, coward" gs. *midlaige*

mífoclad (n., -o-) "bad news, ill omen" ns. *mífoclad*

mifre (f., -ia-) "sadness, faintheartedness" ns. *mifre*

millid "ruins, destroys" pret. 3 pl. *millsit*

milliud (m., -u-, vn. of *millid*) "act of ruining, destroying" as. *milliud*

mind (m., -o-) "crown, diadem" ns. *mind*

mindoíne "warriors" apl. *mindoíne*

mír (n., -n-) "portion" as. *mír*

mo "my" *mo, mmo, m', mm'*

mó "good" *mó*

mong (f., -a-) "hair" as. *moing*

mór "great, big" ns. *mór*; as. *mór, móir, már*; ds. *már, mór*; npl. *móra*; apl. *móra*; cpv. *mó*; as subst. "many" ns. *mór*

móraid "exalts, glorifies" pres. ind. rel. sg. *móras*

mórsaide (m., -io-) "great multitude" ds. *mórsaide*

mórthúath (f., -a-) "great kingdom; province" apl. *mórthúatha*

mos-baim see **baid**

mo-thuittet see **do-tuit**

mruig (m., -i-) "land, region" gs. *mroga*

mug (m., -u-) "male slave" ns. *mug*

múich (f.) "gloom, sadness" gs. *múiche*

muimme (f., -ia-) "fostermother" gs. *mumme*; ds. *mummi*

muir (n., -i-) "sea" gs. *mara*

mullach (m., -o-) "crown of the head" as. *mullach*; gpl. *mulach*

nach "any" ds. *nach*

nár "noble person" ns. *nár*

násad "celebration, festivity" ns. *násad*

nech "anyone, someone" ns. *nech*; ds. *neoch*

nechtar "either" ns. *nechtar*

neim "poison, venom" dpl. *nemib*

nél (n., -o-) "cloud" ns. *nél*; gs. *neóil*

nélbruig (m., -i-) "land of clouds (i.e., Heaven)" as. *nélbruig*

nem (n., -s-) "the sky, Heaven" gs. *nime*; ds. *nim*; dpl. *nimib*

nemnech "venomous, vindictive" ds. *nemnech*

nert (n./m., -o-) "strength, power" ns. *nnert*; as. *nert*; gpl. *nert*

ní (negative particle) *ní, nách, nán, ná, nát, nád, náchit*

ní (neuter of *nech*) "thing" ns. *ní*; as. *ní*; ns. *óenní*

nia (m., -d-) "nephew, sister's son" ns. *nia*

níth (m./n.) "fighting, conflict; wounding, slaying" ns. *níth*; ds. *níth*; apl. *níthu*

nó "or" *nó, ná*

nochtad (vn. of *nochtaid*) "to bare" ds. *nochtad*

noí "nine" *noí*

nónbar "nine people" gpl. *nónbur*; as. *nónbur*; apl. *nónboru*

nós (m., -o-) "manner, custom" ds. *nós*

ó (prep. + dat.) "from" *ó*; 2 sg. *úait, úait-siu*; 3 sg. masc. *úad*; 1 pl. *úand*, 2 pl. *úaib*; 3 pl. *úaib*; *úain-ne*; 3 sg. masc. poss. *óa*; 3 pl. poss. *óa*; with art. *ónd*

oc "at" *oc, 'c, ic*; 3 pl. *accu, oca, ocaib*; 1 sg. poss. *ocom*; 3 sg. poss *oca*; with rel. neg. part. *oconá*; with ds. art. *ocond, ocind*

óc (m., -o-) "young person, warrior" npl. *óic*; gpl. *óc*

ocht "eight" *ocht*

ochtar "eight people" npl. *ochtair*

óchtar (m., -o-) "upper part" ds. *n-óchtor*

óclach (m., -o-) "young warrior" gs. *óclaig*

óen "one" ns. *óen*; dpl. *óenaib*

óenach "meeting, encounter" ds. *óenuch*

óenáilges (f., -a-) "one demand" as. *óenáilgis, óenálgis*

óenar (m., -o-) "singe individual" ds. *óenur*

óenbuiden (f., -a-) "single troop" as. *óenbuidin*

óencharpat (m., -o-) "single chariot" gs. *óencharpait*

óenchlár (n./m., -o-) "one board" as. *óenchlár*

óenchonar (f., -a-) "one road" ds. *óenchonair*

143

óenchossid (-i-) "one-footed person" ns. *óenchossid*

óenchuing (f.) "single yoke" ns. *óenchuing*

óenfer (m., -o-) "one man" gs. *óenfir*

óenguine (n., -i-) "single wound" as. *óenguine*

óenlám (f., a) "one hand" as. *óenlám*

óenlámaid (-i-) "one-handed person" ns. *óenlámaid*

óenmag (n., -s-) "supreme plain" ds. *oínmaig*

óenmarcach (m., -o-) "single rider" as. *óenmarcach*

óenní (n.) "one thing" ns. *óenní*

óensmúit (f.) "one cloud of smoke" ns. *óensmúit*

ol "says" *ol, ar, or*

ól (m., -u/o-, vn. of *ibid*) ds. *ól*

olc "bad" ns. *olc*; as. *olc*; cpv. *messu*

oldaas (*ol* + 3 sg. rel. of subst. verb) "than" *andás, andaas, oldaas*

oll "great, mighty" ns. *oll*

ollam (m., -n-) "master warrior" gpl. *olloman*

olleith (*oll* + *flaith*) "mighty lord" ns. *olleith*

ón "indeed" *ón*

or see **ol**

or (m., -o-) "border, edge" as. *or*

ór (m., -o-) "gold" ns. *ór*; gs. *n-óir*

orc (m., -o-) "lap dog" ns. *orce*

orcaid "slays" pret. pass. sg. *ortae*

órdae "golden" ns. *órda*

óršnáth (m., -o-) "golden thread" gs. *óršnáid*

ort (m.) "destruction, slaughter" as. *hart*

os "and" with disjunctive personal pronoun *os, 's*

ós "over, above" *úas*; 3 sg. masc. *úasa, úasu*; 1 pl. *úasund*

otharlige (n., -io-) "burial place" ns. *otharlige*

popa "sir, master" vs. *phobba, phopa*

pupall (f., -a-) "awning" ds. *pupaill*

ráidid "recites, says" fut. 3 pl. *ráidfet*; augm. pret. 3 sg. *ro raid, ro rádi*

rannaid "divides, distributes" fut. pass. sg. *randfaider*

ráth "surety" gpl. *ráth* (see notes)

ráthaigid "perceives, notices" pret. 3 sg. *-ráthaigestar*

ré (n., -io-) "time, span of a person's life or reign, space" ns. *ré*; as. *ré*; gs. *ré*

recht (m., -u-) "law, justice" ns. *recht*; as. *recht*; ds. *recht*

réidid "rides, drives" pres. ind. 3 sg. *céta-rét* (see notes); ipf. 3 sg. *no réided-som*

réimm (n., -n-) "course, movement" ns. *réim*; as. *réim*

reithid "runs" pres. ind. 3 sg. *rethid*; fut. pass. sg. *resair* (see notes)

remi-tuit "falls before" pres. ind. 3 sg. *remi-tuit*

renaid "sells, exchanges, gives up" pres. ind. pass. sg. rel. *renar*

rí (m., -g-) "king" ns. *rí*; as. *ríg*; gs. *ríg*; npl. *ríg*; gpl. *ríg*

ría (prep. + dat.) "before" *ría, re*; 1 sg. *rium, remum*; 3 sg. fem. *remi, reme*; 3 sg. neuter *riam*; 1 pl. *remaind*; 3 sg. masc. poss. *ría, ríana*; with masc. sg. art. *resin*

ríched (m./n., -o-) "kingdom of Heaven" ds. *ríchid*

ríchtu (f., -n-) ~ *lessa* "act of needing" ns. *ríchtu, ríchtain*

rígain (f., -i-) gpl. *rígan*

rígairech "regal, noble" as. *rígairech*

ríge (n., -io-) "kingship" as. *rígi*; ds. *ríge*

rígeirr "king of chariot-fighters" as. *rígeirr*

rigid "extends; directs; binds; defeats" fut. 3 sg. *riris*; pret. 3 sg. *reraig*

rím (f., -a-) "number" ns. *rím*

rind (n., -u-) "star" npl. *renna*; apl. *renna*

robb (m., -o-) "animal" gpl. *robb*

robud (m., -u/o-) "warning" ns. *robud*; as. *robud*

ro-cluinethar "hears" pret. 3 sg. *-cúala*; augm. pret. 3 sg. *rod-cúala, ro chúala*

rofír see **fer**

ro-fitir "knows, finds out, knew" pres. ind. 1 sg. *ro fetur-sa*; pres. ind. 3 sg. *ro fitir, ru fitir*; fut. pass. sg. *ro fiastar*; pret. 3 pl. *ro fetatar*; with *for* "knows to the discredit of" fut. 1 pl. *ro fessamar*

róg (*ro* + *óg*) "very pure" *róg*

ro-icc "comes" pres. subj 3 sg. *-rrí*; past subj. 3 sg. *-ríssed*; fut. 3 pl. *-ricfat*; sec. fut. 3 sg. *-ricfad, -ricfed*; augm. pret. 1 sg. *ránac-sa*; augm. pret. 3 sg. *ro-n-ánic, céta-ránic*; augm. pret. 3 pl. *-ráncatar, -rráncatar*

ro-laimethar "dares" augm. pret. 3 pl. *níro lámsatar*

rom "early, too early" ns. *rom*

ro-saig "reaches, attains" fut. 3 sg. *ro sía*; pret. 3 sg. *ro siacht, -roacht*

rosc (n., -o-) "vision, eye" ns. *rosc*

rot-bith-mairg see **mairg**

roth (m., -o-) "wheel, chariot; sphere" as. *roth*; gs. *ruith, rotha*

sáebrecht (m., -u-) "false, unjust law" npl. *sáebrechta*

saegul (m., -o-) "lifetime" ds. *saegul*

sáer "noble" as subst. "noble person" gpl. *sáer*

sáeth (m., -u-) "trouble, distress, suffering" gpl. *sáetha*

saidid "sits" ipf. 1 pl. *suidmis*; fut. 3 sg. *seiss*

saigid "approaches, reaches" fut. 3 sg. *sies*; pret. 3 sg. with 1 sg. suff. pron. *siachtum*

sáile (m.) "seawater, the sea" ds. *sáiliu*

sainaltram (n., -n-) "excellent fosterage" ns. *sainaltram*

saincherd (f., -a-) "excellent craftsman" gs. *saincherda*

samalta "comparable to, like" *samalta*

samrad (m., -o-) "summer" gs. *samraid*

samrata (m., -u-) "summery" ds. *samrata*

sant (f., -a-) "greed" as. *saint*

sáraigid "dishonors, insults" augm. pret. 2 sg. *náro sáraigis*; augm. pret. 3 sg. *ro sáraigestar*

scaílid "scatters, disperses" augm. pret. 3 sg. *ro scaíl*

scáinid "bursts, scatters" fut. pass. pl. rel. *scánfaiter*

scarad (m., -u-, vn. of *scaraid*) "separation, split" ns. *scarad*; ds. *scarad*

scél (n., -o-) "tidings" npl. *scéla*

scélach "storied" gs. *scélaige*

sceo "and" *sceo*

scíath (m., -o-) ns. *scíath*; as. *scíath*; gs. *scéith*; gpl. *scíath*; dpl. *scíathaib*

scís (m., -u/o-) "fatigue, tiredness" ns. *scísi;* ds. *scís*

scor (m., -o-, vn. of *scuirid*) "act of ceasing, ending" as. *scur*

sé "he" *sé*

sé "six" *sé*

sech (prep. + acc.) "past" 3 sg. fem. *secci*; 3 sg. masc. *sechai, secha*; 1 pl. *sechund*; 3 pl. *seccu*

secht "seven" *secht*

sechtmain (f.) "week" ds. *sechtmain*

seichid "asserts, declares" pres. ind. 1 pl. *sechmai*

séimid "calms" pres. ind. rel. pl. *sémite*

séis "division, array, rank" as. *séis*

séitid "blows, blows across" augm. pret. 3 sg. *ro sephaid*

sen "old person" gpl. *sen*

sén (-o-) "sign, portent" ns. *séin*

seo (dem. pron.) "this" *seo*

séol (n., -o-) "course" ns. *séol*

sercid "waste away, wither" fut. 3 sg. s*ercfid*

sessam (m., -o-) "act of standing" ds. *ṡessam*

sét (m., -u-) "path, way" apl. *sétu*

sethnu "across" *sethno*

sí, í "she" *sí*

síabarcharpat (m., -o-) "phantom chariot" ds. *síaburcharpat*

síaburchobra (f.) "phantom speech" *síaburchobra*

síabarthae "supernatural, bewitched" gs. *síabordai*

síar "west" *síar*

síd (n., -s-) "peace; fairy mound" gpl. *síde*; dpl. *ssídib* (see notes)

sin (demonstrative pronoun) "that" *sin, ssin, sein, sain*

Sion "Zion" ds. *Sion*

sír "everlasting, eternal" ns. *sír*

sírechtach "sorrowful" ds. *sírechtach*

slab "narrowness, sparseness" ns. *slab* (see notes)

slabrae (f., -ia-) "cattle" gs. *slabrae*

slán "wholesome, healthy" ds. *slán*

slecht "slaughter" as. *slecht*

sleg (f., -a-) "spear" ds. *ṡlig*

slíab (n., -s-) "mountain" npl. *sléibe*

slíasait (f., -i-) "thigh, side" ns. *ṡlíasait*; ds. *ṡlíasait*

slige (f., -t-, vn. of *sligid*) "way, road, path" ds. *ṡligid*

slóg, slúag (m., -o-) "host, army" ns. *slúag*; as. *slúag*; gs. *ṡlúaig*; ds. *ṡlúag*; npl. *slúaig, ṡlúaig*; apl. *slúaig*; gpl. *slog*; dpl. *slúagaib*

snechtae (-io-) "snow" gs. *snechtae, snechtai*

soaltae "well-reared" vs. *soalta*; superlative adj. used as subst. gs. *soaltim*

sochaide (f., -ia-) "multitude, crowd, host" as. *sochaide*

sodain (anaphoric pronoun) "that" *la* ~ "with that, thereupon"; ds. *suidiu, ṡudiu*

soid "turns" ipv. 2 sg. *soí*; fut. 3 sg. *soífid*

somblas "pleasant" ns. *somlas*

sorchae "bright, luminous" ns. *sorcha*

sreith "scatters, hurls, casts" pres. ind. 3 sg. *sreith*

sreth (f., -a-) "rank, line of soldiers" as. *sreith*

srían (m., -o-) "bridle" gs. *sréin*

srón (f., -a-) "nose" dpl. *srónaib*

srúaim (n., -n-) "stream" ds. *srúaim*

sruthbarr "gushing" (see notes) ds. *sruthbarr*

stúagmar "arched, curved" ns. *stúagmar*

súainem (m., -n-) "rope, cord, string" dpl. *súanemnaib*

súas "upward" *súas*

subae (n., -io-) "joy, pleasure, happiness" gs. *subae*

Succet "St. Patrick" gs. *Succet*

suí (m., -t-) "expert, master" gs. *suad*

suide (n., -io-, vn. of *saidid*) "sitting, seat" as. *suide*; ds. *suidiu*; gpl. *suide*

suidigidir "places, seats, settles" past subj. pass. sg. *-suidigthe*

suidiugad (m., -u-, vn. of *suidigidir*) "act of arranging, placing, settling" as. *suidigud*

súil (f., -i-) "eye" npl. *suli*; apl. *súle*; gpl. *súla, súle*

suilig "pleasant, agreeable, favorable" ns. *suilig*

suithchern (m., -o-) "good ruler, generous person" as. *suthchern*

sund "here" *sund*

tabairt (f., -a-, vn. of *do-beir*) ds. *thabairt*

táeb (m., -o-) "side" ds. *thóeb, thoíb*

táesc (m., -o-) "spurt, flow (of blood)" npl. *thóesca*

taidbsiu (f., -n-, vn. of *do-adbat*) ns. *taidbsiu*

taídlech (f., -a-) "shine, sparkle, brilliance" ns. *taídlech*

táin (f., -i-, vn. of *do-aig*) "cattle raid" ds. *tánai*

taircsiu (f., -n-, vn. of *do-fairget*) "offering, effort" ns. *taircsiu*

tairlingid (earlier *do-airling*) "alights, leaps down" augm. pret. 3 sg. *ro thairling*

tairngire (n., -io-) "prophecy" ds. *tairngere*

tairngech "restless, spirited" ns. *tairngech*

tais "gentle, weak, spiritless" ns. *thais*

taiscélaid (*do-scélai*) "introduces, makes known" augmented pret. pass. sg. *ro taiscélad*

talam (m., -n-) "earth, land" as. *talmain*; gs. *talman*; ds. *talmain*

tálcend (m., -o-) "priest" npl. *tálcind*

tan *in* ~ "when" *in tan*; *íar* ~ "then" *íar tain*

tar (prep. + acc.) "over, across" *dar*; 1 sg. poss. *darmo*; 3 sg. poss. *dara*; 3 pl. poss. *dara*

tesargain (f., vn. of *do-essuirg*) "act of saving, delivering" as. *teasarcuin*

tech (n., -s-) "house" ns. *tech*; ds. *tig*

techt (f., -a-, vn. of *téit*) "act of going" ns. *techt*

tecmailid (earlier *do-ecmalla*) "collects, gathers" augm. pret. 3 sg. *ro theclaim*

teine (m., -t-) "fire" as. *tenid*

teist "testimony, praise, fame" ns. *teist*

téit "goes" pres. ind. 3 sg. *téit, -tét, -táet, -taít*; pres. ind. 3 sg. with 3 sg. masc./neut. suff. pron. *téite*; ipv. 2 sg. *airg-siu*; ipf. 3 sg. *na théiged*; augm. pres. subj. 1 sg. *-ndechus*; fut. 1 sg. *regat-sa*; fut. 2 sg. *-rrega; -raga-su*; fut. 1 pl. *raigma*; sec. fut. 2 pl. *-rregthae*; pret. 3 sg. *luid, lluid*; augm. pret. 3 sg. *do-chuaid, -ndechaid*

tét (f., -a-) "string, strand" dpl. *tétaib*

timchell "around" *timchell*

tinnell "plot, treachery, snare" as. *tindell*

tír (n., -s-) "land, country" ns. *tír*; as. *tír*; gs. *tíri*; dpl. *tírib*

tocad (m., -o-) "fortune, fate" ns. *tocad*

tochmarc (n., -o-, vn. of *do-comairc*) "wooing, courtship" ns. *mórthochmarc* "great courtship"

todlach (vn. of to-uss-dloing) "rending, lancing" ns. *todlach* (see notes)

togáes (f., -a-, vn. of *do-gáetha*) "act of deceiving, deception, deceit" as. *thogáis*

togáethaid (earlier *do-gáetha*) "deceives, ensnares, beguiles" fut. 3 sg. *togáethfaid*

tolgda "strong, powerful" ns. *tolgda*

tollaid "pierces" pret. 3 sg. rel. *tollus*

tonn (f., -a-) "skin" gs. *tuinne*; ds. *tuind*

tongaid "swears" pres. ind. 1 sg. *tongu, tongim-se*; pres. ind. 3 sg. rel. *tonges*

torandchless "thunderfeat" as. *torandchless*; apl. *torandchless*

torandchlessach "performing thunderfeats" ns. *torandchlessach*

torbad (m., -u-) "injury" ns. *torbad*

tormaid "resounds, makes a loud noise" pres. ind. 3 sg. *tormaid*

tornochtaid "bares" pres. ind. 3 pl. *tornachtait*

torrama "funeral; act of ministering to, service" as. *torromu*

tost (m., -u-) *i* ~ "silent, at rest" ds. *tost*

tošúgud "baiting trick" gs. *tošúigthi, tošúigthe*

trá "then" *trá*

tráethaid "subdues, vanquishes" fut. 3 sg. *tróethfaid*; augm. pret. pass. sg. *ron-tráethad*

traig (f., -t-) "foot" as. *thraigid, thraig*; dpl. *traigthib*

tráigid "ebbs, causes to ebb" pret. 3 sg. *-tethraig*

tráth (n., -u-) "hour, canonical hour" as. *thráth*

trebaid "inhabits, dwells in" fut. 3 pl. *trebfait*

tréide (n., -io-) "triad" dpl. *trédaib*

trén "strong" gs. *tríuin*; cpv. (for spv.) *tressiu*

trénfer (m., -o-) "warrior" ns. *trénfer*

tres "third; one of three" as. *tres*

tress (m., -u-) "fight, battle" ds. *tress*

tri (prep. + acc.) "through" *tria, tre*; 3 sg. masc. *triit*; 3 sg. fem. *treithe*; 3 sg. masc poss. *tria, triana*; with art. *tresin, triasin*

trí "three" masc. *thrí, trí*; fem. nom. *téora*; fem. acc. *téora*

tríall (m.) "attempting, endeavoring" ds. *tríall*

triar "three people" as. *triar*

tríath (m., -o-) "lord, chieftain" npl. *tréith*

trícha (m., -nt-) "thirty" ns. *trícha*; npl. *tríchait*

trom "heavy" ns. *trom*; cpv. *trummu*

trú (m., -k-) "doomed person" ns. *trú*; npl. *troich, truich*

trúag "wretched, miserable" ns. *trúag*

tú "you" *tú*

túalaing "capable of" *túalaing*

túaslucud (m., -u-, vn. of *do-fúasailci*) "releasing, delivering, setting free" as. *thúaslucud*

túath (f., -a-) "kingdom" ns. *thúath*; as. *thúaith*; dpl. *thúathaib*

túathcháech "blind in the left eye" npl. *túathcháecha*

tuidecht (f., -a-, vn. of *do-tét*) ds. *tuidecht*

tuigithir "covers" pres. ind. 3 sg. *-tuigedar*

tuile (n., -io-, vn. of *do-lin*) "flood, abundance" ns. *tuili*

tuir (f., -t-) "chief hero" ns. *tuir*

tuitim (n., -n-, vn. of *do-tuit*) "falling, being slain in battle" ns. *thuttim*

turbaid "delay, hindrance; disaster, misfortune" ns. *turbaid*

tús "beginning" *ar tús* "first, originally"

úa (m., -io-) "grandson" vs. *uí*

úabar (m., -o-) "pride" gs. *úabair*; ds. *úabor*

úaigthe "united, joined" ns. *úaigthe*

úain (f.) "time" gs. *úane*

úaine (diminutive of *úain*) "little lamb" ns. *úaine*

úainecdae "greenish" ds. *úanicda*

úair "because" *úair*

úanbach (m., -o-) "foam, froth" ns. *úanbach*

úanchenn (n., -o-) "lambhead" ns. *úanchend*

úar "cold" ns. *úar*

úas "above" *úas, ós*

úasal "high, noble" ns. *úasal* cpv. (for spv.) *úaisliu*

úath "a few, one" ds. *n-úath*

úathad (n., -o-) "a few, one" ds. *úathad* "alone"

ucht (n., -u-) "breast, bosom" as. *hucht*

uchtlethan "broad-chested" npl. *uchtlethnai*

ucut "yonder" *ucut, út, sucut, sút*

uile "all" ns. *uile*; as. *uile*; npl. *uile*

úir (f.) "earth, soil" ds. *úir*

uirre (f.) "homage, submission" dpl. *urraib*

uisce (n., -io-) "water" gs. *usci*; ds. *uisciu*

Ulaid (m., -o-) in pl. "Ulstermen" gpl. *Ulad*; apl. *hUltu, Ultu, hUlto*; dpl. *Ultaib*

urchra (n., -io-, vn. of *ara-chrin*) "act of perishing; downfall, defeat" gs. *urchraide*

INDEX OF PERSONAL NAMES

Ádam gen. *Ádaim*

Adarc nom. *Adarc*; gen. *Adarci*

Aífe gen. *Aífe*

Amairgin nom. *Amargin*; gen. *Amairgin*

Aue nom. *Auae*; gen. *Auae*

Badb nom. *Badb*

Cairpre Nia Fer gen. *Cairpri Niod Fer, Corpri*

Calatín gen. *Calatín*

Cathbad gen. *Chathbad*

Celtchair nom. *Celtchair*; gen. *Cheltchair*

Cenn Fáelad mac Ailella nom. *Cend Fáelad mac Ailella*

Conall Cernach nom. *Conall, Conall Cernach*; voc. *Chonaill Chernaig*; gen. *Conaill Chernaig, Conaill*; dat. *Conall*; acc. *Conall Cernach, Conall*

Conchobar nom. *Conchobar*; gen. *Chonchobuir, Conchobuir*

Cormac nom. *Cormac*; gen. *Cormaic*

Críst nom. *Críst*; gen. *Chrísti*

Cú Chulainn nom. *Cú Chulainn, Cúa*; voc. *Chú Chulaind*; gen. *Chon Culaind, Con Culaind*; dat. *Choin Culaind*; acc. *Coin Culaind, Choin Culaind*

Dechtire gen. *Dechtire, Dechtiri*

Derg Drúchtach dat. *Deirg Drúchtaig*; acc. *Deirg nDrúchtaig*

Dub Sainglenn nom. *Dub Sainglend*

Echaid gen. *Echdach*

Eirrge Echbél nom. *Eirrge Echbél*

Eithne gen. *nEithnend*

Emer gen. *Emire*; dat. *Emir*

Éogain Álaind nom. *Éogain Álaind*

Erc mac Cairpri nom. *Erc, Erc mac Carpri, Erc mac Corpri, Erc mac Cairpri*; dat. *Erc mac Carpri*

Feidlimid Fáeborderg nom. *Feidlimid Fáeborderg*

Fergna mac Findcháeme nom. *Fergna mac Findcháeme*

Fergus mac Lete nom. *Fergus mac Lete*

Fergus mac Rossa nom. *Fergus mac Rossa*

Fiacha Foltlebor nom. *Fiacha Foltlebor*

Ísu nom. *Ísu*

Lebarcham nom. *Lebarcham*

Líath Macha nom. *Líath Macha, Líath*; voc. *Léith, Léith Macha*; gen. *Léith, Léith Macha*; dat. *Líath Macha*; acc. *Líath Macha*

Lóeg mac Riangabra nom. *Láech, Lóeg, Láeg, áeg mac Riangabra*; voc. *Laíg, Loíg*; acc. *Lóeg mac Riangabra, Lóeg, lLáeg mac Riangabra*

Lóegaire Búadach nom. *Lóegaire Búadach*

Lug gen. *Loga*

Lugaid mac Con Ruí meic Dáre nom. *Lugaid, Lugaid mac Con Ruí, Lugaid mac Con Ruí meic Dáre*; gen. *Lugdach*; dat. *Lugaid*; acc. *mac Trí Con, Lugthig, lLugaid*

Mess Gegra nom. *Mis Gegra*

Mórrígu nom. *Mórrígu*

Munremur nom. *Munremur*

Níab nom. *Níab*

Rochad Rigderg nom. *Rochad Rigderg*

Scáthach gen. *Scáithchi*

Sencha Sobeóil nom. *Sencha Sobeóil*

Sualtaim gen. *Sualtim*

Succet gen. *Succet*

INDEX OF NAMES OF PEOPLES AND PLACES

Mag Siamrach acc. *Mag Siamrach*
Mairg Lagen acc. *Mairg Lagen*
Midbine nom. *Midbine*
Mumu gen. *Muman*
Muscraige Tíre gen. *Muscraige Tíre*
Roiriu dat. *rRoirind, Roirind*
Síd Nenta íar nUsciu dat. *Síd Nenta íar nUsciu*
Sion dat. *Sion*
Slíab Fúait gen. *Sléibe Fúait*; dat. *Slíab Fúait*
Slige Midlúachra dat. *Sligi Midlúachra*; acc. *Sligid Midlúachra*
Temair gen. *Temro*; acc. *Temraig*
Temair Lóchra dat. *Themair Lóchra*
Tethbae dat. *Tethbai*
Ulaid nom. *Ulaid*; gen. *Ulad, n-Ulad*; dat. *Ultaib*; acc. *Ulto, Ultu*

APPENDIX

H.3.18 Fragments

1. Ro fôghluinnsett na mic druíghecht 7 coimlecht[16] (.i. cocud) 7 admilludh 7 tosúgud. Ro foghluinnsett na hingina fessa 7 dúile 7 amaidecht (.i. glicus).

> The sons studied druidry, slaughter (i.e., war), great destruction, and [magical] enticement. The daughters studied [occult] knowledge and lore and sorcery (i.e., witchcraft).

2. Et ro cóecha uile comtar túathc[h]óecha (.i. láncacha nó clécacha).

> And she blinded all of them so that they were blind in the left eye (i.e., fully blind or blind in the left eye).

3. Robud mór a détide[17] (.i. a dineas nó a dúthreacht) forro díghal a n-athar din cerd hí-sein ro foglannset.

> …to incite their fury (i.e., their pain or longing) (literally, that their fury (i.e., their pain or longing) might be great) to avenge their father through the craft they had learned.

4. "Aca, nírbu gaíne dom athair-si éim tochur (.i. indsaigid nó íarad) fri Coin Culaind; bés (.i. derb) nib gaíne dam-sa cía triallor."

> "No, to fight (i.e., attack or attempt) Cú Chulainn was not a little game for my father. Perhaps (i.e., certainly) it wouldn't be a little game for me either (if I should venture [it])."

5. "Et cuin do-raghtur fris?" ar Erc. "Ni hannsa, co ndernntar tri gaiscidh (.i. tri armud) linde fris,"ar maco Cailitín, ".i. adhmad (.i. obuir no foglaim) .uíí.maine."

> "When will we confront him?" said Erc. "That's easy: when we've made three weapons (i.e., three pieces of battle equipment) against

---

[16] Thurneysen (1912–1913: 15) suggests Latin *conflictus* as the origin of this word. Alternatively, perhaps the word may be identified as *coim[s]lecht* or *cáemslecht* (com-imm-slecht *DIL* C 17.58), appearing in *Cath Maige Tuired*: "eter cáemslecht 7 admilliud 7 amaidichtai" (Gray 1982: 54, §119), translated as "mutual smiting." If so, perhaps *com-* may here be interpreted as an intensive prefix, yielding the meaning "complete or great slaughter."

[17] (*tétige*) f., -ia- abstract noun from *tétach* (*GOI* §257); according to *DIL* (T 161.13–16), *tétach* (*tédach*) is glossed in O'Curry's Law Transcripts (1374) as *merugud* and in O'Clery's Irish Glossary (under *tedaidh*) as *mear* (Miller 1881–1883: 53). *DIL* defines *tétach* as equivalent to *tét*, citing (from Meyer's edition of "The Expulsion of the Déisi") "buí mac tét la ríg Temrach."

him," said the sons of Calatín, "that is, the contrivance (i.e., work or learning) of seven days."

6. "Is mithe dún," ar Erc 7 Lugaid, "erfúacra uán for firu Érend." "Nocha mithigh," ar macu Calitín "úair admad (.i. obair) sechtmaine is admat secht mbliadhan" (.i. ænlá cacha bliadhna do-caith[18] fri dénum na ngai).

"It's time for us," said Erc and Lugaid, "to command the men of Ireland." "No," said the sons of Calatín, "for the work of seven days is the work of seven years." That is, one day each year was spent making the spears.

7. Maine, fer neimnech, is é rodas-innsmasdair 7 ro mheil (.i. ro caith nó ro limadh) íar sin.

Maine, a venomous man, set the spears and ground them (i.e., ground or sharpened them).

8. Ro ordaighsedur Ulaid ord (.i. cinded) comairle do Chon Culaind arná tésed a hEmain Macha amach co thísdís Ulaid imbi.

The Ulstermen set a counsel (i.e., decree) that Cú Chulainn would not leave Emain Macha until the Ulstermen could accompany him.

9. "Do-béra Cú Culaind 7 fa-cialdaid."

"Cú Chulainn will attack. Heed him!"

10. Nídam…indíu] Nidam eirr (.i. gaiscíach-) aighe imtoltanach accobrach (.i. sanndach) imgona andíu

11. Íar sin…fair] Íar sin roling C.C. foragaiscedh (.i. forarmudh) 7 roghab fathi imbe in cetna fath rogabh fair

12. Fortche…Suilig] Foirtce forsa suigmis suide suilig

13. Acc…chath] Aic amae geib leig aLuigh laaraid airitiud laerridh imdegail lacuinnigh comairli lafiru ferrdacht lamná mifre tair remainn donchath

14. Ro fetatar…Emuin Macha] Arofetadur nitiucfadh Emhain Macha doridisi

15. Beochobra ConCulaind isinnlaa fuair bas

16. Ind lám…indib] In lam arogaib 7 intsliasat fontarat rolecht conaroba innert cetna inntibh

---

[18] Impersonal active preterite 3 sg. of *do-caithi*. For another example of this construction see Bergin and Best (1938: 142–143): "co torchaidh .ix. mísa fri haenla" ("so that nine months went by as one day").

17. Cía fhacca dún...] Cia aca dun apuba a Laoigh roraid Laogh conidisbert troich imda 7 corcur mor forn apoba aC.C.

18. Cían...fer nÉrend] Cian adraigsemur meschuiriud fer nErenn

19. At-chíu-sa sund...] Carpat cuclaigid, costaid comairligit comerget arafoilmit arfochlaid aranergit afraigid ri Temrach clofidt- rioth. Ruirsigt- aigthi. Ailfidt- c-na cicsit- roí raindfit- faidb firfidt- fuili fodnaidh naaig-

20. Comérgid...] Comeirgid affraig afiru Erend dofil Cúchulaind cucaibh

21. 7 días...a ainm side] Et dís ocinimserguin doneoch astreisi dontṡluagh 7 caínti cocolluaisc acu. Et corogaibh ailgis diagoiseom feisin .i. blad arbladaibh aainmsidhe

22. Imbred na gaí...for Mag Murthemni] Imbred ingoi 7 insciath 7 inclaidheb 7 nacleasa comtar lir gainemh mara 7 ran- nime 7 drucht cetemain acloicni 7 alethlamha 7 alethchosa 7 acnama derga comscailti iarnanesraidiudh foMagh Murtemne

23. Nirom-aérad-sa...dothchernais] Niromaerasa riam acinaidh modroch tidnaccuil nomodotcernais (.i. modrochtiagernus)

24. Do-bert Cú...at-rubramar] Dobert C.C. ingoi dó arurlainn condechaidh trianacenn 7 gurromarbh danonbur iarndul trianacenn 7 feitid (.i. cuire) triasin mbuidin coforcenn amal remerbramar (.i. amal robrethnaigemair)

25. Do-fuit rí...Lugaid] Dofuit roí dongoí sin armacu Cal- rocuala libh dofaethsat roi dongoi roteilg Lugaidh abuarach (.i. amochrách)

26. La sin do-lléici Erc...Líath Macha] Lasodain doleigi Erc ingoi fair conndemaid isinLiath Macha

27. óenchuing sunda indiu] aencuing sunn indiu

28. La sain...cétna] Iarsin tra dob- achois facenn nacuinge 7 fethid (.i. cuire) triasin mbuidin indinnus cetna

29. Tír ém...ṡáegul] Is fír ón eim or C.C. tír naranacsa ríam nírícfat scela moécnaigh remam. Nuair is bec ata domtṡaegul

30. Amal...ina broind] Amal rainic inloch mescais alamh sethnaidh abronn cofarcaib isindloch ambí na broinn

31. Conid de atá...Con Culaind] Conade ata nitathe buaidh remain indLeth Macha iarmarbadh ConCulaind

32. Benair...dia dígail] Iársin dobenar alam doe doChonCulaind andigail laime dóe Lug-

33. Do-cumlat ass...di úir] Docomlat as íarsin nasloigh doTemraigh 7 b- ait acenn doConChulaind 7 alamh doe leo conad ann ata atorligi acinn 7 alamh dóe 7 lan lainde ascéith douir

34. Do-ceir…Rofir] Docher (.i. dotuit) CúChulaind camtuit trenerr- (.i. trengaisc-) inAirbriu 7 r-

35. Do-fil…úasa] Dofil aenmarcach darsamag oringilla as mór agrindi 7 agripi dotoet andarlat isfeochuine Erend fil uassa

36. Secha…Dé] Dé doiach súd arConall Cernach

37. Int-í dano…fort] Cipé diandles feich tothlaig fair dligim dítsa arConall 7 atu agtriall anaccrai fort

38. La sin do-n-ic…assa thoíb] Iarsin rosginnd intech corogaibh mir afastaib inrí .i. Lug- m-c ConRoi

39. Fé amae…a Chonaill Chernaig] Fé amaé nifír fer sin aChonaill

40. Co rráncatar] Corainic cach daigh friaceíle oUisniuch Mide coCarnnUiNét

41. Tongu-sa a tonges…ocRoirind] Tonga dodía tongus motuath nímidbeine conade ata Ath Midbine forabainn Liffe rolen cobrath

42. Níro dámsat…choscair] Nirodimiset trat Ulaidh in.uíí.main sin isinEamain Macha combuaidh acoscair

43. Úaine…Eomuin] Uaine ortae Emoin ditiu ortae Emoin

44. Ar ba rom ron-tráethad] arbarom (.i. arba dearb) rontraetad

45. Ro fertad fer Aífe] Rofertadh fer Aifi

46. Dia n-epérat…ar flaith] Dianeperat arbuir (.i. slúag) inri roica arflaith

47. A Léith…mairg] ALeith Macha mor nessadh mor ndirsan morngalgat morsirecht

48. Car…gart] Car inmete nasad momiad nometh nogal nogart (.i. eneach)

49. Ar ro fitir…co ngressed] Arrofidur err cain cathbuadhach congreised

50. Gabais…delg] Gabais imbe eochair aratorcair asciath aranimgaib aeach arcumcai adealg

51. Olc lige…óenuch] Olc ligi adbul sluag docer ciarbo aencoisid aenlamaid ditrachtaide aoinech

52. Ro marb…ndíbergach] Romarb Cúculaind cet mulach cet ndíbergach

53. Apraind…bá-so] Aprainn aLeith Macha nabudib nechaib coemaibh focarpat baso

54. Cóemaib] commaib

55. Dursan nách Fíacha…-fallnastar] Dirsan (.i. doile) nach Fiacha foiltlebur fallnastar

56. Dursan nách Fergna…-forcmastar] Dirsan nachFregna mac Finncoime forcmastar

57. Ba méite cach cride…con-bóssad] Bamete cach cridhi rodcar conbossad
58. Ba méite cach dér…bith choíniud] Ba meti cach der nocithe cobrath bad diabithcainiud
59. InBrislech cosin

REFERENCES

Alter, R. 2011. *The Art of Biblical Narrative.* New York: Basic Books.

Barrett, S. 2019. "The Concept of *célmaine* in Blathmac's Second Poem." *Peritia* 30: 11–29.

Beeley, C. 2006. *Gregory of Nazianzus on the Trinity and the Knowledge of God.* Oxford University Press.

Bergin, O. 1921/1923. "The Principles of Alliteration." *Ériu* 9: 82–84.

———. 1928. "Old Irish *ba méite.*" *Ériu* 10: 190–193.

———. 1938. "Varia I. 2. O. Ir. *ecguth.*" *Ériu* 12: 215.

Bergin, O., and Best. R. 1938. "Tochmarc Étaíne." *Ériu* 12: 137–196.

Berlin, A. 2008. "Parallelism." In *Anchor Bible Dictionary,* vol. 5, edited by D. Freedman, pp. 155–162. New Haven: Yale University Press.

Best, R., and O'Brien, M. 1956. *The Book of Leinster*, vol. II. Dublin: Dublin Institute for Advanced Studies.

Bieler, L. 1979. *The Patrician Texts in the Book of Armagh.* Dublin: Dublin Institute for Advanced Studies.

Binchy, D. 1966. "Bretha Déin Chécht." *Ériu* 20: 1–65.

Bisagni, J. 2019. *Amrae Coluimb Chille: A Critical Edition.* Dublin: Dublin Institute for Advanced Studies.

Bourke, A. 1988. "The Irish Traditional Lament and the Grieving Process." *Women's Studies International Forum* 11 (4): 287–291.

Breatnach, L. 1980. "Some Remarks on the Relative in Old Irish." *Ériu* 31: 1–9.

———. 1984. "Canon Law and Secular Law in Early Ireland: The Significance of *Bretha Nemed.*" *Peritia* 3: 439–459.

———. 1989. "The First Third of *Bretha Nemed Toísech.*" *Ériu* 40: 1–40.

———. 1991. "Zur Frage der Roscada im Irischen." In *Metrics and the Media*, edited by H. Tristram, pp. 197–205. Tübingen: Gunter Narr Verlag.

———. 1997. "On the Flexion of the *ā*-Stems in Irish." In *Dán do Oide: Essays in Memory of Conn R. Ó Cléirigh*, edited by A. Ahlqvist and V. Capkova, pp. 49–57. Dublin: Institiúid Teangeolaíocht Éireann.

———. 2005. "Miscellanea Hibernica." In *A Companion in Linguistics*, edited by B. Smelik, R. Hofman, C. Hamans, and D. Cram, pp. 141–151. Nijmegen: De Keltische Draak.

———. 2015. "Legal and Societal Aspects of the Poems of Blathmac." In *The Poems of Blathmac Son of Cú Brettan: Reassessments*, edited by P. Ó Riain, pp. 104–118. Dublin: Irish Texts Society.

———. 2016a. "On Old Irish Collective and Abstract Nouns, the Meaning of *Cétmuinter*, and Marriage in Early Medieval Ireland." *Ériu* 66: 1–29.

———. 2016b. "On the Line Break in Early Irish Verse and Some Remarks on the Syntax of the Genitive in Old and Middle Irish." In *Ollam*, edited by M. Boyd, pp. 151–161. MD: Fairleigh Dickinson University Press.

———. 2021. "Varia Hibernica." *Celtica* 33: 349–372.

Carey, C. 1994. "The Death of Cú Chulainn." In *The Celtic Heroic Age*, edited by J. Koch and J. Carey, pp. 134–143. Aberystwyth: Celtic Studies Publications.

———. 1996. "Obscure Styles in Medieval Ireland." *Mediaevalia* 19: 23–39.

———. 2013. "Muirchú and the Ulster Cycle." In *Ulidia 3*, edited by G. Toner and S. Mac Mathúna. Berlin: Curach Bhán Publications.

Carney, J. 1955. *Studies in Irish Literature and History.* Dublin: Dublin Institute for Advanced Studies.

———. 1964. *The Poems of Blathmac.* Dublin: Irish Texts Society.

———. 1971. "Three Old Irish Accentual Poems." *Ériu* 22: 23–80.

———. 1981. "Linking Alliteration ('*fidrad freccomail*')." *Éigse* 18: 251–262.

Charles-Edwards, T. M. 2000. *Early Christian Ireland.* New York: Cambridge University Press.

———. 2015. "*Táin Bó Cúailnge*, Hagiography and History." In *Sacred Histories: A Festschrift for Máire Herbert*, edited by J. Carey, K. Murray, and C. Ó Dochartaigh, pp. 86–102. Dublin: Four Courts Press.

Corthals, J. 1987. *Táin Bó Regamna.* Wien: Verlag der Österreichischen Akademie der Wissenschaften.

———. 1989a. "Zur Frage des mündlichen oder schriftlichen Ursprungs der Sagen*roscada*." In *Early Irish Literature: Media and Communication*, edited by S. Tranter, pp. 201–220. Tübingen: Gunter Narr Verlag.

———. 1989b. "The *Retoiric* in *Aided Chonchobuir*." *Ériu* 40: 41–59.

————. 1995. "Affiliation of Children: *Immathchor nAilella 7 Airt.*" *Peritia* 9: 92–124.

————. 1996. "Early Irish *Retoirics* and Their Late Antique Background." *Cambrian Medieval Celtic Studies* 31: 17–36.

D'Arbois de Jubainville, H. 1892. *L'épopée celtique en Irlande.* Paris: E. Thorin.

DIL: Quin, G., ed. 1983. *Dictionary of the Irish Language Based Mainly on Old and Middle Irish Materials.* Dublin: Royal Irish Academy.

De Vries. 2015. "Instances of Mirrored Alliteration in the Earliest Irish Poetry." *Australian Celtic Journal* 13: 33–95.

Dottin, G. 1926. *L'épopée irlandaise.* Paris: La Renaissance du livre.

GOI: Thurneysen, R. 1946. *A Grammar of Old Irish.* Dublin: Dublin Institute for Advanced Studies.

Fogarty, H. 2016. "*Dubad nach innsci*: Cultivation of Obscurity in Medieval Irish Literature." In *Ollam*, edited by M. Boyd, pp. 162–171. Maryland: Fairleigh Dickinson University Press.

Gray, E. 1982. *Cath Maige Tuired: The Second Battle of Mag Tuired.* Dublin: Irish Texts Society.

Greene, D. 1972. "The Chariot as Described in Irish Literature." In *The Iron Age in the Irish Sea Province*, edited by C. Thomas, pp. 59–74. London: Council for British Archaeology.

Guyonvarc'h, C. 1966. "La mort de Cúchulainn, Version A." *Ogam* 18: 343–352.

Havers, W. 1956. "Sprachliche Beobachtungen an den Altirischen Glossen." *Celtica* 3: 256–261.

Henderson, G. 1899. *Fled Bricrenn.* London: Irish Texts Society.

Herbert, M. 1996. "Transmutations of an Irish Goddess." In *The Concept of the Goddess*, edited by S. Billington and M. Green, pp. 141–151. New York: Routledge.

Herren, M., and Brown, S. 2002. *Christ in Celtic Christianity.* Woodbridge: The Boydell Press.

Hogan, E. 1910. *Onomasticon Goedelicum.* Revised by D. Ó Corráin. Onomasticon Goedelicum – DIAS.

Hollo, K. 1990. "The Alliterative Structure of Mael Ísu Ua Bhrolcháin's *A Aingil, Beir.*" *Ériu* 41: 77–80.

————. 2005. "Laments and Lamenting in Early Medieval Ireland." In *Medieval Celtic Literature and Society*, edited by H. Fulton, pp. 83–94. Dublin: Four Courts.

————. 2011. "Allegoresis and Literary Creativity in Eighth-Century Ireland." In *Narrative in Celtic Tradition*, edited by J. Eska, pp. 117–128. NY: Colgate University Press.

Hull, Vernam. 1949. *Longes mac n-Uislenn*. New York.

————. 1954. "Celtic Tears of Blood." *Zeitschrift für celtische Philologie* 25: 226–236.

Jakobson, R. 1960. "Linguistics and Poetics." In *Style in Language*, edited by T. Sebeok, pp. 350–377. Cambridge: Massachusetts Institute of Technology Press.

Kelleher, J. 1971. "The *Táin* and the Annals." *Ériu* 22: 107–127.

Kelly, F. 1973. "A Poem in Praise of Columb Cille." *Ériu* 24: 1–34.

————. 1975. *"Tiughraind Bhécáin." Ériu* 26: 66–98.

Kimpton, B. 2009. *The Death of Cú Chulainn: A Critical Edition of the Earliest Version of Brislech Mór Maige Muirthemni with Introduction, Translation, Notes, Bibliography, and Vocabulary.* Maynooth: National University of Ireland.

Lapidge, M. 1985. "Columbanus and the Antiphonary of Bangor." *Peritia* 4: 104–116.

Luibheid, C., tr. 1985. *John Cassian: Conferences.* NJ: Paulist Press.

Lysaght, P. 1996. "Aspects of the Earth-Goddess in the Traditions of the Banshee in Ireland." In *The Concept of the Goddess*, edited by S. Billington and M. Green, pp. 152–165. New York: Routledge.

MacCana, P. 1966. "On the Use of the Term *retoiric." Celtica* 7: 65–90.

————. 1997–1998. "Irish *ba marb*, Welsh *bu farw* 'he died.'" *Zeitschrift für celtische Philologie* 49–50: 469–481.

MacCotter, P. 2004. *Colmán of Cloyne: A Study.* Dublin: Four Courts Press.

Mac Eoin, G. 1977. "The Lament for Cuimine Fota." *Ériu* 28: 17–31.

Malherbe, A., and Ferguson, E., tr. 2006. *Gregory of Nyssa: The Life of Moses.* HarperCollins Spiritual Classics.

Marlow, H. 2007. "The Lament Over the River Nile: Isaiah xix: 5–10 in Its Wider Context." *Vetus Testamentum* 57 (2): 229–242.

McCone, K. 1978. "The Dative Singular of Old Irish Consonant Stems." *Ériu* 29: 26–38.

————. 1984. "*Aided Cheltchair Maic Uthechair*: Hounds, Heroes, and Hospitallers in Early Irish Myth and Story." *Ériu* 35: 1–30.

————. 1985. "The Würzburg and Milan Glosses: Our Earliest Sources of 'Middle Irish.'" *Ériu* 36: 85–106.

————. 1990. *Pagan Past and Christian Present in Early Irish Literature.* Maynooth: An Sagart.

————. 2000. *Echtrae Chonnlai.* Maynooth: Maynooth Medieval Irish Texts.

————. 2006. *The Origins and Development of the Insular Celtic Verbal Complex.* Maynooth: National University of Ireland.

McQuillan, P. 2002. *Modality and Grammar: A History of the Irish Subjunctive.* Maynooth: National University of Ireland.

Meek, D. 1984. "*Táin Bó Fráich* and Other 'Fráech' Texts: A Study in Thematic Relationships, Part 1." *Cambrian Medieval Celtic Studies* 7: 1–37.

Melia, D. "Further Speculation on Marginal .r." *Celtica* 21: 362–367.

Meyer, K. 1912. "Sanas Cormaic." In *Anecdota from Irish Manuscripts*, vol. 4. Dublin: Hodges, Figgis, & Co.

————. 1913–1914. *Über die Älteste Irische Dichtung.* Berlin: Verlag der Königlichen Akademie der Wissenschaften.

————. 1916. "Miscellanea Hibernica." *University of Illinois Studies in Language and Literature* 2 (4): 9–11.

Miller, A. W. K. 1881–1883. "O'Clery's Irish Glossary." *Revue Celtique* 5: 1–69.

Murphy, G. 1956. *Early Irish Lyrics.* Oxford: Clarendon Press.

Nagy, J. 1997. *Conversing with Angels and Ancients: Literary Myths of Medieval Ireland.* Ithaca: Cornell University Press.

Ní Dhonnchadha, M. 2010. "The Beginnings of Irish Vernacular Literary Tradition." In *L'irlanda e gli irlandesi nell'alto medioevo*, pp. 533–596. Spoleto: Fondazione centro italiano di studi sull'alto medioevo.

Ó Baoill, C. 1990. "Person-Shifting in Gaelic Verse." *Celtica* 21: 377–392.

O'Brien, M. 1938. "Miscellanea Hibernica: 122. An Unusual Case of the Old Irish Infixed Pronouns." *Études Celtique* 3: 371–372.

Ó Broin, T. 1963. "What Is the 'Debility' of the Ulstermen?" *Éigse* 10: 286–299.

Ó Cathasaigh, T. 1977. *The Heroic Biography of Cormac mac Airt.* Dublin: Dublin Institute for Advanced Studies.

———. 1977–1978. "The Semantics of *Síd.*" *Éigse* 17/2: 137–155.

———. 1981. "The Theme of *Lommrad* in *Cath Maige Mucrama.*" *Éigse* 18: 211–224.

———. 1983. "The Theme of *Ainmne* in *Scéla Cano Meic Gartnáin.*" *Celtica* 15: 78–87.

———. 2002. "The Oldest Story of the Laigin: Observations on *Orgain Denna Ríg.*" *Éigse* 33: 1–18.

Ó hUiginn, R. 1983. "On the Old Irish Figura Etymologica." *Ériu* 34: 123–133.

———. 1986. "The Old Irish Nasalizing Relative Clause." *Ériu* 37: 33–87.

———. 1987. "Notes on Old Irish Syntax." *Ériu* 38: 177–183.

———. 1989. "*Tongu do Dia Toinges Mo Thúath* and Related Expressions." In *Sages, Saints, and Storytellers*, edited by L. Breatnach, K. McCone, and D. Ó Corráin, pp. 332–341. Maynooth: An Sagart.

———. 1992. "The Background and Development of *Táin Bó Cúailnge.*" In *Aspects of the Táin*, edited by J. Mallory, pp. 29–67. Belfast: December Publications.

O'Rahilly, C. 1976. *Táin Bó Cúailnge Recension I.* Dublin: Dublin Institute for Advanced Studies.

OIGR: McCone, K. 2005. *A First Old Irish Grammar and Reader, Including an Introduction to Middle Irish.* Maynooth.

Pokorny, J. 1919. "Germanisch-Irisches." *Zeitschrift für celtische Philologie* 13: 111–129.

Quin, G. 1974. "The Irish Modal Preterite." *Hermathena* 117: 43–62.

Radner, J. 1982. "Fury Destroys the World: Historical Strategy in Ireland's Ulster Epic." *Mankind Quarterly* 23: 41–60.

Schaffner, S. 2004. "Mittelirisch *fethid* 'geht, macht seinen Weg.'" In *Die Indogermanistik und Ihre Anrainer*, edited by T. Poschenrieder, pp. 277–314. Innsbruck: Institut für Sprachen und Literaturen der Universität Innsbruck.

Schrijver, P. 2005. "The *Roscada* of *Táin Bó Cúailnge* Recension I 2428–2454." In *A Companion in Linguistics*, edited by B. Smelik, R.

Hofman, C. Hamans, and D. Cram, pp. 92–116. Nijmegen: De Keltische Draak.

Sims-Williams, P. 2005. "Person-Switching in Celtic Panegyric: Figure or Fault?" In *Heroic Poets and Poetic Heroes in Celtic Tradition*, edited by J. Nagy and L. Jones, pp. 315–326. Dublin: Four Courts Press.

SnaG: McCone, K., McManus, D., Ó hAinle, C., Williams, N., and Breatnach, L. 1994. *Stair na Gaeilge in Ómós do Phádraig Ó Fiannachta*. Maigh Nuad: Roinn na Sean-Ghaeilge, Coláiste Phádraig.

Sproule, D. 1987. "Complex Alliteration, Full and Unstressed Rhyme, and the Origin of *Deibide*." *Ériu* 38: 185–200.

Stacey, R. C. 2007. *Dark Speech: The Performance of Law in Early Ireland*. Philadelphia: University of Pennsylvania Press.

Stancliffe, C. 1997. "The Thirteen Sermons Attributed to Columbanus and the Question of Their Authorship." In *Columbanus: Studies on the Latin Writings*, edited by M. Lapidge, pp. 93–202. Woodbridge: Boydell Press.

Stevenson, J. 1999. "Altus Prosator." *Celtica* 23: 326–368.

Stifter, D. 2015. "The Language of the Poems of Blathmac." In *The Poems of Blathmac of Cú Brettan: Reassessments*, edited by P. Ó Riain, pp. 47–103. Dublin: Irish Texts Society.

———. 2016. "Metrical Systems of Celtic Traditions." *North-Western European Language Evolution* 69 (1): 38–94.

———. 2018. "An Early Irish Poetic Formula." In *Fír Fesso: A Festschrift for Neil McLeod*, edited by A. Ahlqvist and P. O'Neill, pp. 223–232. Sydney Series in Celtic Studies 17. Sydney: University of Sydney.

Stokes, W. 1862. *Three Irish Glossaries*. London: Williams and Norgate.

———. 1877. "Cuchulainn's Death, Abridged from the Book of Leinster." *Revue Celtique* 3: 175–185.

———. 1898. *Archiv für celtische Lexicographie*, vol. 1. London: David Nutt.

———. 1905. *Félire Óengusso*. London: Harrison and Sons.

Stokes, W., and Strachan, J. 1901–1903. *Thesaurus Palaeohibernicus*. Cambridge: Cambridge University Press.

Suggs, M. J., Sakenfeld, K. D., Mueller, J. R., eds. 1992. *The Oxford Study Bible: Revised English Bible with the Apocrypha*. New York: Oxford University Press.

Thurneysen R. 1912–1913. *Zu Irische Handschriften und Literaturdenkmalern.* Berlin: Weidmannsche Buchhandlung.

———. 1918. "Zur keltischen Literatur and Grammatik: 12. Ir. *tosúgad* 'an-, einsaugen." *Zeitschrift für celtische Philologie* 12: 288.

———. 1921. *Die Irische Helden- und Königsage bis zum siebzehnten Jahrhundert.* Halle: Niemeyer.

———. 1937. "Zwei Irische Etymologen: 2. *art fine* 'Sippenhaupt.'" *Mélanges linguistiques offerts à M. Holger Pedersen.* Aarhus: Universitetsforlaget.

Travis, J. 1944. "Elegies Attributed to Dallán Forgaill." *Speculum* 19: 89–103.

Tristram, H. 1995. "Near-Sameness in Early Insular Metrics: Oral Ancestry and Aesthetic Potential." *Poetics Today* 16 (3): 445–470.

Tymoczko, M. 1981. *Two Death Tales from the Ulster Cycle.* Dublin: The Dolmen Press.

Uhlich, J. 2018. "The Registers of Echaid's Daughter in *Fingal Rónáin.*" In *Fír Fesso: A Festschrift for Neil McLeod,* edited by A. Ahlqvist and P. O'Neill, pp. 233–262. Sydney: University of Sydney.

Walker, G. S. M., ed. and tr. 1957. *Sancti Columbani Opera.* Dublin Institute for Advanced Studies.

Watkins, C. 1979. "Old Irish *saithe,* Welsh *haid*: Etymology and Metaphor." *Études Celtiques* 16: 191–194.

———. 1990. "Some Celtic Phrasal Echoes." In *Celtic Language, Celtic Culture,* edited by A. Matonis and D. Melia, pp. 48–52. Van Nuys, CA: Ford and Bailie.

———. 1995. *How to Kill a Dragon.* New York: Oxford University Press.

www.ingramcontent.com/pod-product-compliance
Lightning Source LLC
Chambersburg PA
CBHW060523130626
46553CB00002B/622